MOTHER —

WITH LOVE TO ANOTHER

LUCKY ONE

JEFF & CHRISTINE

SEPTEMBER 1982

ONE OF THE
LUCKY ONES

ONE OF THE LUCKY ONES

LUCY CHING

Doubleday & Company, Inc., Garden City, New York   1982

Library of Congress Cataloging in Publication Data

Ching, Lucy.
    One of the lucky ones.

    Originally published: Hong Kong: Gulliver Books, 1980.
1. Ching, Lucy.   2. Blind—China—Biography.   I. Title.
HV1624.C5A35   1982   362.4'1'0924   [B]
AACR2
ISBN: 0-385-18105-1
Library of Congress Catalog Card Number: 81-43850

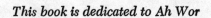

This book is dedicated to Ah Wor

PREFACE ●●

WHILE THE EXPERIENCES in this book are mine, I have had some help with the actual writing. Tina Bailey and I have worked on it together. It has taken us over four years and represents countless hours of discussion and drafting, telephoning, brailling, taping, typing, checking, correcting and editing and without Tina's help I could not have done it. Her help has not been limited to the book and I am not the only one to benefit from her work. Apart from being a volunteer braillist, braille proof-reader and braille instructor, she is one of the regular readers for blind people. I thank her for all this.

My grateful thanks also go to Bill Bailey, Sir John Wilson, Don and Aileen Peake, Anthony Lawrence, Winnie Wong, Emily Young, Phoebe Hsu and Tang Kwan Mei—and to the unknown doctor in the Philippines who started it all!

Lucy Ching
Hong Kong 1980

ONE OF THE
LUCKY ONES

CHAPTER 1 ●●●●●●●●●●●●●●●●●●●●●●●●●●●●●●●●●●●●●●●

WE HELD OUR breath. Had we heard a voice through the static? Perched tense and still on the edge of the bed, we strained our ears. It came again, this time more clearly, in Mandarin but with an accent:

"Hello CY . . . Hello CY . . . This is DU . . . I am in Manila. Are you receiving me?"

"I am receiving you DU . . . ," said my brother into his microphone.

"I am a doctor of medicine and I think I can help you. I know what your sister needs. I will write to some people in America and ask them to send some things to help her. Tell me where to send them."

My brother gave our address as clearly as he could and then asked, "Where do you come from?"

"From New York, but I know Mandarin because I've always hoped to work in China."

Then he said, "Goodbye—and good luck!" and his voice was gone. We sat listening to the crackling static, wondering if it had really happened.

I was eight at that time. Three years before, when I was five, I had discovered that I was blind. Never having seen I did not know until the day my mother told me. It came out when I grumbled about not being able to keep up with my brothers and sisters in a game. "You'll never be able to beat them," she said, "because they can see and you can't. You are blind."

Later I asked why they went to school.

"To learn to read and write so that they can become useful people when they grow up."

"Can I go to school with them?"

"That's impossible. You can't go because you are blind." Mother sounded sorry but very definite. She said I would not be able to see the blackboard or read books.

When plans were being made for family visits or treats I sometimes asked if I could go.

"No, you can't go; you are blind."

I soon learned not to ask.

One day I heard on the radio that blind children in America and England learned to read in some special way with their fingers. Some went to special schools, others went to ordinary schools and studied alongside sighted children. I thought and thought about this and determined to find out somehow.

My older brother, who was sixteen, was very keen on electronics. In his spare time he built himself a transmitter and kept it on a small table beside his bed. After getting his licence as a ham operator he spent hours sending out call signals and talking to people in far-away places. I would sit beside him, listening, and that was when an idea came into my mind: suppose he were to ask if anyone listening knew how blind children could learn to read . . . someone might know . . . and answer. . . . He agreed to try. He spoke in Mandarin and English. He only knew the little of these languages that he had learnt at school, but he did his best. He tried for three weeks but nothing happened. We were nearly giving up —it seemed hopeless. And then DU in Manila answered.

Two months later, soon after breakfast one morning, the doorbell rang. I went and called out to know who it was. It was the postman so I opened the door. He said there was a package for "Ching" and added that he thought it must be for me because he could read enough English to see that it said "Reading Material for the Blind." It suddenly dawned on me that the doctor in Manila must have kept his promise and this package was the result. I called my parents who were doubtful about accepting it, but in the end Father signed the receipt.

I stood in the hall with it in my hands. I could hear my father putting on his shoes and a moment later I heard my mother's sewing machine start up. Then Father called goodbye to everybody and went off to work. I knew the kitchen door was open because I could hear running water and knew that our amah Ah Wor was washing up. I took the parcel into the living-room and set about opening it. The string would not come off so I found some scissors and cut it in so many places that it fell off in bits. All the edges of the paper were stuck down and I could not start pulling it open anywhere. Impatiently I attacked it with the scissors and cut away what felt like wrappings until I came to something that felt like a flat envelope. Inside this I found some very thick small-sized papers with raised dots all over them and some larger papers, several pages bound together, each page covered in hundreds of raised dots. With growing excitement I realised that these must be the things that enabled blind children to learn by touch.

But I had no idea what to do with them. I wished I could get my parents to help me, but my father had gone to work and my mother would not want to be bothered with me. I knew Ah Wor would love to help me but she had the housework to do and she could not read anyway. There was nothing for it but to see what I could find out on my own.

I explored further. There was a small box; in it was a little metal strip with holes in it on one side and tiny knobs on the other. And there was a strange little round thing that felt like a spinning top with the point of a knitting needle sticking out of it. I turned these mysterious things over and over in my hands and felt every inch of them. I could make nothing of them. Then I dropped the metal strip. It landed with a clatter on the floor. I groped about for it and found that it had become twice as long as before. I realised that it was a double strip, hinged at one end so that it opened and shut like a book. I sat at the desk where my brother and sister did their homework, my strange new treasures in front of me, and kept feeling the cards with the dots and opening and shutting the metal thing. I ran my fingers again and again along the lines of holes. I was called to lunch but I did not go. I was terrified that if I went away and left my mysterious new things they might disappear. Nobody came and insisted. My parents—and therefore Ah Wor— often indulged me where they would be strict with the other children and I was allowed to have my way so long as it did not inconvenience anyone. Perhaps it was a small effort to compensate me for my handicap.

Anyway, on this day I sat on in the living-room, pushing my fingers into the holes and wondering. Ah Wor came in with a bowl of rice. I pushed it away and in doing so my hand touched the little round thing. I picked it up. I found I could push it right into the holes—it seemed to fit. Suddenly I wondered what would happen if I put a piece of paper between the two halves of the metal. I ran to the bathroom for some toilet paper and laid it on one half and carefully closed the other half on top of it. Then I tried pushing the point of the round thing into the holes to see if I could make raised dots like those on the cards. I pushed and pushed and then took the bit of paper out. It was full of holes; not dots. I examined the cards and my piece of toilet paper again and realised that the cards were much thicker and stronger, so I went and found a piece of my sister's drawing paper. I checked with Ah Wor that there was no drawing on it and then tried again. This time, to my surprise and delight, there were raised dots.

I waited impatiently for my brother and sister to come home from school. I was so excited I could hardly wait to show them what I had got. They looked very carefully at the papers and told me that one card had all the letters of the English alphabet, which they had learnt at school, printed beside different groups of dots. So I asked them to take my hand and show me how to do them. Luckily I had often heard them doing their English lessons aloud so I did at least know the names and the order of the English letters.

And so I started to teach myself braille—although I never heard this name until two more years had passed. When I was familiar with the letters I switched my attention to another card where there were several letters written close together and the first word I spelled out was b-o-o-k. I asked my sister what it meant and how to pronounce it and she told me. Another group of letters was p-e-n-c-i-l and I was surprised to hear my sister muttering the same word in her own homework. This was marvellous—I felt the world was opening up for me. It was just coincidence that we happened both to be learning the same word at the same moment, but I had been told ever since I was old enough to understand that it was no use a blind child trying to study because blind children and sighted children do not live in the same world or understand the same things.

At that moment, on that evening, I suddenly knew that this was not so. I knew in a flash that it was up to me—that I could do whatever I had the determination to do and I was not limited by arbitrary, pre-set boundaries in the way that my family had brought me up to believe.

CHAPTER 2 •••••••••••••••••••••••••••••••••••

AT THE TIME all this was happening we lived in Canton. Canton is the provincial capital of Kwangtung, the southernmost province of China, and it is only ninety miles from Hong Kong.

Canton—known as the City of Rams from an old legend—and its river, the Pearl River, were the scenes of most of the incidents in the Opium Wars which led in the end to the founding of the colony of Hong Kong. It is also the place where Sun Yat-sen, himself Cantonese, worked to bring about the revolution that ended China's long history of dynastic rule. The party he created, the Kuomintang, was discredited in its turn, but nevertheless it was Sun Yat-sen, using Canton as his base, who was largely responsible for the end of the old system in China. Kwangtung as a province has always been proud of its reputation for independence of thought and action.

But long-established ways of thought die hard. Perhaps I should mention briefly the traditional Chinese background of thought, teaching and belief as it has a direct bearing on social attitudes to disablement of any kind. Confucianism with its system of ethics and Buddhism with its ideals of personal purity provide between them the main framework of precepts, beliefs and customs which have for centuries shaped and directed the lives of ordinary Chinese people. While Confucianism is a practical philosophy of living, Buddhism, by comparison with Confucianism, is a religion. Both are austere and pitiless about human suffering and offer no hope of relief or comfort. The teaching of Buddhism is concerned with human relationships but not with the betterment of social conditions; instead it advocates a personal escape from realities. It is little wonder then, since Confucianism offers no relief from suffering and Buddhism even taught that suffering was a punishment from heaven for one's own sins or the sin of one's ancestors, that throughout Chinese history little effort was made to improve the condition of blind people until after the revolution in 1911, when some of the old ideas began to be challenged.

It was generally believed by uneducated people, right up to the time when I was a child in Canton, that the eyes are the root of all evil and that evil spirits could be released by piercing the eyes with needles or sprinkling pepper into them to cause weeping to wash them out. This would sometimes be done at the command of a temple monk, if the family went for advice on some ailment afflicting the child or some family misfortune, or it could even be prescribed by grandmothers, whose word was always law. Whoever suggested it, the result was wilful destruction of sight. These and other barbaric remedies were carried out in the name of superstition and brought tragedy to many a family.

My father was an architect by profession and had his own construction company, accepting both private and Government contracts. He was reasonably well off and we lived in a fairly large self-contained flat on the second floor of a five-storey building. In 1945 there were eight of us in all—Father, Mother, two boys and four girls. The eldest, a boy, was my ham radio brother. The next child was a girl, my elder sister. I loved her very much, despite the three years difference between our ages, and it was a great grief to me when she died tragically young. I was the third child, the fourth was a boy and the last two were girls.

Like most well-to-do families, my parents were able to afford servants who were called amahs. We had four: Ah Kwun, the cook; Ah Shim, who looked after my elder brother and second sister; Ah Luk, for my younger sisters; and Ah Wor, who coped with my younger brother and me. We children were taught to address our amahs as Kwun Tse, Shim Tse, Luk Tse and Wor Tse. The word "Tse" is used to indicate someone older than oneself. As children we seldom quarrelled or fought; this did not mean we were very well behaved but whenever there was any sign of trouble our various amahs came to the rescue and separated us or took us out.

Perhaps I should explain about names in a Chinese family. Everyone is given a name at birth, but this name is rarely used at

home. It is an official "outside" name or "school" name. At home
one has a "home" name which is used by people older than oneself.
My official name is Man-fai, but my home name was Little Girl
(*Bee Nui* in Cantonese) and I was called that by my parents and
by my older brother and sister. I, however, could only use the
home names of my younger brother and sisters and had to call the
older ones First Big Brother and Second Big Sister. My younger
brother and sisters called me Third Big Sister. Home names tend to
stick to people all through their lives, within their families, but as
they grow up and get to know more people outside the family,
their official names are used more frequently. When in 1977 I
visited America and met my mother and one of my uncles, they
still called me Little Girl.

The amahs did not use either of these names; they had another
set of names for all of us. I was Miss Three. Even now, after all
these years, Ah Wor still calls me Miss Three—*Sam Ku Neung* in
Cantonese. My sisters were Miss Two, Miss Five and Miss Six and
my brothers were Young Master One and Young Master Four.
They had to have the "Young" added on to distinguish them from
Father, whom the amahs called Master. Mother was Mistress.

When we were alone we children liked to call each other by our
home names. This was fun simply because it was forbidden. One
day Father heard us doing it and was very cross. We all got into
trouble and were made to promise never to do it again. I need
hardly say we did do it again—often—but we were careful to do it
when Father was out. Why he minded so much about younger people not showing proper respect to older ones when we were all
children of one family I really do not know, but it was a traditional
attitude and Father was a naturally conservative person.

Our family, like so many others, had been uprooted by the Sino-
Japanese War and later became involved in World War II in Hong
Kong. Canton fell to the Japanese in 1938, when I was still a baby.
Our family stayed on, uneasily, under Japanese rule for a few
months until a friend who was staying with us was raped by a Japanese soldier. Father then became seriously worried for the safety
of his family and decided to take us all to Hong Kong. I have been

told we went by boat in 1938 but I do not remember anything about it.

In Hong Kong we lived in Ho Man Tin and my Third Uncle was able to help Father get work so that he could keep us all. There was an incident on Christmas Eve 1941, when the Japanese were close to Hong Kong and there was a strict blackout. That evening we could hear gun-fire coming closer and closer, but Mother and her friends were playing mahjong and the police banged on the door and said that lights were showing at the window. More paper was added round the edges of the window but the police came back twice more as the light was still showing. There was nearly bad trouble about this because, as we were near the airport at Kai Tak and everyone was jumpy and nervous, we were suspected of being spies signalling to the enemy. In the end Father and Uncle convinced the police we were not. Meanwhile Ah Wor and the other women in the house were busy blackening their faces with soot from the stove so that the Japanese soldiers would not take a fancy to them. They did not want to qualify as the "pretty miss" which the Japanese soldiers were known to be on the lookout for.

Next day, Christmas Day 1941, the Japanese occupied Hong Kong. I do not remember very much about the next three or four years, though people have told me some of what happened. It is not really relevant to my story. I do remember hearing news bulletins about the dropping of the atomic bombs on Japan and the Japanese surrender.

A few days later we went back to Canton. Father had prudently saved the deeds of all the property he owned, and quickly obtained a large income from rent as well as starting up his business again and repairing neglected and war-damaged property. Far to the north of us the Communists were undermining the authority of the Kuomintang, though the last phase of the civil war was not to break out for another two years and we barely knew the name Mao Tse-tung. My family picked up the pieces and got on with their lives. My brother operated his transmitter, and I passed long hours with nothing to do and little company except Ah Wor's.

My life could have been spent in enforced idleness and isolation, cut off from other people and their lives and problems. But I was luckier than that; God had other plans for me.

As I had been blind since the age of six months, I could not remember seeing and did not miss vision or any visual experience. According to Ah Wor, when it was time for me to learn to walk I trailed my hands along the walls and learned my way from room to room. After many bumps and falls I realised that some things were always in the same place, such as doors, steps, bathroom fixtures and pieces of furniture. Before long I was running and jumping with my sighted brothers and sisters and did not realise that I was different. When I was five, one of our favourite games was counting coins. Whenever I dropped a coin I had to crawl on my hands and knees to retrieve it and I was upset when my brothers and sisters were always so much quicker than I was. I pestered my mother to show me how to beat them. This was when she told me I was blind.

I asked Ah Wor how people could see. She told me they see with their eyes. I felt her eyes with my fingers and then my own. They seemed to be the same, but still I could not see. I cried and said I wanted to see. "You can see too," Ah Wor replied, "but in a different way. I see with my eyes. You see with your hands."

Until the end of the Sino-Japanese War, when some people in the Kuomintang Government, inspired by the work of missionaries, began to show more interest in the problem, parents of blind children in China generally got no help or advice or even sympathy from anyone; the community did not want to know about them. They struggled with the situation on their own, feeling guilty and ashamed. They did not want to hear their relatives and friends commenting pityingly on their afflictions so they kept the blind child hidden away out of sight, never going out, learning nothing, growing up totally helpless. The helplessness added to the family's frustration, as it inevitably meant that the blind person would be a permanent burden to the parents or, later on, to brothers and sisters.

It is not surprising that these emotions often developed into an active aversion to any contact with the blind child. Blind people have always been the outcasts of Chinese society, isolated in a tangle of superstition, fear and contempt. In an effort to get rid of them without actually killing them, families would abandon them in places where they hoped they would die undiscovered—hilltops, river banks, deserted houses—or sell them to a range of slave dealers. In the case of a boy, he might be sold or given away to be the property of a sighted or blind fortune-teller so that he could learn fortune-telling. Usually this meant, in practice, becoming a beggar, but some became successful fortune-tellers with a good living. A girl would be sold or given to some blind women who would teach her to sing a few songs and play a musical instrument—usually the *erh-hu*—and send her to beg in the streets. She would probably become a prostitute pretty early on. Blind boys and girls were frequently ill-treated by their slave masters and mistresses. The idea of educating a blind person was unthinkable. There were exceptions, though the better treatment and conditions of some more fortunate blind people were motivated by financial gain, not humanity; they earned more for their exploiters if they were better dressed and better fed. These included sing-song girls in teahouses and restaurants who looked well-fed, wore gaily coloured clothes and were escorted by older women. They were professional entertainers and they performed at parties and celebrations, singing traditional songs. Their male counterparts were usually performers of the *Nanyin,* or Southern Sound, a form of ballad singing much in vogue in Canton before World War II. It is an art form traditionally practised by blind men and takes years of study and great talent to perform well. It was not unusual for people to go to the same teahouse day after day for two years or more to follow the daily developments of a historical romance or a saga of war heroes.

Some of the slave masters and mistresses had the sense to see that a larger investment in food, clothes and tuition for their blind boys and girls would enable them to make more money out of them when they grew up. Good physical appearance and intensive training in Chinese vocal and instrumental music would turn them into adult professionals who could be hired out to perform in teahouses and restaurants, on radio and television and even to make records. But the system of instruction was very hard for the boys and girls. There was no music braille system or tape recording at that time, so the slave master or mistress had to teach the songs or instrumental techniques by endless repetitions, phrase by phrase, sentence by sentence until they were memorised. They sometimes hired an instructor to do the teaching, but whatever the method, they firmly believed in beatings and other punishments as aids to rapid learning, so the unfortunate boys and girls suffered great hardships at the hands of their owners.

When they were trained and able to make money, they had to hand over whatever they earned to their owners. The death of the owners was usually the only way they ever obtained freedom. Sometimes they managed to keep some money back and save up enough to buy their freedom, and sometimes a woman might attract a man sufficiently for him to take her as a concubine to bear and raise his children—though whether this could be regarded as "freedom" is another matter. Sad to say, some blind people who did manage to gather together enough money to buy their way out of exploitation became exploiters in their turn. It took a revolution and the coming of the Communists to break these evil traditions.

One of the traditional occupations of blind people has always been to act as a medium, someone who claims to be able to establish contact between humans and spirits. The living family of the dead person sometimes wants to communicate with him to find out how he is getting along, whether he is happy or unhappy or whether there is anything he wants. They would do this through the medium who may be sighted but is frequently a blind person. The medium starts by burning incense and chanting prayers to the Spirit God to summon the spirit to come up to the earth and lodge temporarily within him. The spirit is then able to speak and answer questions through the medium. In the case of a blind medium, after chanting prayers he would walk up and down tapping his stick on the ground so that the spirit, hearing the tap tap, knows he is to come up. For this reason, to people of the older generation, a blind person's stick was something to be feared, as it could summon spirits up from the depths.

The old convictions that blind men can only be mediums or fortune-tellers and that all blind women, whether they sing in the street or not, are bound to be prostitutes are—or were until recently—serious obstacles to the improvement of blind people's status in the community. There is the belief that if anyone should touch or be touched by the stick of a blind person, it would bring bad luck for three years. For this reason, although there has been a great improvement in recent years, assistance to blind people in boarding buses, crossing roads or finding entrances to buildings is still not offered as readily as it could be. Many people still deliberately move away when they know a blind person is coming in their direction. Superstitions are very contagious and are not easily eradicated.

I consider myself as one of the lucky ones among thousands of blind people in my country, as my parents did not abandon me and did not sell me or give me away. Like most blind children, I was kept in the house and was never included in family outings, but I was not necessarily hidden away from every visitor who came and as I was dependent on voices for all communication, I liked to be with people and listen to their conversation—even when I could not understand what they were talking about.

Sometimes I understood only too well. I still remember an afternoon when a neighbour, Mrs. Chan, called to see Mother. "What a pity you have a blind daughter," she remarked. "You or your husband, or one of your parents, or perhaps even an ancestor must have done something to displease the God in Heaven. Otherwise such a great tragedy would not have befallen you. What are you going to do with her? As long as you are here, of course, you can feed her and take care of her, but you are not likely to live as long as she will, to take care of her until she dies. So who will give her food when you and your husband are gone? You cannot expect your other daughters or sons to take her with them after they are married. And even if your sons and daughters were willing to undertake such a burden, certainly their wives and husbands would not be willing to have her."

Mother blamed all this on her fate and said that she and Father were prepared to feed me as long as they lived; after they were gone it would be a matter of my fate and there was nothing they could do. Mrs. Chan was not the only one who said this. Most of my parents' friends said much the same and it never seemed to worry them that I was in the room, obviously listening. However, it upset me so much to hear such conversations that after it had happened a few times I learned to creep away to the bedroom I shared with my sisters and stay there until the visitor had gone.

Mother's reference to fate sounds hard-hearted but I know she really worried about this. Many times she said to me, "Little Girl, I hope you die before I do—then I shall know you are being well cared for. When you grow up, Father and you and I can live together, but if we die before you, I dare not think what will happen." I know she said this out of love and real concern for me. She and Father both loved me and were anxious about my future, but that was as far as it went. They did not realise that giving me food and shelter was not enough and that the blind child has to develop just like other children. My educational needs were never even considered because it did not occur to them that I could have such needs. They never dreamed in those days that a blind child could be educated.

Fortunately for me, and now for many of my blind friends, Ah Wor was different. She made me the centre of her life. With no formal education and with nothing to guide her except her own commonsense and affection, she helped me to learn how to live blind in a sighted world and to cope with the problems, emotional as well as physical. It meant a hard time for her in many ways. She was still a normal amah in the family with the usual range of domestic work to do, but beyond this she devoted every spare moment to me, guiding my hands to explore new things, fighting my battles with my family, showing, teaching, explaining. She understood my passionate desire to go to school and helped me to get there; used her savings to buy me the essential extras which my parents regarded as extravagant or (later) could not afford; stuck with me through good times and bad and is in fact still with me. Her single-minded devotion earned her no admiration from other amahs or from acquaintances. They scorned her and thought her mad, giving up chances of earning more money for the sake of a blind girl who, they said, would be better dead anyway. It all made no difference to Ah Wor, who plays a larger part in my story than anyone else. To Ah Wor I say thank you for more than can ever be repaid in this life.

CHAPTER 3 ●●●●●●●●●●●●●●●●●●●●●●●●●●●●●●●●●●●●●

ONE MORNING not long after the parcel came I was in the living-room with Ah Wor when there was a scream and a clatter below the window followed by angry voices that rose to a crescendo, then running feet and more shouting. I heard Ah Wor go to the window. A boy had fallen off his bicycle and knocked into a group of amahs so that one had dropped her shopping. Everyone was shouting at the boy who was running away. The commotion died down and then we could hear children laughing. I longed to be down there with them, but I never went out except on occasional necessary outings such as to the doctor or the dentist. That day I suddenly plucked up courage and asked Ah Wor if I could go out.

Ah Wor sounded surprised, but she said she would take me when she had time. I could hardly wait. It seemed hours until she had finished her work, but at last she said she was ready and we would go to the bread shop. She took my hand and we started down the stairs.

I remember every detail. It was the very first time I had gone out simply for the sake of going out. To this day I can vividly recall the sense of revelation—that I could go out like other children, even though I was blind. Until that day I had accepted my fate, but now I began to realise that life held possibilities I had not thought of before.

We walked along, Ah Wor telling me what we were passing but, in my eagerness, I pulled ahead of her and bumped into a group of gossiping amahs. One of them asked Ah Wor if this was a *mang mui* which, literally translated, means "a blind female slave." Ah Wor replied that I was blind but that I was her Miss Three, not a *mui*. The woman said she could not understand how anyone could be bothered to take care of a blind child. She was of the opinion that because I was blind, nothing in life could possibly interest me. She then went on to say that it would be better for me to die rather than grow up.

I tugged Ah Wor's hand. She understood what I meant and we walked quickly away from the amahs and towards where we could hear children playing. To my delight they did not mind my joining them and I played with them for quite a long time.

At last Ah Wor said we must go and buy the bread or there would be none left in the shop. I had never been in a shop before and this one smelled lovely. Ah Wor asked for two pounds of bread and a man's voice asked if she wanted it sliced; Ah Wor replied that she did. I asked her how the man sliced the bread and she took my hand and let me feel gently along the big square loaf, explaining that there was a very sharp knife fixed to the wooden board and this cut the bread into slices of exactly the same thickness, but I had better not feel the knife as it might cut my fingers. I heard the rustling of paper as the man wrapped the bread and handed it to Ah Wor who then gave it to me to hold. Then I heard the chinking sounds of coins and the man said, "Just a minute. I'll get you the change." Ah Wor explained what "change" meant and, as the man handed the money to her, he said, "You are very kind to this blind girl. If everyone would take time to let blind people feel things, then they could find out a lot with their hands."

As we went out of the shop neither of us said anything but I know we were both thinking what a contrast there was between this man and the unsympathetic amahs.

Looking back now, I can see how little, in many cases, attitudes have changed. By an odd coincidence, one day in 1974 when Ah Wor and I were visiting an English friend in Hong Kong, we came face to face with the very same amah who had made the nasty remarks that day in the street in Canton. Later that evening Ah Wor told me that her "friend," who was still working as an amah, had again asked her why she stayed with the same blind woman.

At home that evening in Canton I asked my mother how I became blind. Mother said I was too young to understand and she would tell me when I was older. I could think of nothing else for the rest of that evening and later, when I was in bed and Ah Wor came in to see if I was asleep, I begged her to tell me. At first she hesitated, but when I said I would not let her go to bed until she had told me, she agreed. She said we could not talk there as it would disturb my sisters so we crept along the passage to her room which she shared with Ah Luk. She and Ah Luk had bunk beds and Ah Wor had the lower one, so it was there, sitting on the edge of her bed, that I at last heard the story as she remembered it.

As Ah Wor was telling me the story, Ah Kwun came in. After listening for a while, she told Ah Wor that it was wrong for me to know this. My parents would not want me to know and it was not good for me to know. Ah Wor insisted that I would find out someday and it was better for me to learn the truth than to believe stories that might lead me to blame, unjustly, either my parents or myself. Unconvinced, Ah Kwun shrugged her shoulders and went away.

When I was born, Ah Wor told me, I was a healthy baby with normal vision. My eyes followed lights and people's movements and I could obviously see them. When I was six months old we went to our family village in the Kwangtung countryside near the border with Macau for a ceremony connected with my dead grandfather. While we were there, Mother noticed a red spot in each of my eyes and took me to the local herbalist. He prescribed an infusion of some grasses and leaves to be used as a lotion on my eyes. My eyes became swollen and actually bled; it was obvious that something was badly wrong. They quickly took me back to Canton to see a doctor practising Western medicine who, in turn, advised them to take me to an English eye specialist in Hong Kong. We went by boat and Ah Wor came to look after me because my regular amah hated travelling. Ah Wor carried me into the doctor's office and she said she remembered how both my parents wept when the doctor told them that too much damage had been done to my eyes by the herbal concoction, that the optic nerve was destroyed and I would be completely blind for life.

The doctor was English but fortunately he spoke fluent Cantonese. He told my parents that blindness did not mean uselessness and that it was up to them to bring me up to be a happy and useful person and not to allow me to grow into an emotional cripple. Ah Wor told me that this remark made a lasting impression on her. It was lucky for me that she was there and heard what was said because from that moment on she did everything she could to follow the doctor's advice.

When Ah Wor finished telling me this story, neither of us spoke for a few moments. Then she said she would take me back to my own bed but I said I did not want to go. I suddenly felt I did not want to be alone. Ah Wor quickly sensed this and said I could stay with her but that I had better get up early in the morning as my mother would not like it if she found I had been sleeping in an amah's bed. We soon found that Ah Wor's bed was really too small for the two of us even though I was not very big, so she crept back to my room, took a blanket from my bed and settled herself on the floor while I stayed in her bed.

In the morning she got up at her usual time but I was still sleeping soundly and she did not want to waken me. It was not long before Mother looked into my room and saw I was not there. She called Ah Wor and asked where I was. Poor Ah Wor had to tell her I was in her bed and was reprimanded for it. When I woke up, Mother questioned me but I just said I had wanted to be with Ah Wor and did not say anything about the story of my blindness. I knew I was not supposed to know about that. Mother finally put it down to the fact that I had been listening to ghost stories on the radio; I was forbidden to listen to them after that.

Ah Wor's own life, when she was a girl, had an episode which many people might find strange and hard to believe, like something from a bygone age, and yet it was only in the early 1920s that it happened.

Ah Wor's family lived in the Kwangtung countryside, in a village a little distance from Canton. Her father died when she was two and she was brought up by her widowed mother who worked for a farmer. They lived in the farmer's house, waking up at dawn every morning to the sound of the farmer's wife's cough. That cough was their alarm clock. Her mother would climb out from under the mosquito net that covered the wooden bed she and Ah Wor shared and hurry to the kitchen to start heating some water.

The kitchen was a lean-to structure with a straw roof, made of earth bricks, hard and black with age, which had been tacked on to the house many years earlier by the farmer's grandfather. Against the outer wall, in a pen, was the farmer's ox, his most precious possession. Hearing Ah Wor's mother in the kitchen, the ox would low and grunt and thump against the wall, scratching his side.

It was Ah Wor's job to put just the right amount of water from a storage vessel into an iron pot and then get kindling from the heap of grass and sticks in a corner so that her mother could start the fire in the rough earthen stove, under the iron pot. She lit the fire by striking a flint stone against a piece of iron until she got a spark.

When the water boiled, it was poured into a bowl and a dozen or so curled, dry leaves were carefully taken from a container on the edge of the stove and scattered on the surface. Once, when she was five or six, Ah Wor whispered to her mother that she would like to have some, but her mother whispered back, "We cannot be wasteful. Drinking tea is like drinking silver." Then her mother would take the bowl of steaming tea to her mistress, whose racking cough never stopped until she drank it. The farmer had a bowl of plain hot water, saying that as he had no cough, he did not need tea, which he thought should be for special occasions only.

After breakfast—rice and a little vegetable—the farmer and Ah Wor's mother and some neighbouring workmen all went out to work in the paddy fields, taking the ox along to pull the plough when it was the ploughing season. At noon they all came back for a meal, prepared by Ah Wor as soon as she was old enough to do it. Afterwards the farmer's wife, who suffered from some sort of illness, took a nap and Ah Wor would go out, armed with a wooden rake, to collect sticks and leaves for the kitchen stove and also fodder for the ox.

As she grew up, it was Ah Wor's ambition to attend a study group where she could learn some Chinese characters and be able to write her name. There was no proper schooling in most Chinese villages in those days—it was just a matter of someone who knew a little starting a group and teaching what he knew to others in order to earn some money. However, Ah Wor's mother refused, saying it was not the custom for Chinese women to learn to read and write.

The role of women should be household work and looking after her husband and children, she said.

When Ah Wor was nearly sixteen, drought hit Kwangtung. The rice plants wilted and died in the parched paddies under the blazing sun and at last the farmer told Ah Wor's mother that he had no more work for her.

Ah Wor knew very well how anxious her mother was, though they did not speak of it. Lying in bed that night, silent and afraid, she watched her mother uncover a hole in the earth wall of their tiny room, pull out several pieces of silver and then put the earth back in the hole so that it looked as if nothing had happened. Later, as the two of them tossed and turned, Ah Wor felt a hard lump on her mother and asked what it was. At first her mother would not tell her, but Ah Wor persisted, so eventually the older woman produced a bundle and unwrapped it. In it were the pieces of silver. For thirteen years she had saved her wages from the farmer and had gradually turned them into silver taels. Now they could keep themselves from starving. Ah Wor went to sleep feeling easier in her mind.

But the drought went on and on and still there was no work. They had to leave the farm and go to live with one of Ah Wor's older sisters. This meant sharing a tiny cramped stone house with the sister, her husband and two children, one of whom was about Ah Wor's age. Piece by piece the silver was used up. Ah Wor's mother was desperate and saw only one possible solution—to get Ah Wor married off. Marriage would mean that the girl would be taken care of and some money would come to her mother as a form of dowry from the man's family.

Like all the village mothers Ah Wor's mother approached a marriage broker to find a husband for her daughter. The broker proposed that she be married to a ghost. This is a custom which is certainly dying out today, but I would not like to say it never happens, even here in Hong Kong.

In this instance a youngish man had died unmarried. It was generally believed that such a man was a lonely ghost and that he would be made happier if his parents on earth arranged a marriage for him with either a living or a dead woman. If his wife were liv-

ing, she would then have to go to his parents' house on special occasions to perform certain ritual duties and to worship him. Apart
from these obligations, she would in most cases be free to work. If
the wife were a dead woman, then of course he would actually
have her company.

In the case of Ah Wor, the offer made by the marriage broker
stipulated that she should live permanently in the house of her
parents-in-law, to serve and obey them. This offer pleased Ah
Wor's mother who thought that the arrangement would impose
fewer obligations on the girl who would not have to cope with the
emotional problems of marriage and children. Also it would have
meant that the man's family would pay money to the mother, which
she, as a poor widow, needed very badly.

But Ah Wor found the whole idea completely unacceptable and
said she could not go through with it. She had another sister, married and living in Canton, and so she told her mother she would go
to her sister and get a job in the city and send money home to her
mother to make up for the ghost-marriage settlement. Reluctantly
her mother agreed and Ah Wor went to Canton.

It was her first visit to a city. Electric lights, lifts, water taps,
telephones—all these were new and unbelievable and fascinating
to Ah Wor. She was amazed when she heard village girls who had
come to work as amahs singing cheerfully at kitchen sinks as they
washed dishes under running water. At the farm she had had to
carry water from the well.

She soon found work as amah with a family, but after some years
these people left for New Zealand and she had to seek another
post. That was when she came to our family, about three years before I was born, to look after my older sister. Her mother had died
two years before Ah Wor came to us, but for the ten years or so before her mother's death, Ah Wor had sent her nearly everything she
had earned, keeping barely enough for her own necessities.

When I was born I was looked after by another amah, Ah Sung.
At first she looked after me well, but when I became blind she developed an aversion to touching me and began to behave with pos-
itive hostility towards me. At this time my parents were so overcome with grief and shock that they had lost interest, not just in

me but in all the children, and did not want anything to do with any of us—especially me. Our day-to-day welfare was left in the hands of the amahs.

Whether Ah Sung, taking her cue from my parents' attitude and their obvious misery, may really have thought she was doing them a favour by neglecting me to the point where I might possibly have died, I do not know. What I do know from all Ah Wor has told me in recent years is that Ah Sung would hit me and leave me uncovered at night and would quite deliberately place me on the edge of the bed so that I fell off onto the floor, banging my head. This worried Ah Wor terribly and she and Ah Sung had great arguments about it all. Finally, to Ah Wor's immense relief, Ah Sung had to return home to her own village to nurse her husband who had fallen ill. Ah Wor then asked my parents if she could take charge of me and let another amah look after my sister. My parents, however, said they could not afford another amah as they wanted to have a cook, so Ah Wor agreed to look after both me and my sister. Later, as the family grew bigger and Father's income fortunately also increased, two amahs, Ah Shim and Ah Luk, were added to the household staff.

Ah Shim was a devout Buddhist and a vegetarian. She would spend a long time each morning and evening saying prayers. Buddhists light joss sticks and then pray for as long as the joss sticks take to burn out; often this can take up to an hour or more. Ah Wor often felt that some of this time could well have been spent sharing the duties she and Ah Luk had to perform, but as it was a matter of religious belief, they were very tolerant. Ah Shim, on the other hand, would ask her God in Heaven to send down vengeance on Ah Wor or Ah Luk or anyone else for that matter who offended her!

Her prayer-time had a disastrous effect on my brother's record of attendance at school. He was often late because Ah Shim had to finish her prayers, but my parents, who assumed it was because he got up late, blamed him. Had they known the truth, they would of course never have kept her, but all this was done in the amahs' quarters and my brother never betrayed her.

Looking back, I might be tempted to doubt the truth of the stories about Ah Sung, but it was confirmed to me only a few years ago and quite independently by Seventh Auntie who told me she had seen some of these incidents herself and had tried to warn my mother. Ah Sung, however, was a favourite amah and her word was always believed, whereas Seventh Auntie was a junior member of the family and "suspect" because, although of Cantonese descent, she had been born and brought up in America.

Apart from being blind I was perfectly normal and healthy. Obviously I had problems and frustrations which my sighted brothers and sisters did not have, but at least I had a reasonably good home, a devoted amah and a family who protected me physically though they had no idea of how to cope with my emotional and psychological needs and my natural desire to "see" things with my hands. That side of my life was taken care of by Ah Wor who, uneducated and illiterate as she was, must be one of the kindest and wisest of women. She did by instinct and intuition, love and commonsense all that my parents, perhaps through fear and lack of imagination, never even attempted. She shared my interests, helped me in everything she could and got me out of the scrapes that all children, blind or sighted, get into. One of these sticks in my memory.

It was a wet, windy afternoon. I could hear the rain tapping on the window. Soon after lunch Mother said she was going out with some friends and that I must stay with Ah Wor and be a good girl. She then told Ah Wor to dispose of all the old newspapers which were stacked up in the living-room.

I followed her to the front door and said goodbye. The lock clicked into place as Mother pulled the door shut and the noise of her heels grew fainter as she went downstairs. Ah Wor had gone back to the kitchen to wash up. I stood in the empty hall, wondering what to do.

Suddenly, I remembered Mother's remark about the newspapers. I wondered if I could use them for my raised dots. Sister had said I was using up all her drawing paper, so I had to find something else to use. Perhaps old newspapers would be the answer.

I began to search the living-room, starting at the door and working slowly round, feeling everything. At last I found a big pile of papers on a table by the wall. Overjoyed, I picked them up and hurried to the kitchen to Ah Wor and asked her whether these were the papers Mother said were to be thrown away. Though I could not see her face, I could hear her turn towards me and her voice was pleased and surprised.

"Oh, good girl—are you bringing them for me to throw away?" But when I said I wanted to keep them her voice sounded even more surprised: "Well, don't just tear them up and throw them all over the place!"

I explained that I wanted to try using them to make raised dots, to save using Sister's drawing paper, but Ah Wor said she thought the paper was too thin and the dots would not last.

"Also," she added, "if you keep handling it your hands will get all black."

Black hands did not worry me, but when I slipped a finger under the top layer of paper I realised that she was right—it was very thin. Then I tried putting two or even three layers together and it felt much thicker. With Ah Wor's help I carried the papers in triumph to my bedroom and hid them on the mattress of my bed, under the bottom sheet, where I hoped no one would find them and take them away from me. Then, taking just a few sheets with me, I went to the living-room, feeling on top of the world. I folded each sheet several times until I had a pile of smaller but thicker pieces. I tried some dots. It really did work!

I do not know how long I had been doing this when the front doorbell rang. Thinking it was time for my brother and sister to come home from school I ran and opened the door without first calling out to ask who it was, as I was supposed to do. To my horror there was silence. No one spoke. After a few seconds a man's voice said, "Are your father and mother at home?"

At this I was even more scared as I had never heard this voice before.

"They are out, but who are you? I don't know you. I have never heard your voice before."

Instead of answering my questions he asked, "What's your surname?" I told him it was Ching. Then a second man whispered, "She's blind, so that makes it easier!"

"There's no need to wait—let's get on with it," the first man said.

I was really terrified. I still had the door half open, clutching the lock with both hands. Suddenly I felt the door being pushed open wider and I screamed at the top of my voice for Ah Wor, who came rushing from the kitchen. I could not see if she was as frightened as I was, but I could hear her voice tremble as she demanded to know what they wanted.

The man said, "Mrs. Ching phoned and asked us to deliver a telephone book, so that she would not have to collect it herself. She said she would give us three dollars."

Eventually, after an argument, Ah Wor found three dollars in her apron pocket. That was a lot of money in those days—Ah Wor's wages were seven dollars a month. She gave the men the money and sent them away.

As she closed the door I began to realise what had happened and that it was all my fault. I burst into tears and, although Ah Wor tried to comfort me and told me that everything was all right, I was still crying when my brother and sister came in from school. I managed to calm down enough to tell them what had happened. Sister picked up the telephone book and then burst out laughing.

"It's the old one!" she exclaimed. "Last year's—they sold it back to you!"

The telephone book re-awakened my curiosity about the telephone, which had always been a mystery to me. My wretchedness over the eipsode of the two men began to fade as I thought perhaps I could at last get Ah Wor or my sister to solve it for me. Time and time again I had heard a bell ring and then Ah Wor would say, "Master . . ." or "Mistress . . . telephone for you." Then Father or Mother talked and I never heard any replies. Often I would stand close to the person talking and try to listen but I never heard anything except a faint, toneless sound like a tiny distant voice that came and went.

"Where is the telephone?" I asked. "I can hear it ring but I can't find it. Where is it and what does it do?"

Sister explained that it had wires going to other people's houses so that we could talk to people a long way off, but she said the telephone itself was on a shelf too high up for me to reach, so she could not show it to me.

I asked Ah Wor when the others had settled down to their home-work. She moved a stool near to the telephone shelf, helped me to climb on to it and guided my hands to examine the instrument—the dial with its holes and the receiver that lifted off its rest. I en-joyed making the bell ring when I picked up the receiver and put it back again. Suddenly, while I still had my hand on it, the tele-phone began to ring in earnest. I was so startled that I nearly fell off the stool but Ah Wor steadied me and, as the telephone con-tinued to ring, on an impulse I picked up the receiver. Suddenly I realised that I didn't know what to say. I heard a voice in my ear saying "Hello? Who's there?" I recognised Seventh Auntie's voice and felt less frightened. I told her what had happened and how I had been learning about the telephone at the very moment she rang. She sounded pleased. "Well done! Good girl!" she said.

To receive some praise was an unusual event. Traditionally in Chinese households parents tend to encourage modesty and humil-ity, emphasising a child's weak points rather than praising good ones. As a Chinese and blind as well, I had received scant praise in my short life. But Seventh Auntie, with her American background and different outlook, was not quite as bound by tradition as the rest of the family.

We talked for a few minutes and she asked me to tell my mother to telephone her sometime the next day. At the end we said good-bye and I put the receiver back on the rest. I felt very proud, hav-ing a telephone message to deliver.

After solving the mystery of the telephone I suddenly wondered if I could find out about something else that continually puzzled me—the clock. People talked about the time and I had heard the clock strike the hours, but I could not imagine what a clock was like. So, as I got down off the stool, I asked Ah Wor to let me feel the clock too. I picked up the stool expectantly but she said the clock was too high up for me to reach even with the stool: she would have to take it down from where it was hanging. This she did. I was very disappointed when I felt that its face was only a flat piece of glass. I asked how she could tell the time with that and she explained to me about the two hands, one long and one short, and how they went round. We could not take the glass off and I said, "Why can't they make a clock like my raised dots, then somebody like me could feel it?" Years later, when I went to the Perkins Institution (now the Perkins School) for the Blind, at Boston, I discovered about braille watches and clocks and soon had one of each of my own.

When Father and Mother got home later that evening I told them all about the day's events. Instead of sounding pleased, they sounded upset and told Ah Wor never to let me open the front door again. I defended Ah Wor by explaining that I usually opened the door for Brother and Sister, and Ah Wor told them that today I had opened the door half an hour earlier than the time they were due because I could not tell what time it was. Father simply repeated that I was never to open the door again.

I gave them the message from Seventh Auntie. All Mother said was that next time I must let Ah Wor answer the telephone in case there was something urgent or important. That night I put my head under the pillow and sobbed. Everything I thought I had achieved during the day seemed to have gone wrong. Only Seventh Auntie had told me that I was a good girl.

Second Sister, who was in the next bed, heard me crying and came over to ask what was wrong. I told her that I had been forbidden to open the door for them anymore because I had forgotten to ask who was there that afternoon. She said this would be all right because she and First Big Brother would call out to me every day when they came up the stairs. I would be able to hear that it was them and could open the door for them as if nothing had happened. That made me feel much better.

Then Ah Wor came in to see if we were all asleep. Her kindness started me crying all over again—over the business of not knowing the time. I had really worked myself up into a state over this. Ah Wor promised me that one day soon we would go to the store and

buy a cheap clock and take off its glass so that I could feel the
hands and how they went round. She kept this promise, as she kept
all her other promises to me, and that was how I learned to tell the
time.

CHAPTER 4 ●●●●●●●●●●●●●●●●●●●●●●●●●●●●●●●●

A MEMBER OF the family I have not yet introduced is my paternal grandmother. Usually I could distinguish people by their footsteps, though sometimes it was difficult when they were wearing new shoes, but I could never hear Grandma as she walked very slowly and wore special cloth shoes on her bound feet. These made no sound, so I never knew if she was near me or not until she spoke.

Grandma was born at the time when girls of well-to-do families had their feet bound at about five years of age. The child's mother or grandmother forced the child's toes back under the foot towards the heel and bound them tightly in place with strips of cloth. This was terribly painful and it was many days before the binding was removed even for long enough to wash the feet—and then of course they were bound up again. Once the deformity had become permanent, the binding was removed, but the victims could never walk easily for the rest of their lives. It was a dreadful ordeal and yet it was regarded as an indispensable part of the preparation of an upper-class girl for a good marriage. Girls whose feet were not bound were either slaves or came from a poor family. They could never hope to be the first wives of rich men, only concubines.

This was not the only handicap which women of Grandma's generation had to endure. It was considered inappropriate for them to learn to read and write. There are two famous Chinese sayings: *Nü-tzu wu ts'ai pien shih te* which means "Lack of learning being a woman's virtue," and *Hsien-ch'i liang mu,* meaning "Helpful wife and wise mother." How the second was supposed to result in any way from the first is a puzzle to us nowadays, and both illustrate an attitude now repugnant in an era of equal opportunities for women, but they do show why Grandma, like her contemporaries and like Ah Wor, was illiterate. She could hardly be blamed for re-

taining the narrow, traditional ways of thought in which she had
been brought up.

In her world—which means the old China, before ideas began to
change fundamentally in the decades after the fall of the Manchu
dynasty—everybody wanted sons and it was not unusual in families that already had more girls than boys to kill a newly born girl.
When Ah Wor was born, she was the third girl in a family with no
sons and her paternal grandmother wanted to drown her, but eventually gave way to her daughter-in-law's entreaties to be allowed to
keep her—thereby proving herself to be kinder than some mothers-
in-law who would have insisted on being obeyed; their word was
law. If a woman took a dislike to her son's wife she might even
order her son to get rid of her or find a concubine. It was no good
the poor man objecting—his mother would have her way as head
of the household.

Mother often said that my grandmother was one of the kinder
mothers-in-law. In proof of this she said that on the day of her
marriage to Father, when she knelt to offer tea to Grandma,
Grandma took it immediately. Many mothers-in-law would keep
the young wife kneeling for a very long time before taking the tea.
This inconsiderate behaviour was intended to assert her authority
and ensure obedience and submission. It was believed that kindness
would encourage disobedience and lack of co-operation. It is not
surprising that Grandma shared the general attitudes and prejudices towards blind people.

One morning Grandma came to see my parents, and I have good
reason to remember that morning. Ah Wor was making the beds
and I was washing and dressing a doll. Grandma, Father and
Mother were talking in the living-room. At first my attention was
concentrated on the doll until something Grandma said in a loud
and angry voice made me drop the doll and listen. She could not
understand, she said, why my parents had kept me all these years
and had not given me to the street-singing instructors who would
have taught me to sing and beg in the streets. If they persisted in
bringing me up, I would only be a burden to my brothers and
sisters, who would have to feed me all their lives.

Mother began to cry. She said I was still her child and if they ever gave me away, it would be a disgrace to the family name. Ah Wor had stopped what she was doing and was listening too.

Father then said that he had saved some money and intended to buy a house in my name and let it so that the rent could provide me with a decent income for the years ahead. This would save my brothers and sisters having to provide for me.

I had heard enough. I fled to the bathroom and began to cry. Ah Wor followed me—she was in tears too, the first time I ever remember her crying. While I was carrying on about Grandma and how she hated me, Ah Wor pointed out that at least my father loved me as he was making these plans about a house. This was true and I cheered up a little as I thought about it. To take my mind off it all, Ah Wor asked me to go with her to the market to help carry the vegetables home.

In the market we met some amahs and I boastfully told them my parents were going to buy me a house so that I would have money to live on when I grew up.

One amah, after hearing this, said slowly, "If a war breaks out, you cannot take the house with you if you have to go away. The only way people can provide for themselves is by working—and you cannot do this. You will have to depend on your brothers and sisters to give you rice anyway."

"If someone pays rent for the house, as Father intends, I would have lots of money after a few years and I could take the money with me, wherever I went," I replied.

I felt very clever, having all this worked out. Then another amah joined in and said, "If money is devalued, even if you take it to other places, it won't help you at all."

I asked Ah Wor what "devalued" meant and she explained that if I went only as far as Hong Kong, a dollar from Canton would not be worth the same amount as a dollar in Hong Kong. This did not make sense to me but my child's instinct told me that my ideas about property were no good. I remembered the first amah's words: ". . . the only way people can provide for themselves is by working."

At that moment I determined, once and for all, that somehow I must learn something and so be able to work. The resolve I took that morning—to work and be independent—never wavered and kept me going through the problems and difficulties of the years ahead.

About three months later, Father settled himself on the sofa after breakfast, reading the newspaper instead of leaving for work as usual. Just as I was wondering why, I heard Mother ask, "When will he be coming?"

"Probably about ten," Father replied.

"Is someone coming to see us?" I asked.

"Your Sixth Uncle," Mother said, adding, "little children should not be listening to what grown-ups are saying. When your Sixth Uncle is here, even if you hear what we are talking about, you must not interrupt us by asking silly questions."

Realising that I had talked too much as usual, I made up my mind to be quiet and not to utter a word. I concentrated on pricking my dots and did not even hear the ringing of the doorbell. I heard my name called and knew Uncle had arrived. We greeted one another and then he turned his head away and said, "Ah Yung, this is your master and this is your mistress. From now on, you must do your best to respect and work well for them."

A girl's voice, very low and nervous, said, "My master, my mistress."

I did not hear a response to her greeting and I was aware that she was still standing. For some reason I had not grasped that she must be an amah. I heard myself say, "Is your name Ah Yung?"

"Yes, miss." She sounded very frightened.

I could not understand why she was afraid, so I said, "Why don't you sit beside me? There's room."

She did not move. Uncle said, "This is your Miss Three. If she tells you to sit down, you must do as she says."

Now I realised, from hearing Uncle refer to me as Miss Three, that Ah Yung must be a young amah. She sat down beside me. Uncle then spoke to my parents.

"My fifth brother and fifth sister-in-law, I just don't know how to show my gratitude to you for all that you have done for me and for the financial support you have given me, so I have brought you this slave girl as a gift."

He used the word *mui*—meaning female slave—which I was fast learning to resent when it was applied to me in the phrase *mang mui*.

Uncle then showed my parents a written statement from Ah Yung's parents disclaiming all their rights to their daughter's future and stating that they had willingly sold her to Uncle to employ, use, marry off or give away as he pleased.

None of this made sense to me. I left the living-room as quietly as I could and ran to the kitchen and told Ah Wor all that I had heard. What, I asked her, was the difference between an amah and a *mui*? Ah Wor told me that an amah would be able to decide where she wanted to work and to bargain with her master or mistress about wages. Later, if they were not happy with each other, the amah could be dismissed or she could leave if she wished, whereas a *mui* could not do any of these things. Once she was sold to a family, she would have to work for the same master or mistress all her life, without pay, unless her owners chose to sell her or give her away. She was literally the owner's property. When she grew older the decision as to whether she should be married, and to whom, would rest entirely with her owners.

Now I began to understand why Ah Yung was so frightened. I asked Ah Wor where she was going to sleep and Ah Wor said that my mother had told her to have Ah Yung in her room, to keep an eye on her while she was still new to the household. Ah Shim had left a few months before, so Ah Luk, who normally shared with Ah Wor, had moved into Ah Kwun's room, leaving room for Ah Yung with Ah Wor. Ah Wor said she herself had moved from the lower bunk to the upper one so that Ah Yung would have the lower one and there would be no risk of her falling off the top if she had bad dreams. I said I would show Ah Yung where her bed was. Ah Wor was horrified because she knew I was doing the wrong thing. She tried to stop me but I slipped past her and ran back to the living-room.

"Ah Yung," I said excitedly, "I know where your bed is. Come with me and I will show you."

I realised Ah Yung was standing up but she did not move. I took a step towards the door, sensed that she was not coming with me and turned back. As I started to urge her to come, I heard Uncle say, "Ah Yung, you should do what Miss Three is ordering you to do, but after you have taken your things to your room you should go to the kitchen and ask Wor Tse what you should do to start work." (As Ah Yung was young, she called all the other amahs Tse just as we children did.) Ah Yung then followed me. I asked her how old she was and she said she was fifteen. We went to Ah Wor's room and I showed her the empty lower bunk. I heard her put something in paper down on it. I reached out my hand and felt a very tiny package wrapped in what felt like newspaper.

"What's this?" I asked.

"My clothes," she replied.

I was very surprised, as the package could contain only two dresses at most. "How can you have enough to wear? Why don't your father and mother give you more clothes?"

To my dismay she burst into tears. I asked if she was not feeling well or if she was hungry, but she was unable to say a word. After a few moments I heard footsteps and then I heard Ah Yung muttering through her sobs, "She will beat me."

I listened and assured her that it was Ah Wor who was coming and, as I was saying this, Ah Wor came into the room. She quietly closed the door and said to Ah Yung, "Don't be afraid. I'm sure we shall get along well. Our mistress does not beat people, except the younger children sometimes if they are very naughty. Now you must stop crying, for today is the first day you have come to this family and if Master and Mistress knew that you were crying, they would be very displeased, as sorrow brings bad luck into a house. Now, you come to the kitchen and I will give you something to eat and drink."

When she had taken Ah Yung to the kitchen, Ah Wor came back to me and urged me to go to my own room, for if Father and Mother knew I was spending time with Ah Yung they certainly would not like it. I did not quite understand what she meant but, realising the anxiety in her voice, I did as I was told.

I do not know how long I sat on the edge of my bed. The word *mui* went round and round in my head. I was beginning to grasp why Ah Yung was so miserable—her parents did not want her and

I knew I had said the wrong thing in asking her why her mother and father did not give her more clothes. But *mui*—I was called *mui* too, *mang mui*. To be sure I was *mang*, but my parents had not given me away or sold me and yet I was called *mang mui*. I recalled that amah in the street and Ah Wor's quick retort to her that I was not a *mui*, I was her Miss Three. Why did people call me *mang mui* and how were Ah Yung and I alike? Were my parents planning to sell me as a *mui*? I wanted so desperately to ask Mother about all this, although I was frightened that when she said I was not to ask silly questions, it was because she and Father were planning to sell me.

Then I heard Mother coming towards my room. I made up my mind to ask, but before I could say a word she came in and said that I had been a very bad girl and had made an awful scene in Uncle's presence. I was trying to find words to ask what I had done wrong, but before I could get a word out Mother left the room and went back to the living-room. Next I heard her calling loudly for Ah Kwun. She said they were going out for lunch. I was relieved, as I knew that the amahs, Ah Yung and I would be left in the house on our own. After a few minutes I heard footsteps and voices in the hall as they prepared to go. At last the front door banged shut and everything was quiet.

I ran to the kitchen and told Ah Wor everything. She consoled me and said, "Don't worry—it will soon be forgotten." And she was right. It was.

And what of our slave—our piece of human property? As it happened, things turned out well for her. She soon settled down with us and Mother fitted her out with used clothes that were her size and gave her all the little personal necessities she had never owned before. At the end of each month, when Mother paid the other amahs their wages, she would give Ah Yung some pocket money, which Ah Yung recognised was generous as Mother was under no obligation to give her money at all.

When we left Canton for Macau in 1949, we had to spend a short time in Hong Kong before going on to Macau. Since the possession of slaves was against the law in Hong Kong, Ah Yung told everyone she was a distant relative. She said she really felt part of the family by that time and that she had had a good life in a kind family, unlike some slaves who were beaten, sometimes even to death.

During the years she lived with us she and I became very fond of one another and when I went to school I tried to pass on to her something of what I learned. I tried to help both my illiterate companions, Ah Wor and Ah Yung, to read and write a little. I found some simple primary textbooks and asked a friend to read them to me. I then tried to teach them, but this arrangement was obviously far from ideal as I knew no Chinese characters. However, they learned enough to enable both of them to read street names and shop signs and numbers. Ah Yung, being younger, learned quickly and even managed the English alphabet, which was beyond Ah Wor. However, we all had some fun out of doing it.

On the day of Ah Yung's arrival, Mother came home after lunch and I heard her talking on the telephone to Seventh Auntie. I gathered that they were fixing a day for Seventh Auntie to bring some English friends to our flat to meet my parents and discuss renting the house which Father had bought as an investment for me.

They came a few days later. When they arrived they went into the living-room. I was in my room, but the living-room door was open and I tried to listen across the hall as Auntie translated the conversation. The English couple's names, I remember, were Ann and John but I do not think I ever knew their surname. I believe they were connected with the export and import trade.

They were given cups of tea and went straight to business. My father said the rent would be a hundred dollars a month for the house, preferably in Hong Kong dollars. I expected that the English couple would try to bargain, as Ah Wor would usually do in the food market, but to my surprise, when Auntie translated this, all they said was, "Yes . . . all right . . ." and agreed to everything. I found I could understand those few simple English words from working with my raised dots and the cards with the English words on them. I was delighted when Auntie asked about me and said that her friends would like to meet me. When Mother called me to come and I went into the living-room, I was rather nervous—I was not often called to meet grown-ups.

Auntie introduced me and I was startled to feel both the English people take my right hand and shake it—a custom of which I knew nothing! Chinese adults would not normally shake a child's hand and certainly not that of a blind child. I liked the sensation—it felt friendly. Auntie then said I could call them Uncle and Aunt. This thrilled me because I had learned these words too, and in a moment of insight I was aware for the first time that learning English words was not just something on paper—they were alive and a link with people. Auntie was the only adult person (apart from Ah Wor) who asked to see what I was doing when I was working with my dots. Now, she suddenly asked me to bring my cards and papers and my little pricker to show these friends. I was so proud and happy as they read with me and excited to realise that we were reading the same words together, in print and in dots. It was wonderful to have people taking an interest and asking about the work I had been doing. My parents had never, as far as I knew, even looked at my dots. Admittedly they knew no English, but they took no interest at all and gave me no encouragement. This sounds strange and heartless, but now I can look back over years of experience as a social worker, mainly working with blind people, and I know that this attitude is, unfortunately, all too common towards the blind.

Trying now to analyse in retrospect what my feelings were at that time, I think it would be true to say that I mainly felt a sense of shame that I should be different from others in the family and be limited by my blindness to things which the others, especially my parents, had no interest in and no wish to share. This did not strike me as strange; I never once questioned it. A child accepts the evaluations of older people until something happens to start a process of questioning, and I can honestly say that I felt no resentment at my parents' indifference to my struggles to learn English and do my dots, despite the contrast between that indifference and their interest in what my brothers and sisters did.

But the seed of change was sown that day. It was a critical day in my life because someone actually treated me as a person worth taking notice of, someone whose little interests were worth discussing and looking at. We read through all the cards together—it must have taken us about half an hour. The gentleman patted me on the head and the lady bent down and kissed me. No one had ever kissed me before. It is not usual for Chinese parents to kiss their children, unless they are very Westernised. Though we could not say very much to each other, I had the impression that these people liked me. I was so overwhelmed that I made up my mind to work hard and learn all the English I could so that I would be able to talk easily with them and maybe with other English people as well.

Father and Mother had left the room to fetch some papers and Seventh Auntie asked me in a low voice if I would like to go out to tea with them and then spend a few days with her. I jumped at the idea. Seventh Auntie then told me not to say anything until she had talked with my mother.

Soon Father and Mother returned and, after a short discussion about the lease, the English people signed the papers on the big table. Seventh Auntie then asked Mother if she could take me with her for a few days. Mother had no objection but sounded surprised that Auntie could be bothered with me.

Auntie, Ah Wor and I went to my room to pack the things I would need. I could not believe what was happening—I had never gone to stay with anyone before. Ah Wor told Auntie that I was able to manage most things for myself and could learn a new place quickly and easily. At last everything was in a suitcase (one lent to me by Ah Wor) and then Ah Wor said I should change into a better dress, so I went and felt along the things in the wardrobe until I came to the one I knew was my red dress. I took it out and put it on. Seventh Auntie said it looked good and suited me. When she asked why I chose red for my best dress, I replied that Mother had told me red is the colour of good luck.

When we were finally ready to go, everybody said goodbye in the hall. Ah Wor whispered in my ear that if I was suddenly not sure where I was or could not find the bathroom, I must not be afraid to ask Seventh Auntie or my cousins.

Seventh Auntie took my hand and we went downstairs and out to the English couple's car. Seventh Auntie opened the door and took my hand and placed it on the top of the doorway so that I could feel how high it was and so avoid banging my head. Once I was in, Auntie followed and sat beside me. The engine started, the car moved forward; we were on our way.

CHAPTER 5 ●●●●●●●●●●●●●●●●●●●●●●●●●●●●●●●●●●●

WE DROVE INTO Central Canton. I could not believe that this was really happening to me, the blind child who never went anywhere. It was like a dream. Auntie translated almost everything that was said, encouraging me to join in and translating what I said into English. I felt very important but also very confused. At home I was taught never to join in the conversation of grown-ups. This was a strange, bewildering experience. The English couple said to me, through Seventh Auntie, that I could call them Ann and John. At this I was even more confused, as it was absolutely forbidden to call a grown-up by name.

They asked me what were my favourite things to eat. I said I had never been to a restaurant, so I did not know what I would like there. Auntie mentioned sandwiches, cakes, biscuits, hot and cold drinks. None of these meant anything to me but I said I would love to go to a Western-style restaurant. Soon the car stopped and we got out. It was exciting to be in a street so different from the market streets I was used to with Ah Wor. There were new noises and new smells—food smells but different from home cooking.

We entered what I sensed was a big building and Auntie told me we were coming to the lift. While I was still puzzling what this meant, I felt we were entering a small room with lots of other people in it, all standing close together. I heard a sliding noise and had the sensation that the room was moving up; then, all of a sudden, it seemed to be going down. Actually, of course, it had stopped, but to me it felt as if it was falling down and the whole building with it. I was so frightened that I frantically clutched at Auntie's arm. She realised I was afraid and put her arms round me and for the first time in my life I knew the comfort and security of being held tightly by a grown-up. Despite our close relationship, Ah Wor never did this to me even when I cried. She naturally followed the example of most Chinese parents who are strictly undemonstrative towards their children.

As soon as we had sat down at a table in the restaurant, Auntie gave me a cup of hot tea and I felt perfectly all right again. She asked me whether I had been in a lift before. This was the second time she had used the word "lift" and I asked what it was. She explained how it worked and I realised that it was the first time I had been in one. I was excited about it and wanted to go in it again.

We had what I now know was an English afternoon tea and I loved it. The English lady asked if I would like sandwiches. I had never heard of a sandwich but I was ready to try anything new, so I said, "Yes, please." I heard a waitress put things down on the table and Auntie guided my hand to something and told me to take one. I did not know what "one" was, so I took hold of what I touched first. The result was a collapsed sandwich, half on my plate, half on my lap and the ham on the tablecloth. I was dismayed as I felt it fall to pieces but Auntie came to my rescue and then asked if I had ever had a sandwich before. I said no and asked what exactly it was. She described it and I said that we had bread at home but only used it as toast at breakfast.

Slices of cake and a cup of hot chocolate were equally strange and delicious. To me the word "chocolate" meant chocolate bars and I was amazed to find it hot, in a cup. And I learned for the first time about stirring; when Auntie put sugar and milk in the chocolate I heard a curious little grinding noise which had to be explained to me. Feeling carefully what was on the table I found a metal thing and picked it up—and was horrified to find I was holding what seemed to be a small, cold, hard hand with prickly fingers. When the others had stopped laughing, they told me it was a fork and described how Europeans eat with knives and forks. My knowledge of tableware, limited hitherto to bowls and chopsticks, expanded immediately to take in these new and fascinating things.

As we were talking, I asked what else was in the building. Auntie said it was a big department store with different goods on each floor. I said I would love to go to some of them. The English lady said they needed to buy some things for the new house and asked if I would like to go with them. I said I would love to. Secretly, I knew this meant going in the lift again and I was thrilled at the idea of the big shopping floors.

One of the waitresses, who was making out our bill, called another waitress and whispered to her, "Look, this *mang mui* wants to go with these people to the shop. I wonder what she can get out of it when she can't see what there is!" The other waitress whispered back, "Are you sure she's a *mang mui?*"

I was listening to them, feeling humiliated, and did not hear Auntie say we were ready to go. She touched my arm and I realised they were all standing up. My indignation about *mang mui* quickly left me as I found myself back in the lift again.

How I wished I could have let those waitresses know how much I enjoyed the afternoon, even though I could not see. Seventh Auntie and the English people guided my hands to feel and examine and explore things I had never imagined. I then realised that I could "see" a great deal with my hands if only sighted people would be thoughtful enough and patient enough to show me round. At last the time came to go home. The English couple took us in their car to Seventh Uncle and Auntie's house and we all said goodbye.

That evening at Auntie's house, I sensed a great difference in the relationship between my three cousins—all girls—and their parents as compared with the more formal atmosphere of my home. They were much more relaxed and did not have to stand on ceremony. For instance, as we played together, we laughed and giggled to our hearts' content without being told to be quiet. And at the supper table my cousins just went and helped themselves to bowls of rice without having an amah to wait on them.

One thing that struck me specially was that they did not have to go through the long traditional greetings in order of seniority which we were obliged to observe at every mealtime. This consisted of each of the children, in turn, starting with the eldest, saying to everyone senior to himself "I wish you a good meal." First Brother said it first to Father and Mother; then Second Sister said it to Father, Mother and First Brother; then I said it to Father, Mother, First Brother and Second Sister and so on down to my poor youngest sister who had to say it to seven people. This was done every time Father and Mother were present at a meal—even breakfast. If we children were on our own, of course we did not bother. But such formalities found no place in the easy-going atmosphere of Seventh Uncle and Auntie's house.

After supper and playtime my cousins had to do their school work. Uncle was working and Auntie was giving me some new English words to take down in raised dots. I wanted to learn as many words as I could so that I could study them back at home. She encouraged me to talk and I told her how I was often referred to as a *mang mui* and how I hated it. Auntie was shocked. She said she could understand *mang* as I was certainly blind but she could not understand *mui*, as my parents had not sold me to be a slave. I insisted I had heard it many times—from the amahs in the street, from people coming to our house, from the waitresses that afternoon—and I was sure I was not making a mistake. She said she would ask Uncle, just to be sure. Soon afterwards Uncle finished his work and came to sit with us, so Auntie told him about it. He confirmed that I had heard correctly. He went further and said that most Chinese people, instead of referring to a blind person by his or her given name, would address them or speak of them as *mang mui* (blind slave girl), *mang kung* (blind old man) or *mang jai* (blind boy). He added that the reason a blind person like me was not given a cane, as I would be in America or Britain, was because the cane is regarded as the symbol of the blind beggar or prostitute. Auntie was horrified and she quickly realised what this meant to blind people, relegating them to the lowest status of society and making them feel crushed and humiliated. She thought for a moment and then suggested that perhaps Uncle could write a letter to the local newspapers to try to make people aware of what they were doing by thoughtlessly using this phrase, but he said that even if he did, it would not make any difference. He explained that there are several interpretations of the phrase and that if people were suddenly challenged with it, they would always deny that they meant "blind slave girl" even if they had used it with that exact intention only a moment before. They would try to argue that the word meant simply "a blind girl" or "woman" or, at the worst "a blind singing beggar." They would also assert, usually, that they were saying the word for "sister."

It is true that the word *mui* can be said in two different tones, one rising and one falling. These tones make a great difference. The rising one is inoffensive and means "little sister" or "girl," while the falling one means "slave" whatever anyone says.

For many years now I have checked with my blind friends how they react to the phrase *mang mui* and every one of them, without exception, was certain that the speaker meant "blind slave." We blind people are conscious of being regarded as social outcasts by sighted people. This is proved over and over again for all of us by the fact that in public places, from buses to churches, from restaurants to cinemas, people can be heard moving away from us. Speaking personally as a blind woman, from time to time when I have accompanied one of my male colleagues to some official occasion, people have actually come and asked my companion, in front of me, how much this *mang mui* would need to be paid to sing a song. I do not find this amusing.

There has been some improvement in recent years. Certainly since my schooldays there has been a genuine effort, especially in the past ten years or so, to educate public opinion into a more enlightened attitude, and things are improving. Not only are canes, including the up-to-date long cane, accepted as routine equipment for blind people, but also blind youngsters can go into ordinary schools where facilities are provided for those who can cope with the academic side.

I felt so completely at home with Auntie, who was taking such a sympathetic interest in my problems, that I told her about something which had been worrying me. I explained to her that I listened as hard as I could to what my brothers and sisters said aloud when they were doing their homework and took down what I could in dots. The difficulty was that this only worked for English words. I did not know how to put Mandarin or Cantonese into dots and I wondered if there was any way of doing this. If only there was, and I could learn it, I could take down what I could overhear of all their subjects instead of only English.

Auntie and Uncle thought about this; then Auntie had an idea. She asked Uncle to look in the telephone directory to see if he could find anything under "Blind." I could hear him flicking over the pages and at last he said he had found something that looked useful—there was a home for blind women called the Mo Kwong Home. It was too late to ring up that evening but Auntie said she would do so next morning.

The next day she telephoned quite early and explained about me and it was arranged that we would visit them the following day. I was so excited that night that I could hardly sleep. I hoped and hoped that there would be a Chinese dots system and that the people in the Mo Kwong Home could teach it to me.

Auntie said we would have to go by bus to the Home as it was a long way off. This was my first bus ride. We waited at the stop and when the bus came Auntie held my arm firmly and steered me up the steps and into a seat. She described the conductor and explained that the little ringing noise I could hear was made by a machine which punched a hole in the tickets. She gave me the tickets to hold and I could feel the holes. She told me what we were passing and at last she said we had to get off the next time the bus stopped.

We climbed off and the noise of the bus engine faded as it drove away. Auntie said she could not see anything that looked like the Home so we would have to ask the way. She spoke Cantonese quite fluently, but with an American accent which upset the tones, so she sometimes hesitated to speak to complete strangers in case they did not understand her. She could not read Chinese characters at all. She stopped some people who were passing and whispered to me to ask them about the Home. They walked on without replying, so Auntie was surprised and said a woman was coming and we could try her. The woman giggled and instead of answering the question said to me, "You look well dressed. Why do you want to go to the Home? Tell your mother to look after you." Then she walked on, still laughing. Auntie was amazed at all this rudeness. I did not want to ask again so Auntie suggested we go to a store and buy a fruit juice and ask there.

We had our drinks and Auntie brought out the money to pay. As she gave it to the woman, she asked where the Home was. The woman turned towards me instead of answering Auntie and said, "Don't go there with your mother. That's what happened to a lot of the blind women there—their mothers took them and left them and never came back again." Auntie kept her temper and said we were only going there to see somebody, so at last the woman showed her which way to go. When we got there, the gate was not locked, so we went in. There were some blind women walking in the garden, but when we tried to speak to them, they ran away without replying. Auntie guessed they were not used to meeting strangers and were frightened of us. She said there was what looked like the main entrance and led me towards it. She rang the bell and as we stood waiting I could hear a piano playing and voices singing. I suddenly felt I wanted to learn to play the piano. The door opened and a woman's voice asked us to come in. She said she would take us to the office. We went into a room and the woman asked us to sit down and wait. She went away and after a few minutes the superintendent came in. Auntie whispered to me to stand up as she did so herself. Later I asked her why we did this and she explained about politeness and social etiquette.

The superintendent greeted Auntie, who introduced me. Then the superintendent shook my hand. This was the second time in three days that I had had my hand shaken. It gave me a feeling of warmth and friendliness and I felt less nervous.

The superintendent told us that the Home was founded in 1909 by a group of American missionary ladies who were concerned about the plight of blind beggar girls and prostitutes in the streets. Many of the present adult residents had arrived as children years ago, and as they had nowhere else, this became their permanent home. This severely limited the number of new applicants they could accept as the Home was unable to hold more than thirty residents. They were trying to raise funds in America to enlarge the place, but that would take time and new buildings could not be ready for several years.

Auntie asked what kind of training was available. The superintendent replied that residents were taught about washing, ironing and personal skills necessary for looking after themselves and their clothes; and there were classes in knitting, Cantonese braille* and piano playing. Cantonese braille and piano playing—the two things I wanted! But for once I remembered that I must not talk and ask questions in the presence of grown-ups, so I kept quiet. However, the next moment Auntie asked me to tell the superintendent how I began learning English braille. It was such a surprise that she should ask me to tell my story instead of telling it herself that for a moment I did not know how to start. Auntie encouraged me and said I could take my time. At first I was very nervous and stammered badly, but as the superintendent asked questions and talked directly to me, I began to feel better and finished by talking quite naturally and confidently. I felt quite grown-up all of a sudden, taking part in a conversation with two grown-ups who were interested to hear what I had to say. Then I asked if I could be taught Chinese braille. The superintendent did not reply for a moment and I waited anxiously.

She said they would love to do it but there were problems. For one thing, the Home was full up and for another, all the women were twenty or over and I was only eight. When Auntie suggested that perhaps I could go each day like a pupil at day school, the superintendent said she was afraid I would still be lonely and left out because I was so much younger than everybody else. I said that at home I was mostly with the amahs who were much older than I, but the superintendent still seemed uneasy. Auntie realised we were not going to be able to make any definite arrangement then, and suggested leaving it so that we could talk about it at home. She assured me that some arrangement would be made for me to learn Chinese braille. She said she noticed that I always referred to Chinese braille whereas the superintendent spoke of Cantonese braille and she asked what was the difference. The superintendent explained that there were two braille systems in Chinese—Mandarin

* The word "braille" is used here and subsequently for convenience. Chinese has no exact translation; both in Mandarin and Cantonese the system is called "raised dots." I first heard the word "braille" when I went to the Ming Sum School; see Chapter 15, pp. 138–40.

braille and Cantonese braille, both being phonetic systems based on the sounds of words and their tones but varying considerably in detail.

At Auntie's request the superintendent showed us round the Home. We met the staff and the residents. I wanted to talk to the blind ladies but they were very quiet and reserved and would not talk much. I was fascinated to examine the heavy books in braille in which each sheet was made up of several layers of paper. I asked the superintendent if that was because the dots would last longer. When she said yes, that was exactly the idea, I whispered to Auntie that it was what I did too, using several layers of newspaper. Auntie told me to tell the superintendent this, so I did and was both surprised and pleased when she praised me for being resourceful and said that if I got the chance of an education, I would probably do well.

While I was still looking at the braille I heard Auntie ask the superintendent whether there were any books giving advice to sighted people about dealing with blind people. The superintendent said that they had a pamphlet, but it was in English. Auntie said she spoke English, so the superintendent gave her one. We said goodbye and left the Home.

As we waited at the bus stop, Auntie looked at the pamphlet and saw that the recommended method of walking was for the blind person to hold the arm of the sighted person and walk about half a pace behind, so that she could feel when the sighted person began to go up or down a step and so on. She asked if I would like to try this. I did and realised immediately that it felt as easy as when I walked with Ah Wor.

That evening, when we had told Uncle about the day's adventures, Auntie said I must do my best to get my parents to let me learn Cantonese braille. She said she would like to help me but she thought it would be better all round for me to try to get what was wanted by my own effort and only ask her to help if I was desperate and felt I was getting nowhere. She gave me her telephone number and said she would be thinking of me and wishing me good luck. That was the last evening of the happiest few days I could remember.

The next day Auntie took me home on the bus. Although I had enjoyed myself so much, I was impatient to get home and start trying to persuade my parents.

CHAPTER 6 •••••••••••••••••••••••••••••••••••

ON MY FIRST evening at home I told my parents about the Mo Kwong Home and tried to convince them that I was serious about wanting to learn. They said I was too young and that I could wait a few more years. I argued, with a determination that I think surprised them as well as myself, that I would much rather the money Father was saving for me from the house rent should be used now and not saved for the future, if by using it I could begin to learn something. The amah's words—"one must work to live and money can lose its value"—were never far from my mind.

My parents thought at first that it was a passing fancy, but I was so persistent that at last they realised I meant it and began to listen to me seriously. They discussed various possible schemes, but these all involved using teachers who could see and who would therefore not know braille. This, as I pointed out, would not help me as I could not take down in braille anything told to me in Chinese unless I could learn Chinese braille. Father thought I would be able to memorise some of what I was taught, but it would obviously be a very unsatisfactory arrangement.

Father and Mother were afraid that by concentrating on braille I would only emphasise the difference between myself and the seeing world. They did not seem able to grasp that braille was the only possible way for me to learn. But at last I did succeed in demonstrating this by showing them that, by using braille, I had learned the same English words that my older brother and sister had been repeating aloud to themselves. Father and Mother knew no English but they asked my brother and sister to bring their books and check whether I had learned the words and spelling correctly. I had, and this impressed them.

They actually went to consult the teachers at a small school nearby and discussed the problem with their friends, but it all came to nothing as everyone agreed that it was unheard of for a seeing teacher to teach a blind child. Also, no one could really see the point of it, because who had ever heard of a blind person doing anything except singing or playing an instrument in the street? It was not as if I could ever work like other people and support myself when I grew up, they said.

However, they did eventually agree to arrange for me to learn Cantonese braille. This was done more to humour me and to keep me happily occupied than to help towards genuine education, but whatever their motives, they did contact the Mo Kwong Home and ask that one of the residents be allowed to come and live with us and teach me to read and write Cantonese by the blind method. They undertook to pay my teacher a salary and to make a regular contribution to the Home.

Once this was fixed I begged them to let me learn to play the piano as well. To my delight and amazement, Father not only agreed to this but bought me a piano, which duly arrived and was put in the living-room. All this was exciting and wonderful, not least the fact that Mother was evidently anxious to make my teacher welcome and comfortable and made my sisters and me turn out of our bedroom so that my teacher could have a room to herself. We girls went in with the boys and it was very crowded, but it all helped to convince me that my parents were really taking an interest in my affairs and this made me feel more secure.

When the day arrived for my teacher to come and Mother had gone to the Home, I waited breathlessly in the hall, my ear pressed to the front door, straining to catch the first sounds of them coming upstairs.

At last I heard voices, indistinct at first, then coming nearer. I heard Mother say there were more steps and then counting them aloud. There was a brief pause as they reached the landing and the bend halfway up; I knew they were almost at the door so I opened it and greeted my teacher as Mother introduced me to her. From the start Teacher called me by my home name and I always called her Teacher.

Ah Wor came from the kitchen and took my teacher's suitcase

from Mother. I insisted I would take Teacher to her room. I asked her to take my hand but when I moved she stood still. I sensed she was worrying about steps, so I assured her there were none and that I would guide her safely. She came with me slowly, saying nothing. I felt uncertain and anxious at her silence—perhaps she had taken a dislike to me. However I discovered later, as time passed and she gradually became more relaxed, that she was desperately nervous and scared at being in a private home as the only other one she had ever known was her own, of which she had terrible memories.

During the time she lived with us I pieced together her story—of parents who ill-treated her and considered killing her because she was blind, and who eventually abandoned her near the Mo Kwong Home in the small hours of the morning.

Her parents worked for a rice farmer, but she never knew the name of the village, let alone details of the street or the house number. Early one morning when she was seven years old and had been totally blind for two years, her father took her from home. They went by train to what she eventually found out was Canton. When they got off the train they walked for hours. At last her father said he would go and get her some rice. He said she must wait for him patiently and must not move or utter a sound, otherwise a policeman would come and take her to the lion and the lion would eat her. It was raining hard and bitterly cold. She was terribly frightened but dared not make a noise, so she just stood there in the pouring rain. Next morning a lady from the Mo Kwong Home found her. This lady asked a missionary to come and see her. They took her into the Home and gave her dry clothes and food and let her go to sleep. For the first week she was very ill but the missionaries took her to the doctor and looked after her until she was well.

They notified the police and attempts were made to contact her parents. Advertisements were put in the press and appeals made on the radio, but in vain. By the time she came to us she had been in the Home for over fifteen years. Her story was very typical and showed clearly why the residents were all adults, ranging in age from about twenty years to a few who were much older.

We got on well together, though she was always quiet and reserved. It was wonderful companionship for me to have someone
who shared the same handicap and understood the problems.

Ah Wor still took me with her in the evening after supper when
she went to the bakery to buy bread for breakfast. I loved going
for the walk but was worried about leaving Teacher by herself in
her room, so one evening while we were out I asked Ah Wor if she
thought she could manage to take both Teacher and me. I was
afraid she would feel that having two of us would be too awkward,
but I need not have worried—she said she would be glad to, adding that Teacher really ought to get out and have some fresh air
and exercise instead of just staying in her room. As soon as we
were home I told Teacher this and thought she would be very
pleased. But to my surprise she did not sound at all pleased and
said that she had no desire to go out. I asked why, but she did not
seem to want to talk about it. I was not going to be put off as easily as that. I not only wanted her to come but I wanted to know
why she would not, so I persisted and asked again and again until
finally she told me she was afraid of steps.

She said that from the time she became blind at the age of five
she never went out of the house at all until the day her father took
her on the train to Canton. He made her walk ahead of him and as
she could not see and he did nothing to help her, she constantly
fell up and down steps and over things on the ground, but her father continued to push her ahead.

I told her that when Ah Wor and I first went out together she
took my hand and I had had a few falls because I could not tell
what was ahead. Then, one day, Ah Wor was carrying a big package of clothes from the dry-cleaner and had no hand free, so I took
her arm instead. We walked along quite comfortably. When we arrived home Ah Wor remarked that although we had just been
along unfamiliar streets I had managed all the steps and corners
without any trouble. We tried again the next time we went out and
found that it really made a tremendous difference. We wanted to
see why this way of walking together was easier. We soon discovered the reason—being closer to her, I could follow the movements
of her body as she walked half a step ahead of me and did not

need to be told what was coming unless it was some unexpected obstacle. Then she had to warn me. We had discovered for ourselves, through trial and error, the internationally accepted method which Seventh Auntie told me was described in the English pamphlet given to her by the superintendent at the Mo Kwong Home.

Teacher listened to all this with interest and the next time Ah Wor and I asked her to join us in our evening walk she said she would like to come. The three of us set out, with Ah Wor in the middle and Teacher and me on each side of her. We strolled along quite easily, talking as we went and enjoying the cool, spring evening. Teacher had never been so cheerful and happy before, which made me glad.

As we were on our way home I whispered to Ah Wor that there were footsteps behind us, following us. Ah Wor looked back and whispered that it was just a group of four children and we need not worry. Teacher stopped talking. Suddenly Ah Wor said to the children in a loud voice, "Don't throw that stone at us! If you do we will report you to the police and they will punish you." The children were giggling and chanting, "One *mang mui*, two *mang mui*, one's not enough, you have to have two. One fell in the well, One fell in the sea, The silly old amah just cried 'help me.'" They were still following us and chanting. Then a man who must have been a relative of one of them came running up, slapped one boy and took him away, telling him angrily that he should not tease blind people as it might bring bad luck to him and his family. The rest of the children ran away.

Ah Wor said, "Teacher, don't look so sad. They are just ignorant people so we need not take any notice of them." Ah Wor's comment caught my attention. As I had never seen, I could only detect happiness, sadness and other emotions in people's voices. It was the first time I ever realised that their faces showed these things as well.

Teacher said she felt bad about the children sneering at Ah Wor and she would rather not go out for any more walks for fear of it happening again. I was feeling the same and said that as Ah Wor had taken me to the bread shop so many times, I knew the way well and Teacher and I could go by ourselves. Ah Wor said this would not be safe. The children might throw things at us and we would not be able to avoid getting hurt. Nor could we identify the culprits and she doubted whether we would get any help from sighted people, even if we called out. She thought that if the three of us went out together regularly, everyone would get used to seeing us and the children would lose interest and stop jeering at us. She finally overcame Teacher's objections and we continued our walks and, sure enough, after a couple of weeks the children stopped following us and making fun of us and we did not hear many silly comments from adults. Although we occasionally heard whispers and suspected that some people were staring at us curiously, this did not upset us any more.

I loved our lessons. I was fascinated by the initial and final symbols which indicate the tones of Cantonese and I was thrilled because Father and Mother began to take more interest in my work and would ask me what new things I had learned.

However, this interest did not last very long. The raised system was so different from the written characters they knew that they could not understand any of it. I suspect that they felt more acutely than ever that I lived in a different world from my brothers and sisters—a world in which they had no part. This was brought home to them one day when, as a little test, they dictated a few sentences to me. When I had pricked them out in dots they took the paper to Teacher, who was in another room. She of course read it at once. This made them realise that I had a means of communicating with other blind people which they could neither share nor understand. This made them feel "left out" and their interest faded.

Why they never made any attempt to learn even a little about the raised system I do not know. The fact remains that my blindness formed a total, insurmountable barrier between us—a barrier which they believed they could not overcome and therefore they never tried. But this need not be so. If only the parents of blind children would try to learn a little braille with them, it would help the children to feel accepted and less odd, less different.

Music provided us with some common ground. They would listen when I had learnt a new tune, but it was all at such a simple level that it did not create much in the way of an intellectual bond. Teacher could only teach me tunes by ear. She knew a little of the braille music code, but it is immensely complicated and as she only partly understood it herself she certainly could not teach it to me. So I contented myself with learning a few easy pieces and memorising them.

My teacher taught me for four or five months. At the end of that time she had taught me all she knew, so she went back to the Mo Kwong Home and I struggled on alone.

One evening I was sitting as usual with my brothers and sisters, listening to what I could catch of their lessons and doing my own work. I heard my younger brother reading a verse from the Bible, "For God so loved the world . . ." Did it really mean what it said? Who was this loving God? Would he love a blind girl? Almost everyone said it was better for the blind to die than to live. Did God regard blind people differently?

I asked them this. No one said anything. I had evidently asked something they could not answer. Second Sister broke the silence at last and said she was certain God loved me too because the Bible said God loved the world and I was one of the people in the world, so I must be included. To me, this reply was comforting. I then asked them to tell me more about this God, but they said they did not know enough, so I asked my younger brother if he could find out more from his teacher. The next evening he told me his teacher suggested we should go to church, so we did, just the two of us, the next Sunday. However, before we went to church we tried to think of a way of getting our parents' permission to go.

Our family, like most Chinese families, worshipped our ancestral tablets and my parents were anxious that when they were dead we would continue to do this, worshipping their tablets, offering them food, paper money and furniture and observing all the usual rites. For this reason they often said they strongly objected to Christianity.

But I wanted badly to go to church. What could we do? We put our heads together and finally I remembered hearing a hymn, "What a friend we have in Jesus." On Sunday morning I told my parents that Younger Brother and I were going to see a friend. Fortunately they did not ask us the name of this friend. In fact, I overheard them saying they were glad that Younger Brother would take the trouble to go out with me. In this way we went to church for three Sundays. On the fourth Sunday, as I listened to the sermon, I realised that by telling our parents we were going to visit our "friend" and deliberately refraining from telling them who this "friend" was, we were acting as if we were ashamed of Christ and this certainly would not please Him. We prayed and asked Christ to forgive us and asked Him to help us witness for Him.

We went home and told Father and Mother that the name of our friend was Jesus Christ. Upon hearing this they were very angry. Father said that if we wanted to believe in Jesus Christ, then he would leave it to Jesus Christ to give us our Sunday meal and he would not have to feed us. He did not carry out this threat. But he often said that if Jesus is God and God is all-powerful, why didn't he work a miracle to enable me to see and go to school and, later, earn my own living?

I knew the reason he said this was because he thought it was an impossibility. However, years later, when I started to work and to contribute to the family expenses, he often told our relatives and friends that he had come to believe in God, for without God's help I would never have been able to do it.

My younger brother and I went to church together, just the two of us, every Sunday. After a few months we both accepted the Christian faith and became members of the Southern Baptist Church. I shared my Christian faith with Ah Wor and she accepted it. We became prayer partners, though she did not become a church member until many years later, in Hong Kong. My Christian faith was one of the great milestones of my life and has been the guiding force in all I have done ever since.

I have had three of these milestones—three moments at which I suddenly knew not only that I could go on coping with my problems, but why. These events, each in turn, gave direction and purpose to my life. They were like releases of adrenalin, giving me fresh energy and an incentive to keep going. The first was the answer to my brother's ham radio appeal for me and the subsequent arrival of the braille material; the second was when I became a Christian; the third was my meeting with a blind beggar girl—a chance encounter which, beyond any question, determined the course of my life.

CHAPTER 7 ●●●●●●●●●●●●●●●●●●●●●●●●●●●●●●●●●

THIS IS HOW it happened.

One evening when Ah Wor and I went for our usual walk I heard a voice calling "*Mang mui, mang mui,* come and sing." All my resentment at the hated phrase flared up and I was surprised to hear a meek voice say, "Yes, coming."

The clack of wooden clogs and the tap-tap of a stick came nearer and then a girl's voice began to sing. She sang one song and asked for money, but the women (Ah Wor said they all looked like amahs) would not pay till she had sung some more. After three songs she asked again and they still would not pay. She began to cry, saying if she did not take thirty cents to her instructor she would be beaten, but the heartless amahs laughed at her and did not pay.

I was mystified, but one thing was clear—she desperately needed thirty cents. I had money at home but none with me, so I asked Ah Wor if she would lend me thirty cents to give the girl. Ah Wor said we had better give her forty cents if we were going to keep her talking, so she gave me the money and we went to where the girl was whimpering and pleading with the women.

"We have forty cents for you, so don't cry," I said.

She immediately stopped crying and said, "Thank you very much and may God in heaven bless you."

I asked her if she would stay for a little while and tell me about her instructor and why she was frightened of being beaten. She was on her guard at once and said, "People who can see never understand us."

"But I'm not a seeing girl. I'm a blind girl like you."

I sensed she did not believe me, so I told her quickly how I became blind. At last she decided to trust me and we moved away from the crowd.

She told us her story. She became blind from measles when she was six or seven—about six years before we met her. Her parents thought that keeping a blind girl would bring bad luck to the family so when they heard of a blind woman who made a living out of training and exploiting blind girls as singing beggars, they gladly got rid of her.

Every day she had to earn at least thirty cents before she dare return "home," as otherwise she would be beaten and made to stand and sing all night, without food, and be sent out again early next day.

I had my Chinese New Year "lucky money" at home so I asked the girl to come each evening so that we could talk and I would give her forty cents. She agreed to this but said she dared not stay longer now, so we said goodbye.

After that we met each evening and she told us about her life and her "slave mistress." When she spoke of this woman she used the Cantonese word *see-fu* which actually means "instructor," but in the context of blind people and their exploiters, the additional interpretation "slave master" or "slave mistress" is always taken for granted. The blind people were not only treated as slaves; for all practical purposes they *were* slaves.

I asked her why her instructor treated her so cruelly as she herself was blind and might have been expected to be more sympathetic. But the girl explained that as the woman had endured the same treatment herself as a girl, she was quite deliberately getting her own back by treating her girls in the same inhuman manner. It evidently gave her some satisfaction and I have since found out that she was typical of most slave mistresses.

I asked Tse Tse (which is the form of address anyone my age would use to an older girl) how many meals she had a day. She said she had only one, and that was when she returned in the evening. Ah Wor told me she looked terribly thin and ill. I asked Ah Wor if we could secretly bring her some hot rice from home. I said I could easily eat less to save some for her. Ah Wor said we could not do that as it would be a form of stealing, but she said there was a small food stall not far away and she could buy her something to eat and drink from there when we met each evening. For the first few evenings, when Ah Wor bought food for the girl, some of the amahs made sarcastic remarks about her virtuousness and others sneered at her and said she was a fool. They said she must have been a blind person in her past life as she did not seem to be ashamed of being seen with blind people in this life. Ah Wor just ignored them.

One evening I asked Tse Tse how she managed to find her way about by herself and if it was difficult for her. She told me that when she was first sent out into the street she was very frightened as she was never shown how to find her way and had no idea where to go. After wandering aimlessly for a few days she was beaten for not bringing any money back, and realised that if she was to survive at all she had to work out her own method of finding her way. She set about memorising all the landmarks she could and getting to know the details of the feel of walls in her locality. She learned to know where she was by particular landmarks, by the special smell of certain shops, by groups of steps and the shapes of corners and ledges. As she became better at it she realised that at the beginning she had quite often spent a whole day groping her way up and down the same street.

Everything was difficult. If she asked the way, she heard people moving away without answering her. Sometimes she would get caught up in a crowd of people and find herself having to cross a road and going where she did not want to go. At other times, people who meant well would push her to some strange place and she would have a hard time finding her way back again. People shouting and traffic noise often drowned the smaller sounds she depended on for knowing where she was; so did gusts of wind.

At ground level there were a thousand hazards, from hawkers' baskets to dog leads, from badly parked cars to roadmenders' holes; wire and brambles from hedges snatched at her clothes and overhanging tree branches, wet with rain, slapped her in the face. Fast-moving traffic and dawdling people were both difficult to avoid. Window shoppers forced her to leave the comparative security of contact with the wall.

One great problem was that people tried to move silently out of her way, so she never knew where they were. Of course she had her bamboo stick to help her and when she was forced to walk in the middle of the pavement she went slowly, tapping loudly with her stick, but it was no use. It seemed as if the people around her were seeing and hearing nothing; they bumped into her and allowed her to bump into them. Then they screamed and shouted and swore at her, saying they would have three years' bad luck because they were touched by the stick of a *mang mui*. Such encounters left her confused and disoriented, and standing trying to get her bearings again just made her the target for more insults and cursing. Many people obviously thought that because she was blind she was mentally defective as well.

One evening we waited at the usual place; we waited and waited but there was no sign of her. Then I heard the voice of a girl singing and playing the *erh-hu*. Ah Wor told me that this girl was blind too and she looked pale and thin, just like Tse Tse. I wanted to find out about her and I asked Ah Wor if we could talk to her, but she said no, because we had no money to give her if we delayed her in her begging. We only had the regular forty cents with us and if we gave it to this strange girl we would have nothing for Tse Tse if she came late. I realised Ah Wor was right. Then, all of a sudden I heard the familiar voice singing and pleading for money as she came in our direction, but it sounded to me as if she was crying at the same time. As she came up to us Ah Wor asked what had happened to her, and then explained quickly to me that she was barefoot and had bloodstains on her arms, her forehead and her ankle. Tearfully she told us what had happened that afternoon.

As she was walking slowly along, someone suddenly grabbed her arm and yelled "look out!" throwing her off balance so that she lurched forward and cracked her forehead against a lamppost and then fell to the ground. At first she did not realise that she had cut herself quite badly. She lay still for a few moments, till the first shock had worn off; then she felt blood running down her nose and realised that she was hurt. Also, as she fell her wooden clogs had come off. She sensed that there were people standing round staring at her but no one offered to help her up. With an effort and feeling sick and dizzy she managed slowly to get to her feet. She made herself ask if anyone would be so kind as to show her where she could find her clogs, but the onlookers just laughed and gave her no help whatsoever. She then tried to walk around the area, hoping she would find the clogs, but in vain. The only fortunate thing was that she did not lose her stick.

I tried to think of something to say to comfort her, as she was crying again, but could not find anything to say. Ah Wor then said that the man who grabbed her had probably meant well but it would have been much better to leave her alone, even if she appeared to be heading for a lamppost, because as she walked slowly, tapping ahead with her stick, she might bump into the lamppost but it would not be a violent collision. It was the shock of the unexpected interference that had caused the accident.

She then said Tse Tse needed a plaster for her forehead and a new pair of clogs. On second thought, she said it would be much better to get her a pair of shoes. Tse Tse did not know what "a pair of shoes" meant as she had never had anything but clogs. I let her examine my shoes with her hands. She thought they felt much more comfortable and less likely to slip off.

Ah Wor, realising we were going to need more money after all, told us to stay where we were while she ran home to fetch some. We were quite close to home, so it would not take her more than ten minutes. She found some steps for us to sit on and hurried away. She was back again very quickly, somewhat out of breath.

We went to several shops but they refused to let Tse Tse try on any shoes because her feet were dirty from walking barefoot. Finally a shopkeeper said that if her feet could be washed he would let her try on some shoes. Ah Wor took her to the washroom and helped her to clean up. After trying on several pairs she chose the most comfortable ones, and Ah Wor said they looked very nice on her. I shall never forget her delight and pleasure as she walked out of the shop in her new shoes. She told us that she knew people wore other things on their feet because she could hear the clicking noise, unlike the clonk of clogs, but she never knew what a difference they would make or how much easier it would be to cross the road in them as there was no danger of them coming off.

Then all of a sudden she came back to reality and wondered what she could tell her instructor about the new shoes. I said she did not have to tell her anything, but Ah Wor said the instructor would know at once by the different sound. We were all worried about what to do. We walked in silence, trying to think of an answer, and then we passed the bread shop and Ah Wor said she had an idea. She suggested to Tse Tse that if she took some fresh bread back with her and gave some to the woman, saying it had been given to her and that she would like to share it with her, then perhaps the instructor would not be too hard on her. This seemed like a good solution and we felt relieved.

While she was buying the bread, Ah Wor suddenly said, "Hello, Mrs. Choi." I remembered with dismay that Mrs. Choi was a friend of Mother's and was sure to tell Mother that she had seen Ah Wor and me with a strange blind girl. I felt equally sure that Mother would not be at all pleased. When Tse Tse had gone, carrying her bread, I told Ah Wor I was worried what Mother would say and she agreed that almost certainly Mother would regard it as a disgrace for me to be seen in the company of a street-singing beggar. She thought I would probably be severely scolded and made to promise never to see Tse Tse again. She did not think Mother would beat me, but I said I would rather be beaten than not be able to meet my friend any more.

Then I realised with horror that Ah Wor would certainly get into trouble too, for allowing me to meet Tse Tse. I asked her what she thought Mother would do to her, and she said she would probably get a bad scolding and might even be fired. This was a terrifying thought. I wept with fear and anxiety at the thought of being separated from Ah Wor and was afraid, in addition, that she would blame me for getting her into trouble. Instead she comforted me and told me to try not to worry as things might not be as bad as I thought.

That night I was so worried that I could not sleep. And the next day, every time I heard the doorbell I thought it must be Mrs. Choi. She did come finally, in the late afternoon, and as soon as I heard her voice I ran to the kitchen and closed the door as I dared not listen to what she and Mother were saying. After what seemed like an age, but was actually only about half an hour, she went. I heard the front door bang shut and Mother's steps coming to the kitchen. Tears were streaming down my face as I opened the kitchen door and walked towards her. "Why are you crying?" she asked, but amazingly her voice was not angry. "I was coming to give you some money to give to your street friend. But if you are crying, I'm not going to give it to you."

I just could not believe my ears. I tried to stop crying but did not know what to say. Mother then asked Ah Wor to tell her about this blind friend. As Ah Wor was telling the story her voice sounded a bit shaky. I think she too could hardly believe what was happening.

By the time she had finished I had calmed down enough to speak and said to Mother that I would like to give the money to my friend. I also asked if we could take her some cooked rice every night. Mother gave us permission but told Ah Wor to mark a bowl for Tse Tse and keep it separate so that it did not get washed up with the family rice bowls, as many girls like Tse Tse were ill. For the same reason she said we should not stand too close to her. Such unexpected understanding from Mother was more than I had ever dreamed of or hoped for.

One evening when all the rest of the family had gone to Third Uncle's birthday feast we took Tse Tse into the flat and gave her a good meal. She and I thoroughly enjoyed ourselves, but poor Ah Wor was in a terrible state of nerves in case we were caught. We felt sure that, despite her unexpected sympathy, Mother would probably feel that bringing a beggar girl into the flat was going too far. Father would certainly not stand for it; he would consider that doing such a thing as having a beggar girl sitting at table, even in the kitchen, would be a shame and a disgrace. But all was well— we were not found out. The other amahs did not join in; they stayed disapprovingly in their rooms and Ah Kwun said Ah Wor should not disgrace the family name.

Tse Tse talked of the visual memories she had of the time before she lost her sight. She said she could remember the faces of her parents and her brothers and sisters and she spoke of sunsets and rainbows and of how, sometimes, a sound or a smell would reawaken a dormant impression so that a whole scene would be re-created in her mind's eye. To me, with no visual experience, this was all strange and I wanted to know more.

Suddenly I realised she had never told me her name, so I asked her. Sadly, she replied that she did not have a name any more, because everyone, including her parents, called her *mang mui* after she became blind. I then asked her what her name was when she could still see. She said her home name had been Ah-mei, meaning "beautiful" and her official name was Po-yuk, but her parents said that she could not be called by either of these names once she was blind. (Ah Wor later confirmed that she certainly was not beautiful as she had no eyeballs and her eye sockets were sunken and hollow.) Her official name would not do either because Po-yuk means "precious jade" and she, being blind, was just a common human being of no value.

As this question about her name had cast a shadow over our previously cheerful conversation, I changed the subject and told her the story about my ham radio brother and how I received the parcel from America which started me learning English braille, and how my teacher had taught me Cantonese braille. She brightened up then and I showed her my raised dots and the slate and stylus. I offered to teach her and she said she would love to learn, but then she realised that it was time for her to go back to her slave mistress.

Before we parted she said, "Try to learn as much as you can so that perhaps later you can teach all of us blind people to read with our hands and then we needn't be blind slaves in the street and be called *mang mui*." I promised her I would try.

We met for twenty happy evenings. On the twenty-first evening we waited for her but she did not come. For about ten days we waited and hoped; we walked all over the district and asked people if they had seen her, but it was no good. We never saw her again. We never knew what had happened to her. But those twenty days had a profound and lasting effect on my life.

In my despair when she had gone I prayed to God to tell me what to do. I believe He guided me to remember what she said about teaching blind people and I made a solemn promise to Him

that I would give my life to helping and teaching blind people if
He would help me to learn enough to do it. I found myself filled
with a great determination to learn, and in one of those strange
moments of inner certainty I knew that with God's help I would
succeed.

CHAPTER 8 ●●●●●●●●●●●●●●●●●●●●●●●●●●●●●●●●●●●●●

IT WAS SUMMER, 1946. Term ended and my brothers and sisters all came home from school. They were happy and relaxed. The final exams of the year were over and they would not have to worry about school work for a good two months. I asked them about the questions in their exam papers and found that I could answer most of them.

At the supper table Father and Mother discussed how the family would spend the summer vacation. Hiking, picnics and similar activities were mentioned and then Father, who had evidently been waiting to get the best effect with his announcement, said they might all fly to Hong Kong to spend the entire summer there. There was tremendous excitement and the young ones could hardly stay in their chairs. The possibility of flying in an aeroplane and swimming on the Hong Kong beaches sounded exactly what I would love to do. However, it was of no use for me to make the slightest suggestion that I wanted to join this exciting family trip, for I knew well by this time that they would not take me. From the conversation I gathered that there would be eight of them going— Father, Mother, my five brothers and sisters and the amah Ah Luk, who had been with us for about eight years and looked after my younger sisters.

Soon after supper I ran to the kitchen where Ah Wor and the other amahs were having their meal. They had their food after we had ours and much of it consisted of what came back from the dining table. Sometimes I wondered what the food was like by that time; it must have been quite cold. Nevertheless, this was what happened in most households. And even if the food was a bit cold and congealed, I think they enjoyed their mealtimes in the privacy of the kitchen, as this was the time when they could have a good gossip about everything and everybody. I loved to join them and they seemed to accept me as one of them and went on talking in front of me without reserve.

This time when I went in they were saying how badly they felt about the fact that I probably would not get the chance to go to Hong Kong. Ah Luk said that as they were going to take an amah with them, why didn't they take Ah Wor instead of herself, then I could go and Ah Wor could take care of all of us. In fact, Ah Luk actually went to the living-room and suggested this to my parents, although Ah Wor warned her that it would not work. I listened to this with surprise, for I thought Ah Luk only cared about my fifth sister, who was her special charge, and now I realised for the first time that she cared enough about me to risk her job.

To divert for a moment to Ah Luk's own story, only a few months before this time she had gone through a period of great sadness. She had come to work in the family in 1938, just before we all went to Hong Kong during the Japanese occupation of Canton. My parents had agreed that she might bring her adopted daughter, then about six years old, with her.

Ah Luk's husband had died when they had been married only a short time and her mother-in-law had insisted that she adopt a girl —her motive undoubtedly being to provide herself with someone to look after her in her later years. Until this moment in 1938 Ah Luk genuinely did not know that the child was mentally retarded, as she had been looked after by the grandmother, Ah Luk's mother-in-law, since she was a few months old. The grandmother never told her daughter-in-law about the child's mental state because she was afraid Ah Luk would stop sending money for her support. Suddenly, however, the grandmother had what sounded like a stroke and died. Ah Luk was sent for to collect the child and made the appalling discovery that her daughter's ability was severely limited and she could only repeat, parrot-fashion, a few words over and over again. At first sight, however, she appeared quite normal.

This daughter, Ah Fuk, stayed in our house until we all fled from the Japanese and went to Hong Kong. When Hong Kong itself later fell to the Japanese my parents realised that they would have problems in feeding their own family and Ah Fuk was one too many. They suggested to Ah Luk that she might get a relative to look after the girl, but none of them would, not even for money. So, with no other alternative, Ah Luk, hearing that a couple was looking for a girl of Ah Fuk's age to bring up as their daughter-in-law, seized this opportunity and somehow managed to obtain payment—ten dollars then, worth about fifty dollars now—from them before they discovered the girl's limitations.

Ah Luk really loved Ah Fuk despite her mental disability and parting with her, especially in such distressing circumstances, was a great grief to her. She was terribly worried about what would happen to Ah Fuk and her fears proved to be well-founded. All contact was lost with the other family and when we returned to Canton in 1945, Ah Luk made all possible enquiries. She even placed advertisements in the Hong Kong newspapers, but with no result. To this day she does not know what happened to her poor daughter.

On that evening in Canton in 1946, when Ah Luk had so bravely queried my parents' plans about the holiday in Hong Kong, my parents, not surprisingly, were irritated and warned Ah Luk not to put ideas into my head. They obviously believed that it would never have occurred to me to want to go on a holiday unless someone gave me the idea. They said that if Ah Wor went along, saddled with me to look after, she would not be able to do as much work as Ah Luk would do because she would have to show me every new place whenever they went sightseeing. They added that as I was unable to see I would not get much out of such a trip.

I wanted so much to tell them that although I could not see I could enjoy myself by listening to people's descriptions, by touching things when I could. I had heard people talk about walking on smooth sand or on rocky paths, smelling new and different smells, hearing the sound of waves on the beach, and I wanted to try all these things. I had heard stories on the radio with seashore sound effects and I longed to be there and hear the real thing. Several times I went to the living-room but in the presence of the family I

could not get a word out; I was afraid I would displease them, as
Ah Luk had already failed. Also I knew only too well that they
would have no time to spare to take me round and show me things.

The day came when they all left for Hong Kong. I stood in the
hall saying goodbye and wishing them all a good time and trying
not to cry. For the first few days I felt lonely and very sorry for
myself. However, Ah Wor, Ah Yung and I were free to do what we
liked and new interests soon occupied my mind. Most days I listened early in the morning to a radio programme of simple conversational English and tried frantically to keep up as I put it all into
dots. Then we had breakfast and Ah Wor did whatever housework
was necessary. After that we were free to go out.

We went for walks, exploring parts of the city we had never
been to before. We walked through the parks, on grass, under trees
that rustled overhead in the wind, but the thing we came to love
most was to go, especially in the evenings, to the bridge over the
Pearl River and listen to all the noises. Ah Wor told me it was an
iron bridge and that when big ships came up the river two sections
of the bridge lifted up, like arms in the air, to let them through. It
was not very far from our flat and it was a place that stimulated
my imagination. I had heard a few programmes on the radio about
other countries, and by listening to the ships on the river I felt a
sort of contact with the world beyond China. Sirens hooted; ropes
creaked; big engines thumped; little ones chugged; oars splashed;
things bumped and scraped against each other and against the
quaysides; people shouted and swore. One day we were all to sail
down the Pearl River but I did not know that in 1946.

We had to shop for food so Ah Wor would deliberately take me
to shops further away than our usual local ones. One morning, on
one of these outings, we found a cool place under some trees and I
suddenly realised that I could hear the unmistakable sound of children study-chanting. It is customary in Chinese schools for children
to chant phrases and sentences and spelling in chorus after the
teacher. It was a summer morning school. I was so fascinated that I
asked Ah Wor to take me as near as possible to the window of the
classroom so that I could sit down and listen to the lessons. I was

able to hear the teacher's explanations and the responses of the children.

"Now, we are going to have a test, so put your books away and tidy up your desks," the teacher said. How wonderful that they all had desks of their own—secretly I admired and envied them. I strained my ears to hear the test questions but all I could hear was a curious, regular, scratchy-squeaky noise, then the teacher's voice saying, "Can you read what is on the blackboard? If anyone can't, please raise your hand." I did not hear anything more but I remembered Mother had said I would not be able to see the blackboard when I asked her a long time ago why I could not go to school. Now I realised she was right and I still did not know what a blackboard was, or that the funny noise I had heard was chalk writing on it. I longed to feel the blackboard and find out how people wrote on it—and feel the desks too, and see what the children sat on. Did they sit on the floor, like me?

I listened to this for two mornings; then I decided to bring along some sheets of newspaper and my dot-making things so that I could take down as much as I could hear. Ah Wor found me a small, flat piece of wood to use as a portable table. She saw me settled on the ground under the window before going to a nearby market to do her shopping.

As I was working like this one day I noticed there was someone standing a little distance from me. I knew this because I could sense a shadow falling on me and also the person was altering the current of air blowing on me. I could tell that the person was looking at me for a long time. The next day several people were standing watching me—whether women or men or how many I could not tell.

The following day was Sunday, so there was no class for me to listen to. I told Ah Wor I wanted to go to church. I knew my way very well—just a few turns on the same side of the street without having to cross to the other side. I insisted that I would like to go there by myself. She said she would not be worried about me if I could use a stick to feel my way, but as a stick would only be used by street-singing blind beggars I certainly could not do that. Then

I had an idea. "Could I use your umbrella?" I asked. I explained that I could use an umbrella to feel my way just as poor Tse Tse did with her stick.

Ah Wor insisted on following behind me just this one time and if she saw that I could manage all right then she would stop worrying and would let me come home by myself after church. We set out together and with the aid of the umbrella I found I could move quite easily and felt happy and proud. Seeing that I found my way without difficulty, Ah Wor watched me go into the church and then went back home.

I walked confidently in, feeling my way with the umbrella. The tip of it struck the end of a pew so I turned in without thinking that someone might already be sitting there. To my dismay I sat half on someone's lap. I said, "Oh, I'm very sorry—I can't see." But all I could hear was the noise of several people moving hurriedly away leaving me alone in the pew. I felt afraid, left there all by myself, so I crept out into the aisle again, and then someone took my hand and said kindly, "Here's a seat. Would you like to sit by me?"

I sat down with relief. I was too young to realise then the irony that even in church most people had no charity in their hearts for a blind person. After church, when I stood up and moved out into the aisle, I was nearly knocked off my feet by the people streaming out. The lady who had befriended me said, "It's very crowded. Can I help you?" I said it would be all right if she would just help me to the door. When we got there she said there were still a lot of people and suggested we sit down on a bench in the church porch for a few minutes.

Suddenly, she asked me what I was doing every morning outside the classroom window when I looked as if I was punching holes. Then I knew she must be one of the people who had stood watching me. I explained to her exactly what I was doing and she sounded very thoughtful. She told me she was a teacher of religious education at the Pooi To Chinese Middle School, teaching Primary 5 and 6. I was aware of a small voice inside saying urgently, "Go on, speak up—here's your chance!" I summoned up all my courage and told this teacher the entire story of how I had learnt the touch system of reading and writing in English and Cantonese and how I no longer had a teacher because she had taught me all she knew. I begged and pleaded for the opportunity to study with other children. She said she could understand how anxious I was to learn, but that certainly in China, and probably in the whole of Asia, she had never heard of an ordinary school that could cope with a blind student. Even if the teachers would give me a trial period, they would not know how to teach me. None of them knew the raised system and I could not read print. I pleaded to be given a desk and a seat in the classroom so that I could listen to the teachers and take down as much as I could in dots. In this way, although I could not study with my eyes, I could study with my ears and hands.

The teacher was most sympathetic and promised she would do all she could to help me. She said the whole situation was so unusual that she would have to talk with other teachers to see what could be done.

The days passed slowly. Every day I was hoping against hope that the teacher would have some news for me. On the tenth day I felt I could not contain myself any longer. That morning after I had listened for a time at the classroom window and the time for break came, I asked Ah Wor to take me to the school to look for the teacher. We went round the building and in at the gate to the playground.

There were children everywhere, shouting, running, laughing, pushing. We stood back against the wall hoping we wouldn't get knocked down. We tried to ask where we could find the teacher who was teaching religious education, but we could not make ourselves heard. At last we attracted the attention of two or three who stopped and asked what we wanted. I asked again where the Bible teacher was. No one said anything for a moment and I sensed they were looking at me curiously.

Then one of them said, "Are you blind?"

"Yes," I answered.

"Why do you want to see our teacher? Surely you don't think you can come to school like us, do you?"

"I hope I can," I replied.

By this time I could hear that one or two more students had joined the group and heard the conversation. An older boy said, "You said you can't see but you want to study like us. You can't be serious. How can you study like us?"

I was getting anxious and nervous and I could feel from the tenseness of her arm that Ah Wor was too. I started to ask again, "Please tell us where we can find . . ." but before I could finish the question the bell rang. The children ran off giggling and one or two of them chanted *"Mang mui, mang mui,* come and sing . . ."

Within seconds they had all gone: the playground was deserted. I stood there feeling angry, bewildered and at a loss. But I had no time to dwell on this—all I wanted was to see the teacher. At that moment, just for once, even *mang mui* seemed less important. But it upset Ah Wor.

"Perhaps it is not the best thing for you to go to school with children who can see. They are too young to understand and be kind," she said.

"I don't want to think about this now. If the teacher could get me in to study here and if I don't argue with the other children, they may not be too bad to me. But everybody's gone. Where can we find someone to ask? Is there anywhere we can go to find out where the teacher is?" I asked.

"Perhaps we could go inside and try, and hope for the best," Ah Wor suggested.

As we went inside the school I felt even more nervous. I was dreading meeting some more children and being called *mang mui* again. But I didn't tell Ah Wor this as I knew it would upset her. I had got this far and I did not mean to give up now. As we walked along, Ah Wor said the doors of all the rooms were closed. We could hear study-chanting in some of the rooms; others were very quiet and I thought they must be doing paperwork or a test. We decided to walk along until we found a room with its door open or met someone we could ask.

Finally Ah Wor saw an adult woman ahead of us. We caught her up and asked her to help us. She mumbled something we could not make out and then just walked away. We asked several people but they either ignored us or mumbled something and fled from us. Ah Wor said they all stared at us.

We almost felt like giving up and going home, but I was determined not to be beaten. We found a staircase and went up to the next floor. Ah Wor saw a woman coming in our direction: we walked towards her and repeated our enquiry. To our great relief she was pleasant and helpful. She took my hand and let me walk with her. She said she would take me to the Bible teacher and Ah Wor could come with us. We went up another flight of stairs, round several corners and finally reached a big room. She put my hands on the back of a chair and let me sit myself, and she told Ah Wor to sit down too. She told me she had seen me pricking dots outside the classroom window, and now she would go and find Teacher Mak for me. I was glad to know the Bible teacher's name. We thanked her for her kindness.

"It's no trouble. Anyone would do this for you."

She left the room, unaware of the irony of her words. We sat in silence, I thanking God for having sent her to our rescue.

Within a few minutes footsteps approached, the door opened and the familiar voice of the Bible teacher greeted me.

"Well, here you are. I'm glad to see you," she said as she sat down by me. I asked eagerly whether she had any news for me about coming to the school.

Her tiny but perceptible hesitation was enough to tell me that there was no good news. I repeated the question, and I could tell from her voice as she started to reply that what she had to say was not easy.

She told me that she had talked with the other teachers and with the school principal. They had contacted other schools and also the Education Department, and the general opinion was that as there was no precedent for a blind child attending school, no one believed it could be made to work. She said she sympathised with me, but it was impossible to help me in my situation.

I was desperate. I pleaded and begged. I said I had heard a radio programme about someone called Helen Keller who was unable to see, hear or speak and *she* had managed to go to school and finally learnt to speak too.

Teacher Mak seemed to be impressed by my passionate desire to study. She promised me that she would talk with the school authority again and see if they would at least give me a seat in the classroom, and said she would let me know as soon as they had reached a decision.

That day I went home with a feeling of foreboding.

I wanted to study like the others—not just to be listening in the classroom and taking no part. I talked this over with Ah Wor. She said it would still be better for me to have a desk and a seat inside the classroom than to be sitting on the ground outside the window. Perhaps if I was able to answer the questions in class, the teachers would let me join in with the other children more. I agreed. But I prayed every day, telling God that if He could make this happen, which everyone said was impossible, I would faithfully keep my promises to Him and to Tse Tse.

My anxiety never left me; it was always at the back of my mind. But suddenly the excitement of a new adventure gave me something new to think about. Ah Wor's sister Ah Ping came and suggested taking the three of us, Ah Wor, Ah Yung and me, to the Cantonese opera. At first I did not much want to go because Father and Mother had always said that as I could not see, I would not be able to get anything out of it. But Ah Wor said that even if I could not see what was happening on the stage, I would still be able to follow it by listening to the dialogue and the singing. This was something I had not thought of before. It was worth trying. Also, Ah Wor said that if I was bored, we could leave the theatre at any time. So it was decided—we went to the opera that afternoon.

At the opera house the beating of drums and gongs was exciting but made me feel nervous at first. People around us were talking, eating, laughing and moving about and someone in the row in front of us was even snoring. All these noises made it very difficult for me to follow the story. However, people quietened down after a while and I began to pick up the story and follow the voices of the actors and actresses. Ah Wor and Ah Ping described the costumes, the scenery and the action and I was thrilled with it all; I almost felt I could see it. Though I have never had visual experience of colours I love to be told about them. I began to realise that the speed of the drum beats and gongs, which make me jump at first, could tell me what was happening on the stage—for instance, that someone was deep in thought or an important person was coming onto the stage or there was a boat or a horse or a battle. My companions were surprised that the dialogue and singing told me so much about the story that I was able to tell them some of the details of the action. The reason for this was that I had listened so often to my brother and sister doing their school work that I had picked up some of the literary terms used in the stage dialogue but not used in everyday Cantonese and therefore unfamiliar to my illiterate companions. Also, being unable to see, I probably concentrated more on the words of the songs and the conversation. Later, when my parents came home and I told them about this visit to the opera, they accepted with some astonishment that it gave me real pleasure and after that they sometimes took me with them when there was something they wanted to see.

When we came out of the opera that evening it was almost supper time. Ah Wor asked whether I would like to eat out for a change. I was all for this. Ah Ping suggested a teahouse where she had been before and said we could get there by rickshaw. They decided we would need three rickshaws, one for Ah Ping, one for Ah Yung and one for Ah Wor and me. I had often heard people calling for rickshaws but I had no idea what they were like. Remembering the frightening experience of getting into a lift for the first time, I asked Ah Wor to tell me about rickshaws. She told me it was like a big chair with two shafts sticking out in front. The rickshaw-puller, or coolie, would stand between the shafts holding one in each hand, like a horse between the shafts of a cart. He would then run and pull the rickshaw behind him. When he stopped he would lower the shafts to the ground so that the passenger could step out. This sounded fun.

Soon we found three rickshaw-pullers with their rickshaws. Ah Ping and Ah Wor tried to bargain with them. As I listened to them arguing and heard the rickshaw-pullers say how high their living expenses were, I felt we should give them what they asked for, so I whispered to Ah Wor not to try to beat them down. Ah Wor whispered back that they usually asked for more, as here it was the custom to bargain and they never expected to get what they first asked for. I insisted that if we were not going to pay the full amount, I would rather not use them. One of the men heard this and said to his fellows, "This *mang mui* is indeed kind-hearted." As I felt my hackles beginning to rise, another coolie said, "Don't refer to this young mistress as a *mang mui*. You heard how she defended us. Such a good-hearted person must be protected by heaven and would never be suffering as a slave." Ah Wor said, "That's right— she's our Miss Three." Now the coolie who called me *mang mui* came up to me and said, "Miss Three, I'm sorry for what I said. I'll never use that phrase again. Now I will take you wherever you want to go without pay."

His voice sounded so honest—I wanted to say something in appreciation but could not find the right words. Then I heard Ah Wor say the nicest thing: "We will pay you according to your price." When we got to our destination Ah Wor offered the coolies the full amount. They did not want to take it and tried to give her back the difference between the amount and the amount she had offered when they began bargaining, but Ah Wor insisted they take the full amount as she knew I wanted them to have it. In the end they accepted it and we all parted friends.

As we walked towards the teahouse, I could tell it was a very busy street by the number of people pushing all round. The teahouse was crowded too and I could smell all kinds of good food —things Ah Wor made for us at home sometimes. We found some seats and as none of us could read the menu, Ah Wor said we would wait a minute or two and look round to see what other people had ordered. The others told me what they could see people eating. We made up our minds and gave our orders and the waiter brought a pot of tea and teacups. As we were drinking our tea, two men came and sat at the same table. It is customary in Chinese restaurants not to have to ask permission to share a table with people already sitting there, as long as there are some empty seats. The two men talked loudly and one of them was coughing almost continuously. Ah Wor told me to hold my cup close to me instead of leaving it on the table; she whispered to me that they were all holding their cups like that as the man was opening his mouth very wide and coughing right at us across the table. Soon the other man sneezed and I could feel raindrops landing on my head. Ah Wor told us all to take our cups and chopsticks to another table.

I asked Ah Wor if this was where my parents usually took my brother and sister for meals. She said no, they would never come to a place like this; they would go to a more stylish restaurant. I thought of the restaurant where I had had my English afternoon tea; Ah Wor explained that that was a Western-style place and would normally be used by more sophisticated and well-dressed people. The waitresses would wear uniforms and the menus would be in both Chinese and English. The restaurant where my parents took my brother and sister was different again, Ah Wor added— more polished than the one we were in that day, but all Chinese.

Then she said something that made me realise for the first time that clothes had a social aspect. The reason she could not take me to a good restaurant, she said, was not only the expense but the fact that she was wearing amah's clothes which would not be acceptable in such a place.

This immediately made me curious about amah's clothes and I wanted to feel Ah Wor's dress all over and examine the collar and the buttons and the material and be told about the colour and the pattern and everything. Ah Wor laughed and said she was sorry she had never thought to tell me all this before. She said she would make herself some smarter clothes so that she could take me to a better restaurant. That gave me something to look forward to. I said I had loved our meal at the teahouse—which was true. We had had a marvellous day and I went home tired and happy, my head full of the opera.

CHAPTER 9 ●●●●●●●●●●●●●●●●●●●●●●●●●●●●●●●●●●●

DAYS PASSED AND I became more and more anxious because I had heard nothing from Teacher Mak. Then one afternoon I heard the bell ring. Ah Yung went to the door and opened the little window to see who it was.

I heard her say, "There's no one with that name here."

"But she does not see, and she came to our school with her amah long ago."

I recognised Teacher Mak's voice and ran into the hall calling out to her at the same time. At this Ah Yung immediately opened the door and I took Teacher Mak's hand and led her into the living-room. My feelings were a confused mixture of joy and anxiety, wondering what kind of news she had brought me. I hardly dared ask.

Ah Yung brought a cup of tea to Teacher Mak, just as she would do when Father and Mother had guests. I felt very grown-up. I had a guest visiting me, the first time such a thing had ever happened.

To my delight Teacher Mak said she had good news for me. She said the teachers were impressed by the fact that I obviously had a quite unusual desire to learn and they were sympathetic. Although they were doubtful if it would work, they were willing to give me a trial period of three months. They thought that to begin with, anyway, I should work at my own pace and need not try to keep up with things that were too difficult for me. She went on talking about plans but I was not listening—I was imagining myself sitting in the classroom with the seeing children, with a desk and chair of my own. One bit of my dream had come true. Silently, I thanked God.

Teacher Mak finished her tea and said she must go as she had work to do at school. We both stood up and she took my hand. We walked into the hall where she stood for a moment and I realised she was looking round. She asked where my bedroom was, and agreed to come and see it. We went past two doorways and in at the third which was my room. She turned to me and said with obvious relief that I seemed to be able to find my way about all right. She explained that she and the other teachers were worried that I would get lost and not know where to go, but I assured her I could learn my way around places quickly. Then we went back to the front door and she held my hand for a moment as we said goodbye.

I shut the door after her and rushed to the kitchen to tell Ah Wor and Ah Yung this unbelievable, marvellous news. Ah Wor, of course, was very happy for me. She insisted we go straight out to the shops to get something special for supper as a celebration. However, Ah Yung was unusually quiet and I could sense she was upset over something, so I asked her what was wrong. She said in a very small voice that she was sorry for not letting my teacher friend in immediately but she had not recognised the name Teacher Mak used for me. Teacher Mak had asked for me by my Chinese name, Man-fai. Poor Ah Yung—she had never heard my full name: she only heard me called Miss Three, Little Girl or Third Sister. Once I entered the school I was called Man-fai, but up to that point no one ever used it so Ah Yung could not be expected to know it.

On our way to the market Ah Wor suddenly cut in on my excited chatter, saying, "You must let your father and mother know as soon as you can because they will have to give you money to pay your school fees." This brought me down to earth with a rush. Suppose they did not agree to my going to school. . . . Suppose they refused to pay my fees. And how could I let them know, for even if I wrote a letter to them in Hong Kong, they would be unable to read my dots. I was in despair. Ah Wor suggested that I could ask a street letter-writer to write a letter for me, just as she did when she wrote to her sister. This sounded like a way out of the problem, but I said I would not like just to tell the letter-writer what I wanted to say and have him put it in his words—I would want to write the

letter out in dots and then read it to the letter-writer to write down
for me, word for word. I was no longer interested in getting something special for supper; the treat could wait. All I wanted was to
go home right away and write my letter.

An hour later we set out again, I with my precious letter
clutched in my hands. Ah Wor wanted to find a particular letter-
writer who had done letters for her. When we found him there was
a group of amahs already waiting so we had to wait our turn. An
amah who knew Ah Wor asked if she was writing another letter to
her folks in the village, because she had had one written only a
couple of days ago. Ah Wor said no, it was her Miss Three who
was going to have a letter written.

"You mean this little blind child wants the letter-writer to write a
letter for her?" the amah asked in surprise.

"Yes, I want to write a letter to my parents."

"What are you going to say to your parents then?" The amah was
even more surprised.

"I want to ask them to pay for my school fees."

"Is there a school here that a blind child like you can go to?"

I did not answer her question as I wanted to re-read my raised-
dots draft yet again and make sure that I was saying everything I
needed to say. As I was reading, I realised that the group of amahs
had pushed closely round me. They were saying it was useless for a
blind person to know these raised dots when no one else could read
them or understand them and I could not even write to my parents.
One amah suggested that they let me go ahead of them, out of my
turn, so that they could watch me with the letter-writer and see
how I used my raised-dots paper. I was too intent on getting my
letter written to be bothered by what the women were saying.
They pushed Ah Wor and me up to the front of the line. Slowly I
dictated my letter, phrase by phrase, sentence by sentence. Occasionally the letter-writer suggested to me the substitution of other
words and I agreed because they sounded better to me. The amahs
watched this performance with amazement—I could hear them
muttering and exclaiming among themselves. At the end the letter-
writer said that in all his years in this business my letter was the
easiest he had ever had to write because it was all worked out for

him and he did not have to listen to a maze of confusing thoughts
and facts and then try to sort them out into sentences. I heard the
amahs saying that perhaps my dots were not so useless after all,
which did me a world of good. We went home feeling much more
cheerful.

The next day was Sunday. I wanted to go to church, so I asked
Ah Wor if I could borrow her umbrella again. To my delight she
said she would go with me, as she only had to cook dinner for the
three of us and she could do that when we got back. It was good to
have her with me for, although I knew my way, I did not want to
sit on someone's lap, as had happened last time, or hear people
shuffling away from me.

We got there early and I could hear quiet meditative music. Ah
Wor whispered that someone was playing the piano. I listened to it
with growing pleasure and wished, as I had wished ever since
Teacher left, that I could go on learning to play. I loved music.
Then Ah Wor whispered again that Teacher Mak was coming towards us. Before she finished saying it Teacher Mak spoke and
asked if she could sit with us. She sat beside me.

That morning it seemed as if the sermon was aimed at me personally. The subject of the sermon was the parable of the talents
from St. Matthew's gospel. I sat listening to the story—so familiar
to me now, but that day I was hearing it for the first time. I heard
the preacher telling how the master came back and took away the
one talent from the third servant and gave it to the one who already had ten talents. All of a sudden I felt as if something opened
in my mind and I understood. I felt that if I could think of the seeing people round me as the people who were given five talents,
then I, who could not see, would be the servant who was given the
two talents. God did not expect the two-talents servant to do as
much as the five-talents servant did, so even if I could not do as
much as people round me who could see, but could make the best
use possible of my hands, my ears and my brain, how wonderful it
would be if one day, seeing God face to face, I might hear Him
say, "Well done, good and faithful servant." At that moment a clear
distinct voice inside me said, "I am proud of you, child." It seemed
to me that this voice was the voice of Jesus—the same inner voice

that had prompted me to speak up when I first talked to Teacher
Mak and started the course of events which had led to the golden
opportunity for me to go to school. Then I remembered the day in
the school playground and the taunting voices—"*Mang mui,* come
and sing." I tried not to think about this. I knew I would have
problems, but I prayed silently that God might help the other children to be kind and not call me *mang mui.*

When the service was over and we were walking out, Teacher
Mak asked if I could stay behind for a few minutes because she
had something to tell me. I was afraid she was going to say that
the teachers had changed their minds about accepting me. However, to my relief she said she had been thinking that it would be
better for me to go to Junior I (which is Form I these days) instead of going to Primary 5 or 6. She explained that if I went into
Primary 6 I would have to work for the graduation exam into the
Middle School, whereas in Junior I, I could adjust gradually to
school life and the curriculum and not have any graduation exams
hanging over me. Above all, the students in the Middle School
might be a little more understanding and kind.

"You mean," I said quickly, "that in Junior I they might not call
me *mang mui?*"

Teacher Mak was horrified and asked if they had said this in
front of me. She wanted to know the whole story, so I told her. She
said she was glad, after all that had happened, that I had not been
put off but had perservered until I finally found her at the school.
Now I remembered how only a little while ago, in church, I had
asked God to help the girls to be kind and not call me *mang mui.*
The fact that I was to go to the Middle School and work with older
girls was an answer to the prayer. Teacher Mak promised that she
would talk to the girls and make them understand that they must
never use that phrase.

She asked me to go to the Middle School building on the coming
Friday. There would be someone to meet me and take me to
Teacher Lee's room, where the entrance examination questions
would be read to me so that I could answer them orally. I asked if
I would still be allowed to go to school if I could not answer some

of the questions. Teacher Mak assured me that whether I passed or failed the exam, the school had decided to give me a trial period of three months. This entrance exam was a means of finding out my academic background as I had never been to school before.

For the next few days I studied frantically all the notes which I had taken from listening to the homework of my brother and sister and outside the classroom window during the summer school. I was also holding my breath to know whether my parents would agree to pay my school fees.

Friday morning came and I took my gadgets for making dots and a small pile of newspapers, each sheet folded into two or three thicknesses. Ah Wor took me along to the Middle School building. To my surprise it was quiet and orderly compared with the noise we had encountered when we went to the Primary School. Then I remembered Teacher Mak saying that the students in the Middle School were older and more mature. Also, it occurred to me that since the summer school was over, all the girls who were at the school that day were taking entrance exams and were probably busy doing last minute review. In fact, I heard murmuring voices and the sound of books and turning pages. Then a man's voice asked if we were looking for Teacher Lee. Ah Wor said he must be the messenger from the school office. He led us along corridors and up a couple of flights of stairs till we came to Teacher Lee's room. I found out later that there was a board downstairs showing the whereabouts of the rooms on each floor, but that would not have helped either of us.

Teacher Mak met us at the door; as always, her voice was warm and smiling. She said that the test would probably take about three and a half hours, so we could let Ah Wor go and she would take me home. As we walked into the room she said Teacher Lee would come over in a few minutes to read me the questions which I was to answer orally. I asked if Teacher Lee could read the questions to me so that I could take them down in dots. I also asked to be allowed to do the answers in the same way and read them to her at the end. During all this, I had been wondering about the room we were in. From the resonance of our voices it did not seem a very big room and from what I had heard when I was listening outside the window, the classroom sounded bigger than this. Finally I asked if it was a classroom and Teacher Mak said no, it was an office. Since Teacher Lee had to read to me, they decided it would be better to do it in an office, so that we would not disturb other candidates.

Soon Teacher Lee came. Teacher Mak told her that I wanted to do my questions and answers in dots. Teacher Lee sounded surprised and asked why. I explained that when I was listening outside the classroom window during the summer school I had heard the teacher writing the questions on the blackboard and asking the students if they could see them. Then, after a long period of silence, I heard her tell the students to hand their papers in. I had worked out that the students were writing down their answers and therefore had more time to think about them than if they were answering orally. Teacher Lee agreed to do it my way. My first exam was to be Chinese language.

Teacher Lee started to read. I tried to do my dots as fast as I possibly could. It must have taken me about fifteen minutes to take down all the questions. I was in a panic about the time as I had been told the exam was to last an hour. I asked Teacher Lee if I could have extra time to make up for what had already been used. She said she thought this would be fair but as there were no provisions or regulations for dealing with blind students, she would be afraid to take a decision on her own responsibility. This meant I would have only forty-five minutes to write down my answers. Then the two teachers left me alone to get on with it.

I felt much better when I was left on my own. I carefully read over the ten questions. To my relief I found I knew the answers to six of them because I had heard my brother and sister chanting them aloud in the evenings. But I did not know how to answer the other four. There was no time to be lost—I had only forty-five minutes and could not afford precious time to worry about four unknown questions. I had my work cut out writing down the six answers I did know. I was wrestling with the problem of working at a small desk in a room with an electric fan which blew all my loose sheets of paper onto the floor. I crawled about trying to pick them up but could only find some of them and, knowing that time was running out, I gave up looking for them and decided to concentrate on answering what I could. Before I had quite finished I heard the bell ring and time was up. Teacher Lee came back and said it was time for me to read my answers. She said that some of my papers were on the floor and she collected them up and gave them to me. I sorted them into order as fast as I could and then read her my answers.

She was surprised that I knew the complete answers to six of the questions. This gave me sixty marks out of a hundred which was just a pass.

Just as we were finishing I heard footsteps. I could not recognise the steps and knew it was not Teacher Mak. Teacher Lee said it was Teacher Leung who was coming to give me my English exam. I stood up to greet her. She said hello and took my hand. This conveyed a feeling of kindness and helped me not to be so nervous.

Teacher Leung explained that the exam was in three parts. In the first part she would read me English words and I was to give the Chinese equivalents; in the second part she would read me English words and I was to give their opposites in English. In the third part I was to make sentences using English words I was given. She suggested it would be much easier if she just read me the paper and I gave the answers as we went along. I said no, I would rather do it the other way, so that I would have time to think, to which she agreed. I started work and almost immediately realised that my papers were flying off the desk again. Teacher Leung was still in the room—I could hear her writing—and she suddenly said, "You've dropped some of your papers on the floor." She picked them up for me and stood watching as I sorted them out. She realised I did not have enough room on my little desk, as I needed space to separate the used sheets from the unused, so she suggested I go and work at her big desk. She led me to the other end of the room. I was surprised to feel this big desk: although she was working at one end and I at the other I had plenty of space. She gave me a paperweight to stop my papers blowing all over the

room but it was something so heavy that I knew it would completely flatten my poor dots. I told her this, so she laughed and
gave me a small book which did the trick.

The bell rang again. This time I had only done two-thirds of the
paper and no matter how frantically I stabbed away at my dots I
could not have finished the paper in time. There were many words
I did not know, and in any case I had not the least idea of how to
make an English sentence. All I had heard my brother and sister
chanting were single words. I knew nothing about how to construct
a sentence or use tenses. I tried to answer a few, but I knew they
were not right. As I read my answers to Teacher Leung I realised I
must have done badly and I dared not ask her the result. However,
I did ask her nervously if I would still be able to go to school, despite not knowing much English. Thank goodness she said the
same as Teacher Mak had said earlier, that whatever happened,
the school would have me.

The last period came; it was Arithmetic. Yet another teacher,
Teacher Hui, came to give me the questions. Now I was really in
trouble. I had heard my brother and sister use the word "arithmetic," but I had not the slightest idea what it was all about. I made a
desperate attempt at three questions out of the ten, and I am certain they were hopelessly wrong. I think Teacher Hui realised
pretty soon just how far I was out of my depth—it must have been
all too obvious as my hands went over and over the questions and I
wrote almost nothing. But she was very kind and told me not to
worry. For someone who had never been to school, I had done much
better than they had expected, she said. Arithmetic is regarded, she
continued, as a difficult subject even for seeing students and I
could leave it out if I wished to. At that moment I felt too discouraged to say anything, but inside I felt, obstinately, that I would do
Arithmetic if it killed me. The radio programme I had heard which
had started everything had said that blind children in England and
America studied all subjects, so there was no reason why I could
not do Arithmetic.

It was all over. For better or for worse, I had done my entrance
exam. Teacher Mak came and asked if I was ready to go home. I

asked if we would pass the church on our way because if we did, I could find my way from there, but she said it was no trouble to come all the way with me and she would be glad of the walk anyway. We set off and she asked me how I had got on. I told her everything that had happened and particularly my dismay over the Arithmetic paper. She was sympathetic and said this was natural enough, because my brother and sister, like most students, would do their Chinese and English language out loud but would work silently when doing their Arithmetic problems, so it was hardly surprising that I had not managed to pick up any of it.

The days went by and there was still no letter from Father and Mother. There were only a few days left before term began. One evening at bedtime I just could not keep my anxiety to myself any longer. I asked Ah Wor what I could do if Father and Mother did not agree to pay my school fees. Ah Wor reassured me, saying that since the school had agreed to take me, she felt sure my parents would pay, but I was still worried. So Ah Wor told me to come with her. We went to her room where she opened a drawer with a key and took out some more keys which rattled on a ring. She went to her bed and I heard her pull her trunk out from under it and fit a key into the lock. It was a metal trunk and the hinge creaked as she opened the lid.

She took out something and gave it to me. It was a small bundle wrapped in a towel. Inside the towel there were several little objects like coins, but much heavier. She told me these were gold. She had bought them with the money she had saved since her mother had died and she no longer needed to send much money home. She said that if my father and mother refused to pay my school fees she would sell the gold and pay my fees.

Child though I was, I realised the significance of what Ah Wor was saying to me. These were all her savings. I then asked her if it was important to her for me to go to school. She said that it was, and that although she did not have the opportunity to learn to read and write, she had come to realise that it was important for everyone to go to school and that it mattered just as much for me as for my brothers and sisters.

At that moment I felt that Ah Wor really loved me more than anyone else in the world did. Impulsively, I threw my arms round her neck and cried and told her I loved her and would never be parted from her.

CHAPTER 10 ●●●●●●●●●●●●●●●●●●●●●●●●●●●●●●●●●●

A FEW MORE days went by and then the telephone rang while we were having lunch. Ah Wor answered it—it was a long-distance call from my mother in Hong Kong. She said they would be home around six o'clock the next evening.

Next day, as soon as I heard the clock strike six, I stood near the front door and listened. I had been forbidden to open the front door, but I still wanted to hear the first signs of their return as I was consumed with anxiety about my fees and hoped to ask about them the moment my parents arrived. Like all children with one idea occupying their minds, I innocently assumed that the matter of my fees would be uppermost in my parents' thoughts as it was in mine.

I stood straining my ears, as I had done the day my teacher came. There were voices and footsteps but not the ones I was waiting for. Ah Wor was busy away in the kitchen and time crawled by. Then, at last, I caught a familiar tone of voice—my brother's, far away at the bottom of the stairs, arguing with my sister. Excitedly I called Ah Wor from the kitchen to come and open the door. I heard voices coming nearer, the sound of feet, the bumping of suitcases, and then they were on the landing and exclaiming with surprise that the door was open. Ah Wor's explanation was drowned in the commotion of their arrival. The family was home again.

There was a great carrying-in and opening and unpacking of suitcases, everyone so excited at finding the things they had bought in Hong Kong that they did not even stop to drink the cups of tea brought to them by the amahs. Everybody talked at once—about clothes bought or made by tailors, books, shoes, materials; someone said the pink dress material looked better than the blue, and the black and white ones went well together. Then they were talking about the lovely beaches, the places they had gone to for Chinese and English meals, the beautiful department stores, how they enjoyed going up and down in the lifts in the hotel, how strange it felt when the aeroplane took off and landed, and what they had to eat during the flight.

I listened to all this with wonder and admiration but felt that none of it mattered as much as the all-important question of my school fees. I was dying to ask about them but I knew it was no good trying until some of the chatter and excitement had died down and Father might be willing to listen to me.

Suddenly Mother called to Ah Wor and told her there was a piece of dress material for me. Ah Wor held it out for me to examine as she said, "Look, it's very beautiful. It's pink." I felt it but I was not very enthusiastic as my mind was still on my fees. Ah Wor handed it to me so I went and put it away in a drawer in my room and then returned to the living-room. A few minutes later Mother called Ah Wor again and asked her to give her back the first piece of material and have another one instead. I fetched the first piece and handed it to Ah Wor, who took it to the living-room to Mother. Evidently Mother gave Ah Wor a less attractive piece because I heard Ah Wor say in an unusually loud voice, "We don't like this piece of material. We don't have to have a piece of material at all." Then she headed for the kitchen. I was astonished to hear Mother say in an equally loud voice, "Are you the king or the mother-in-law in this household? Here, have the first piece back, no one's going to take it away from you." (By tradition in Chinese homes the mother-in-law is very much "the boss" and what she says goes.) I heard Ah Wor go to Mother. She must have taken back the first piece and marched off to my bedroom. I followed, not knowing what to say and thinking Ah Wor would be very upset, but as soon as we reached my bedroom she pushed the door shut and roared with laughter.

"Mistress said was I the mother-in-law," she chortled. "Well, I'm only an amah, but at least she finally decided not to take this lovely piece of stuff away from us, and I'm so glad." As Ah Wor was saying this, I heard Mother's footsteps coming towards the room and I was frightened that she might hear what Ah Wor was saying. However all was well. She said, "You're quite right, Ah Wor—that piece is much better for Little Girl." Then she turned to me and said she would ask her tailor to make me a nice dress.

Everyone gradually calmed down and the household slowly returned to normal. Soon after supper Brothers and Sisters said their sunburn was sore and they were tired and wanted to go to bed early. Now the living-room was quiet, with Father and Mother reading the newspapers. I felt I had no time to lose; feeling agitated and breathless, I asked whether they had received my letter. They said they had but that obviously I couldn't possibly have composed the letter—the letter-writer must have done it for me. I told them that I had written the letter myself, in raised dots, and dictated it to the letter-writer. They said they could not believe it. I said I still had my raised-dot copy and I could read it to them. I went to fetch it as Father went to find the one I had sent him. I read my copy to them and they were amazed that except for the change of three or four words which the letter-writer had suggested to me they were identical. I further told them that the teachers had let me take the entrance examination and that I had just passed in Chinese and English language but had failed in Arithmetic, and that they had told me to go to school next Monday. I was to start in Junior I and I was to have a trial period of three months.

I could hear Father and Mother saying to each other that it was incredible that I could have written that letter and that I must be about Primary 5 standard. They also said they were worried that because I would be the only blind girl, the other children might tease me and knock me about. They were obviously disturbed and uncertain about the whole idea. But finally they said that although it was unheard of for a blind person to earn her living by doing socially acceptable work, since I wanted so much to learn and since the school had agreed to take me for three months, they must pay my fees. They made it depressingly clear that they thought I would give up the whole crazy idea at the end of the three months, by which time I would have found out for myself that I really could not do the same work as sighted students.

"Do you mean you are going to pay my school fees?" I asked.

When they said yes, I rushed to the amahs in the kitchen and told them the good news, so happy that I was laughing and crying at the same time.

CHAPTER 11 ●●●●●●●●●●●●●●●●●●●●●●●●●●●●●●●●●●●●●

I woke up before dawn. The excitement of going to school for the first day was too great—I could not go back to sleep. I lay with my eyes wide open, straining to detect the only thing I could see—the difference between darkness and light. The darkness thinned a little and I listened intently for some sign of life in the silent house. At last I heard a sound in the kitchen. I slid out of bed and crept along the hall past the other bedrooms. It was Ah Wor. She said it was too early for me to get up. I told her that I wanted to fold more newspapers to write down notes in class. With her help I stacked up a big pile which would be more than I needed for the day. She put a rattan bag into my hand and said it was her gift of a school bag for me. For months I had been playing with Brother's and Sister's school bags, pretending I was going to school. Now the game was over.

I went back to my room and dressed, putting on a white cotton Chinese dress (a *cheongsam*) which Ah Wor assured me would pass as school uniform until she could make me new ones.

I asked Second Sister to take me with her to school and she agreed. But when I told her I had to go to Junior I, she said she could not help me because she had to go to Primary 6 which was in another building. This must sound odd as Sister was three years older than I, but she had missed school through illness and was about a year behind, whereas I was going into a form where I would be considerably below the average age. Ah Wor said she would take me until I knew the way well enough to go alone. We all three set out together but separated when we came to the Primary School, which was where I had sat outside the window on the grass.

As we entered the gate of the Middle School I suddenly realised

I had not asked Teacher Mak where I should go, and now I did not know where to find her. We asked many girls where the new students should go but no one bothered to answer until finally a girl showed Ah Wor where it was. We went in.

I thought there would be desks and chairs for a class but Ah Wor told me there were several long tables and benches and some girls were sitting writing, but there did not seem to be a teacher with them. Many girls were lining up at a desk at one end of the room to collect some papers from a lady. When I asked them if they were new students and what they were doing, they only said yes, so I still did not know what they were doing. At a loss, I decided to join the line and do whatever they did. Ah Wor stood beside me. After a long wait my turn came and I arrived at the desk. As soon as the lady handed the papers to me, the girl behind me tried to push past me to the desk, but I knew I must find out what to do with the papers before going away. I eventually made myself heard over the noise and the lady said these were forms I had to fill in and return to her. Taking them in my hand, I followed Ah Wor to an empty place on one of the benches and we sat down. The only thing I could do was to ask someone to read the papers to me, but each time a girl came and sat near us and I asked if she would be so kind as to read them to me, she left and went to another bench until at last Ah Wor and I were left with the whole bench to ourselves.

After a long while someone sat down at our bench and Ah Wor whispered to me that she was a much older girl, probably Senior II or III. Expecting another rebuff, I asked her if she could help me. To my intense relief she said she would be glad to fill in my forms for me. She told me they were called "registration forms." She read me the questions one at a time and wrote down my answers and then took me to the clerk to hand in the forms. I was given another piece of paper which she told me was the book-list for the coming year. She asked how I would manage about the books, so I said I would have to ask someone to read them to me. She replied that it might not be necessary for me to buy all the books myself as whoever read to me could probably do so from her own copies. But Ah Wor whispered to me to ask where we could buy the books because she had worked out that the reader might not be in my class. I repeated this to the girl and she agreed and offered to take us to the bookstore. She explained that we could go and do this immediately because this first day was called "registration day" and there were no classes, and now that I was registered I was free to go home.

My new friend told me her name was Wong Wing-tze. She asked if I would like to walk with her. I took her arm and thought how lucky I was to find someone so understanding and kind. In those days, according to custom, we were not supposed to call anyone older than we were by their given name, so I decided to call her Big Sister Wong. That day was the beginning of a friendship which has lasted ever since. When she left school she studied medicine and later specialised in ophthalmology. She worked for many years with the Hong Kong Government as an eye specialist and she is now in private practice as a consultant. Her friendship proved to be of the utmost importance to me since she helped me to overcome some of the seemingly insurmountable problems in my school work, which I shall describe later. Once she was in practice as an eye doctor and I had started my social work, whenever she encountered a patient who was blind or going blind she would put them in touch with me, telling them I was her schoolmate.

However—back to school. The next day, the first proper day of term, Big Sister Wong waited for me at the school gate and took me to the right classroom. She said I had better stay in the front row until the teacher came to assign our seats. I sat there, feeling happy and excited until I heard the girls talking about me quite loudly, wondering why I was there. I knew they must be staring at me. I wanted to tell them I was there as a student, but as they referred to me as "she" or "that blind girl," I did not think they sounded very friendly and I was not sure they would like it if I talked to them.

Footsteps came briskly into the room and there was a rustling sound of general movement. The teacher had arrived. The girls said "Good morning, Teacher Lee." I realised that their voices came from above my head, so I stood up. "Sit down please." I sat down and recognised the voice of Teacher Lee who gave me the

Chinese language exam. This made me feel a tiny bit less nervous. The girls behind me were muttering to each other that I stood up later than they did and did not even know that I should sit down after greeting the teacher. They wondered why I had not learnt all this in primary school.

Teacher Lee introduced me to the class. She said that although I could not see and had not been to school before, I was eager to learn and she hoped that the girls would help me and be friends with me. She then outlined the work of the term ahead and explained that she wanted us all to keep a diary of three days in each week, describing what we did in our spare time, as this would help in our Chinese language lessons. She then said we were all to prepare the first lesson in our textbook for our next class, two days later.

I thought about the textbooks we had bought the day before. They felt quite thin to me, nothing like the thick notes I had taken down during the summer school. Surely, I thought, I could ask Brother and Sister to read to me and it would not take much of their time.

The bell rang and the class was dismissed. The girls started talking and laughing and I heard them leaving the room. I stood up, not knowing what to do. From their voices and other noises, I could tell that the door was to my right. I stood up and walked slowly, touching the edge of my desk, until my hand reached the edge of the next desk and then the next. There were six rows of them. "Ah," I said to myself, "next time I come to school and come into this room I shall be able to find my seat. But I wonder how big the room is." Talking to myself I walked in a straight line counting how many desks there were in each row. There were seven. I counted them carefully and found that it came to forty-two altogether. Forty-two students, I thought. Then I heard voices and people coming upstairs. I was afraid they might not like to find me wandering round and feeling their desks so I quickly dashed back to mine. I had a moment of panic that I might have made a mistake in counting and be in the wrong seat, but I hastily felt what was on the desk and found my familiar things, so I knew all was well.

The girls all came back to their desks and I heard one of them say that the next lesson was Geography. This time I listened carefully to hear when they stood up. The teacher—a man—said that he would call the roll so that he could begin to learn our names. This way I found out that Chan Yin-hing was on my left and Lee Lai-ying on my right. The lesson began and I tried to take notes as quickly as I could while the teacher talked, but I missed many things. I knew the teacher must be pointing to some sort of drawing when he said that this is Asia and this is Europe and this is America. I was hopelessly lost. He said that if anyone didn't understand, they should raise their hands. I wanted to raise mine but no one else asked a question and I was afraid to be the only one.

During the recess at the end of the Geography lesson I intended to speak to the girls near me, but before I could think what to say they had all rushed out. I was left alone again, so this time I found my way to the door. I could hear that the stairs were to my right, so I trailed my hand along the wall on that side, counting the doorways and memorising the distance. After passing two doorways I reached the top of the stairs. Then I turned back with my left hand on the wall this time. After passing two doorways I was about to turn into the third room, knowing it was my classroom and feeling triumphant that I could now find my way from the stairs right to my own desk, when suddenly an older, unfamiliar voice spoke, making me jump. She asked what I was doing. Timidly I explained and told her I was finding my way around. "Here," she said, "let me take you back to your classroom. Don't wander round by yourself. You could easily fall downstairs and hurt yourself." I felt somewhat mortified at being steered back into the room I had already found perfectly successfully myself, but I did not dare say anything except a meek thank you.

When school finished that first day, Ah Wor came to look for me and found me at the top of the stairs. We walked home together and she asked me how I had got on. I was dying to tell her everything, but oddly enough some instinct of caution held me back—all I told her was how I had charted my course from my desk to the stairs and back. I felt a sudden fear that if I described the difficulties, they would all regard this as proof that it would not work and would stop me going.

Back home, I told Brother and Sister what lessons I had had that day. I asked if they could read to me from my textbooks. They said they must do their homework first, but after that they would read to me. Father heard this and said that each day they were to read to me for up to an hour, depending on how much school work they had to do themselves. I found it encouraging that Father was interested enough in what I was doing to make this arrangement.

By the time Brother and Sister had finished their homework it was nearly bedtime and I was worried whether I should ask them to read or not. I thought they must be tired and wanting to go to bed. We had been given several lots of work to do, but the one that really worried me was the preparation for the next Chinese language lesson. I asked Brother and Sister if they could each read to me for a little while. Although they read to me for quite a while, they could not finish the lesson because I could not work fast enough at my dots. I covered sheets and sheets with dots and thought this must represent about half the textbook. I was very dashed when Brother told me I had taken down just over one page of the printed book.

Sitting on my bed and reading my lessons and notes after the others had gone to bed, I realised rather hopelessly that of the four subjects I had been given to prepare I could not even do one whole lesson. Brother and Sister had their own work to do and I could see that I was going to need much more help than they would have time to give me. It came as a shock to discover that one page of my little textbook meant five or more pages of my dots. I only had three months to prove that I could do it. What would happen if I could not get all the lessons read to me? And how was I going to know what the teachers wrote on the blackboard? Some teachers read part of it aloud, some did not. Could I ask the girls to read some of it to me? But how could I get to know them? They talked among themselves about me but so far none of them had spoken to me. If I made the first approach, would they resent it? Would I always have to stay behind in the classroom during recess, not knowing anyone to go out with? I did not want to worry Ah Wor as it would really upset her and Father and Mother would probably seize on my difficulties with relief, saying, "I told you so." I did not know what to do, so I cried from sheer frustration and anxiety, all over my precious sheets of dots which were on my lap, making them almost unreadable. I thought I had better stop crying and do some thinking instead. I came to a firm decision that the next morning I would make the first move and speak to the girls sitting near me. I had heard them say they were afraid of blind people, so perhaps if I talked to them I could show them that I was just ordinary like them and they would get used to me.

The next morning, before the teacher came in, I heard some girls talking about me. They were saying I had found my own way to my desk. They found this incomprehensible. Taking a deep breath and trying not to look or sound as nervous as I felt, I said, "Hello, do you want to know how I found my way?" And I told them how I used the edges of the desks and the wall to work out my surroundings. There was a moment's stunned silence. Then a voice said, "Oh, you can talk can you? We didn't think you could."

When the next recess came the girl on my left asked why I was making dots. I said, "You are Chan Yin-hing." She asked how I knew, so I said I heard her name when the roll was called. This attracted the attention of some of the other girls and in no time at all they were all standing round telling me their names, asking about my dots and begging me to write their names down in dots for them. We were all so busy chattering that I did not at first realise that they had not left the classroom as they usually did. I began to feel more confident and started to ask them some of the things that puzzled me. One was how they knew what the lesson was going to be before the teacher came in. They all laughed and explained to me about the schedule of classes. The next minute they were reading it to me and watching with fascination as I put it into dots. They could not understand why it came out so much bigger than the printed one up on the wall.

That second morning was a turning point. From then onwards they accepted me as just another of them. They showed me round the washroom and the dining room and helped me to learn my way from the bottom of the stairs to the school gate. We all had a lot of fun doing this and they worked out a sort of guessing game, finding out if I knew who they were until I had sorted out their names and voices properly.

Most of the girls were older than I. It was Form I in the Middle School so they were eleven or twelve, while I was only nine. As a result, after a short time they nicknamed me Youngest One, Ah Sai, which I liked.

One day I asked Yin-hing, who was very friendly, to tell me why they said they were afraid of blind people. She told me my eyes looked very strange and rather frightening; they were very red and looked swollen and always had tears running from them. This was the first time I had ever been told this, so when I got home I asked Ah Wor what I could do to make myself look better and more like other people. She thought about this and then said I could ask Mother to buy me a pair of sunglasses. I did not know what sunglasses were so she fetched a pair from Mother's room and showed them to me. I put them on and Ah Wor immediately said I looked much better. She said they hid my eyes and made me look just like any ordinary sighted person wearing sunglasses. I wore them to school and all the girls complimented me and said how good they looked. This made me realise the vital connection between personal appearance and social acceptance—something that is not readily obvious to a blind person. I have always kept it in mind with my blind clients and friends and have encouraged them to wear dark glasses when their blindness causes any sort of disfigurement.

CHAPTER 12 ●●●●●●●●●●●●●●●●●●●●●●●●●●●●●●●●●●

As I CAME to know the girls better I asked some of them if they could read to me when they were doing their homework. The first one I asked said she was never very happy about reading aloud and did not think she would be a good person to do it. Another said she would be glad to read to me for a little while if I could go to her home after school. Still another said she would rather come to work with me at my home. Quite early on, two of my girl cousins who lived in Canton agreed to read to me regularly, for which I was very grateful. So, each day after school, someone would be reading to me for about an hour at my home; then, after supper, Ah Wor would take me to the home of another reader for another hour or so. She would go home to do some work and come back in time to take me on to someone else's house for another hour. At times, if the home of the girl was too far away, Ah Wor would bring some sewing or knitting to do while she waited for me and would then take me on to another house. Usually, by the time I returned home, Brother and Sister would have finished their homework and were ready to go to bed. If they were still up I would ask each of them to read to me for a little while; even twenty minutes each was a great help. With the time spent in travelling and in putting the lessons into dots, it was already late at night, with the household asleep, before I could begin to read through what I had taken down and make some attempt to learn it. I became terribly tired.

One day there was an air of excitement in the classroom, with a medley of voices repeating passages, asking and answering questions, all talking together. Soon Teacher Lee arrived. We put our books away and there was silence. We were going to have a Chinese language test. Teacher Lee wrote the questions on the blackboard and then asked if anyone had any questions. No one said a word. I could hear the little sounds of pens on paper. I was afraid to be the first one to speak but I knew I had to ask Teacher Lee to read the test questions to me. I raised my hand. In order not to disturb the rest of the class she had almost to whisper the questions to me as I put them down in dots as quickly as I could.

When the bell rang I waited until all the girls had handed in their papers so that I could go and read her mine. But I heard Teacher Lee's footsteps going towards the door. I quickly ran after her, calling her name. She turned back and said she had forgotten about me. By the time I had read my answers to her and she had written them down, recess was over. She said I had the complete answers to eight out of the ten questions. She praised me for listening intently in class, saying that the test had been based on classroom teaching as well as on what we had studied in our textbooks. She asked me to leave my raised dot answers with her. I did not know what she wanted them for, since she had taken my answers down in writing, but I was afraid to ask her the reason so I just did as I was told.

A week later when we had our next Chinese language lesson we were all eager to know the results of our test. Teacher Lee said that apart from four who had failed, most of us had done quite well. She then went on to say that one pupil had earned eighty marks. We were dying to know who it was and I think everyone else was as amazed as I when my name was called. I stood up nervously. She asked me to come forward to her desk. She handed me my answer papers and told me to turn round to face the class; then she asked me to read them aloud slowly. I started to read in a very small voice and she told me to read louder. I was very relieved when I had read the last question and was able to go back to my seat. From then on the girls asked me to explain Chinese language lessons to them and I often had a small group gathered round my desk.

When we came to the first English test it was another story altogether. I was worried as I knew very well that I had not been able to do all the work properly. The stories in the textbook were so long that it had not been possible to put them all into dots—the other girls had not been able to spare the time to read them all to me. I could not pick up everything in class and I kept coming across grammar patterns which were unfamiliar to me but which the girls did not want to take time explaining to me as they knew them from primary school. I managed only a third of the questions and I knew I could not have passed. I badly needed someone to read and explain to me the English lessons which I should have had in Primary 5 and 6. Everybody, including my brother and sister, was so busy with their own work that I could not find anyone to help me. I had exactly the same problem with Arithmetic and in the first test I completed less than a third of the questions. I was seriously worried.

One afternoon as I was on my way to the playground during recess Big Sister Wong came up and asked how I was getting on. I told her about my difficulties over English and Arithmetic. She was very sympathetic and said she could help me with my English. So, once or twice a week she taught me the grammar and the new words I had missed by not going to primary school. She also showed me how to pick out the important points of a story and retell them in simple English without memorising every single sentence from the lesson. In this way, even if I was not able to put the entire lesson into dots, I would have enough of the main points necessary for tests and exams. With her help, I had pretty well caught up with the others in English after a few weeks.

But I was still hopelessly behind in Arithmetic. Then, by pure chance, I overheard Lee Lai-ying say she had a cousin in an upper class who was looking for private tutoring to help with her school fees. From what Lai-ying said, her cousin was evidently good at Arithmetic. I felt sure that if only I could have private tutoring for a while I would be able to catch up and then I could keep up with the class. But how could I find the money to pay for a private teacher? I thought about asking my father and mother, but was afraid they would say this proved that I could not do the work and would see it as an opportunity to make me give up the whole project. Then I remembered Ah Wor saying that she would help to pay my school fees if necessary. If I told her I would need only a short period of tutoring, she would probably agree to help me out.

I could pay her back when I grew up—but could I be sure of this? My parents told my brother and sister that if they worked hard they would be able to make a good living when they grew up. Could I be sure I could earn money when I grew up? To me, this was an insurmountable problem. That evening Ah Wor asked me if I had some problems, because I was unusually quiet and looked worried. But I did not say anything then. I made some excuse about a headache and waited for a suitable chance to ask her.

On Sunday afternoon, as usual, the rest of the family went out for a meal. Now was my chance. I asked Ah Wor to come to my room where we would not be heard by the other amahs, and said I had something very important to talk to her about. When she came in I closed the door and asked her to promise that, whether or not she agreed with what I was going to say, she would not tell anyone else in the household about it. Then I told her about my hope of having private lessons in Arithmetic for a little while. I thought she might not understand about this, as she had never been to school. But she understood all right. She said she would give me money for private tutoring for as long as I needed it and no one would know. I said I would pay her back when I grew up, but then I suddenly lost my confidence and asked how she would feel if I could never earn enough money to repay her. She laughed and said she hoped she and I would be together for the rest of her life, as she had no family except me, and that what was hers was mine too.

The next morning I asked Lai-ying to tell her cousin that I could pay her to help me with my Arithmetic. Lai-ying was excited and went to find her cousin right away. However, she returned disappointedly and told me that her cousin, Lee Wai-wan, did not think she could teach me because I was blind. I asked Lai-ying to take me to see Wai-wan, hoping that I might be able to persuade her to change her mind. Lai-ying introduced us and I greeted her, but there was silence—she did not speak. I began to feel edgy but I explained what I wanted. Instead of talking directly to me, Wai-wan turned to Lai-ying and said, "Tell her I really can't teach her as she can't see how I work out the sums and problems on paper, and I can't teach her how to do all these in dots." I said that if she would just read me what was written down and then explain the steps in words, I thought I would be able to follow and would work out the Arithmetic signs in dots myself. Whenever I got lost I would ask questions. I sounded as if I was full of confidence, but I had no idea whether I could really work out a system of Arithmetic signs in dots. However, since the day of the entrance exams I had determined to learn Arithmetic somehow, and getting Wai-wan's help seemed the only chance of doing it. I was desperate to persuade her. Finally, and very reluctantly, Wai-wan agreed to try it for one or two weeks.

At that time I could not understand why it was that when I first met people they usually tended to talk to me through a third person, as if I was a baby or an idiot. Later I found out the reason for this.

Since I had never been able to see I was quite unaware of the visual mechanics of conversation which sighted people learn from infancy without even thinking about it. I knew nothing of the vital part which eye contact plays in all social encounters. As a result I did not look at people when I was talking to them, which meant that they were in doubt as to whether I was responding to them. Therefore they would use my sighted companion as a sort of interpreter. Ever since I began to understand this problem I tried to overcome it, but it is a skill which is very hard for a blind person to acquire.

For the first few days of our Arithmetic lesson I felt lost and very tense with Wai-wan. Whenever I asked a question she would just answer me briefly. She avoided giving me the really basic explanations I needed, and said she did not see why I should bother too much as my teacher would probably make allowance for my not being able to see. Several times Wai-wan checked my homework and said all my answers were right, but when I read them out to the teacher I found they were all wrong. I told Wai-wan about this and insisted that she must treat me as she would a seeing student.

In the end she gave in and agreed to work seriously with me. That was the turning point and at last I began to get a grasp of the subject. After three months I was able to manage on my own and stopped having the private lessons. However, I must admit in all honesty that I have never been very brilliant at Arithmetic. But, oddly enough in view of the unpromising start to our relationship, Wai-wan and I became friends.

As for the problem of Arithmetic signs—all the code and signs in dots that I was using were my own invention and they served me well throughout my school-days. Later, however, when I went to America, I learned the proper braille Arithmetic code and had the painful process of unlearning what I had used for so many years.

CHAPTER 13 ••••••••••••••••••••••••••••••

IT WAS AN exciting week in our household. Third Uncle had announced that he was coming to see us on Saturday. Mother was busy superintending the amahs in a frenzy of cleaning, washing, scrubbing, tidying and polishing. The house had to be decorated with vases of flowers, bowls of fruit and red paper ribbons with lucky characters on them. We children were told to put all our belongings away and make our rooms perfectly tidy; everything must look its best. Because of the extra work, Mother said that Ah Wor could not be spared to take me from house to house for my reading sessions. What could I do? How was I to get the work I needed read to me? My brothers and sisters were too busy to help. If I could not be read to I would certainly fail my weekly test. As always I asked Ah Wor for help and it was she who had an idea.

She knew that at the school there were some boarders—girls who for various reasons lived at school all the week and went home at weekends. She suggested that I ask some of the boarders if they could read to me for about half an hour each and I would pay them some money. This worked out wonderfully well. The girls, knowing they were being paid, did not fool around and I completed a tremendous amount of work, all in a few hours at school with no time wasted going from one house to another. Ah Wor arranged with an amah at school to give me something to eat when the boarders had their supper, and she saved some proper supper for me to eat at home. And, of course, she paid all these extra expenses.

But back to the visit. Third Uncle was the head of the entire Ching family. In families of my father's generation the sons and daughters were usually numbered in separate sequences. This avoided the undesirable circumstance (which would have applied in my father's family) of having to acknowledge a girl as the eldest member of the family.

My father's family originally consisted of two daughters, one of whom was the eldest child, and seven sons. My grandfather had a concubine—known as "Little" Grandma—who bore two boys. These were my fourth and sixth uncles. All the rest of the family, seven children in all, were born to my legal grandmother. Little Grandma died quite young and so proper Grandma brought up the whole family of nine.

My first uncle died when he was in his early twenties, somewhere about the turn of the century, and Second Uncle turned out not to be of the stuff of which family heads are made. So the responsibility fell upon Third Uncle who was willing and well able to carry it.

When Third Uncle was seventeen his father, my grandfather, died. In order to support his younger brothers he left his village (Chung San, near the Macau border), which offered little scope to an ambitious young man, and went to Canton to look for a job. He first worked as a shop assistant in a store selling imported merchandise, and he went to night school to study written Chinese and English conversation. He was obviously intelligent and hard working and was soon promoted to a post of greater responsibility in a bigger store belonging to the same owner. He lived in a very frugal way and scrimped and saved until he had enough money to bring his four other brothers and his mother to Canton. They all settled down together and jobs were found for numbers four, five (who was my father) and six. Number seven was too young to go to work and was sent to school. His graduation from secondary school a few years later impressed on Third Uncle the value of education and made him realise how much he and the other boys had missed. He had by now established his own business, so it was too late for him to try to catch up on his own education, but he did what he could to encourage the other three to fill in some of the gaps. He also decided to send my seventh uncle to America.

So, as you see, Third Uncle held a very special and important place in my father's eyes. Hence all the preparation.

Before he came Mother lectured us all on manners and how we

were to behave. I was especially singled out and told "not to talk." Our hair and finger-nails were inspected and we were told to be quiet and keep tidy and to leave the grown-ups alone in the living-room when all the greetings were over.

We children were in awe of Third Uncle. By now he had become a senior Government official in the Kuomintang and we felt quite frightened of him. We stood in a line in the living-room, listening to the noises of arrival in the hall. Then Third Uncle came in and sat down. Mother brought him a cup of tea while we stood silently in line. Then at last she presented us, saying all our names in order of age, and we bowed and muttered "Uncle" and then scuttled out to our own rooms, glad to escape. However, I had noticed one little thing. I was the third to be presented; when my mother presented my older brother and sister Uncle made no reply—I assumed he acknowledged their bows with a slight inclination of the head, per-haps a smile—but when my name was called he said, "Little Girl, I'm so glad to see you," and patted me on the shoulder. I was very surprised and thought about this as I ran off to my room.

I settled down to do some homework. After a little while, my older sister, who slept in the same room and was evidently listening by the open door, came over and pulled my arm and said, "Listen, Uncle is talking about you." I was amazed and crept to the door-way to listen. Uncle was saying that he knew I had come third in a class of forty-two and had been given a little badge for it. I did not hear Father or Mother say anything. They must have been some-what embarrassed, because I had never told them, thinking they would not be interested. Of course I had told Ah Wor about it. Uncle went on to explain that a colleague of his had a daughter at the school and she had talked about the blind child in Form I. The colleague had thought this unusual enough to be worth mentioning to Uncle, who in turn said it must be his niece. Then Uncle said he would like to see how I worked.

Next moment Mother came across the hall calling my name and told me to go to the living-room. Remembering the warning about not talking I wondered nervously what I ought to do. However, Uncle was very nice and soon made me feel fairly at ease. He asked to see my books. He then asked how I could put the text into dots, so I told him. He then asked if I could really put all the text into dots. I said that usually I could only get one third of it done. He then put some money into my hand and said I could find myself some readers to read to me for as many hours a day as I felt necessary and pay them accordingly. I counted the money and was amazed to find it was ten dollars—more than Ah Wor was paid for a month's wages. I had never had so much money all at once before. As I was thinking how much reading it would pay for, I heard Uncle asking me how I knew which coin was which, so I showed him how easy it was to recognise dollars, fifty-cent and ten-cent pieces by their sizes and different weights. He asked what I would do with notes, as all the different values felt the same, so I said I thought I would fold them in different ways. (I still do this—so do my blind friends.)

Uncle said he would give me this amount of money every month. Father said he could manage this amount himself and Uncle should not bother but Uncle, evidently anxious to remove any suggestion that Father could not afford to give me ten dollars a month, said quickly that he would like to do this as I had brought honour to the Ching family name and he was proud of me and proud to be able to help me.

These words turned my whole world of beliefs and attitudes upside down. We children had been taught to believe that Third Uncle was a fine and important man who brought honour to the Ching name. I, on the other hand, had been left in no doubt that my blindness was a disgrace and a slur on the family, which was why I had always accepted my dreary fate of having no social life and of being left out of nearly all family activities. This was why I had never told my parents any details about my school work. They had never shown any interest in it. Having indulged me to the extent of allowing me to go for a trial period, they made no further enquiries about it, regarding it, I suspect, as a way of keeping me occupied and out of mischief. I was used to hearing my brothers and sisters receive restrained approval (as much as traditional Chinese modesty would permit) for doing well and bringing home good reports—and getting into trouble when they had bad marks. I was never scolded but I received no approval either, as no one in the house except dear Ah Wor knew anything about my little troubles and triumphs. So, suddenly to be told in front of my parents, by this admired and respected uncle, that I, the shameful incubus of the family, had brought honour to it was quite unbelievable.

Uncle's remark confounded everyone and an embarrassed silence followed. It was broken by Uncle himself who went on to say, as if in anticipation of my parents' unspoken objections, that he saw no reason why I should not be able to find a job to support myself. He said that he had read of blind people in other countries (he mentioned America and England) who did all sorts of jobs and added that he would willingly consider sending me abroad later on, for special training, after I had finished my secondary education.

I sat there listening, barely able to believe my ears. I was still in a chair close beside Uncle—I could hear his movements and his breathing. He was really there, close beside me, saying these astonishing things in a calm, matter-of-fact tone, probably quite unaware of their effect on me.

But that effect was so profound and so lasting that I look back on that day as one which helped to settle the eventual course of my life. Until that moment it had never entered my head that I might go abroad, and the idea of doing a real job had been no more than a dream. The problem of paying back Ah Wor the money she was spending on me hung over me, and now, suddenly, the unbelievable sounded possible. The idea of a job and of earning my living began to take shape and I was filled with curiosity to know more about what work blind people did and how sighted people accepted them in these other countries.

One thing that happened was that I began to have a tiny bit of confidence in myself. It was not much, but it was there—Uncle had planted it and his continuing interest and kindness during the rest of my school-days helped it to grow.

Actually, that day marked a point at which a lot of changes began to happen. First I went to Teacher Mak and asked her advice about finding readers. She said she thought the girls in the school were bound to be undependable because of the demands of their own school work, so she suggested that as I was able to pay, I would do better to employ grown-up people, probably housewives, who would be glad of some extra money. This sounded a good idea and I was glad when she said she thought she might be able to find some suitable people. Before long, she had found some married women, former pupils of the school, who agreed to rotate and come to the school each afternoon and read to me for a total of four hours. This arrangement was soon started, and before long I was doing far more work than ever before. On Teacher Mak's suggestion, I had the material read to me in advance, so that I had my version in dots to follow when the whole class was reading with the teacher. Two people came each day, one from three-thirty to five-thirty and one from five-thirty to seven-thirty. At seven-thirty, Ah Wor came and took me home and gave me supper, after which I could settle down to doing my homework. (It was often nine-thirty or ten o'clock before I started.) All this made my work much more orderly and satisfactory, but there was one snag—making my dots every day, using a handframe and stylus, rubbed my knuckles raw till they bled. No Perkins Brailler in those days.

When this arrangement had been working well for some weeks, a new and difficult situation arose. My father had evidently been doing well in his business, running his own company as an architect and builder. One day he told all of us during the evening meal that we were going to leave the flat and go to live in a much bigger house, on the outskirts of Canton. We children were excited but not sure just what a big house would be like, and we dared not ask. We found out quite soon. Only about two weeks later Mother met us after school with a car and a driver and we were taken for quite a long drive. At the end of it was the new house. The move had all been done while we were at school that day, and we never went back to the old flat on the second floor again. We felt sad that we had not even said goodbye to it.

The car stopped and we all climbed out, but instead of going straight into the house we walked quite a distance in the open before coming to two steps and going through a doorway. Then we went up one long staircase and then another and round what seemed to me miles of passages before reaching a room that I was told was mine.

Mother left me standing in the middle of this totally strange room and went to show Brothers and Sisters their rooms. I felt completely lost and wondered how I was going to find my things and how I could ever learn to find my way. I listened for voices, to know where Second Sister was. When I heard her, I tried to go in that direction. My hand found a doorknob which I turned, hoping it would lead me to Sister's room. Instead, I walked into a lot of clothes. I put up my hand and felt coathangers and recognised the collar of a dress, so I knew I had found a wardrobe with my own clothes in it and my shoes on the floor. I wondered where all my raised-dot papers were.

I carefully closed the cupboard door again and, following sounds, found the door out into the passage. Trailing the wall with my right hand I set out to find Sister and nearly jumped out of my skin when close beside me Grandma's voice shouted. "When you can't see, why do you run around? If you want something, why don't you press the bell?"

I had not even known Grandma was in the house. In her cloth shoes she had come right up to me without my hearing a thing. How she thought I was to find a bell in the first few minutes I do not know.

I gave up trying to find Sister and took refuge from Grandma back in my room. If there was a bell, I should be able to find it. I guessed it would be on the wall so I began systematically feeling all round the room. The first thing I came to was a chest of drawers, so I opened the top drawer and to my joy found in it all my raised-dot papers safe and sound. Next came my bed, so I walked round that and back to the wall on the other side of it, and quite close to it I found what felt like a bell. Nervously I pressed it and listened but could hear nothing, so I pressed again and in a minute or two heard the welcome sound of Ah Wor's footsteps coming. I told her how I had managed to find the things in my room. She was pleased and said I was a clever girl. Her praise made my anxiety and frustration worth while.

Second Sister came running along the passage from her room, wanting to see mine. She stopped in the doorway exclaiming, "Oh —it's dark!" I heard Ah Wor switch the light on and Sister came into the room, saying that she did not like to go into an unfamiliar place where there was no light. From that time on I tried to remember to turn on the light whenever I went to my room and to turn it off when I went to bed. I realised that although it made no difference to me whether it was light or dark, it mattered to seeing people and later (though I sometimes slip up even now) I took special care to check whether the light was on whenever I had visitors in my room.

Ah Wor had to go to tidy up the dining room. Mother came in to tell us to go downstairs for supper when we heard the bell. Grandma, who was evidently hovering within earshot, shuffled over and said wouldn't it be better if Ah Wor brought me my supper to eat in my room. Mother did not say anything and I knew better by now than to protest. Ah Wor was already on her way downstairs and obviously she heard what Grandma said. She stopped and came back quickly into my room and said to Sister and me that if we would go to the dining room as soon as we heard the bell, she was sure she would not be told to bring my food to my room. That sounded better to me. In the end Sister and I decided to go down well before Mother rang the bell. I was afraid Grandma might complain to Father about this, but she did not say anything—then.

After supper the amahs went to their quarters for their meal. Grandma, Father and Mother went into the sitting room. They said they didn't want us children there listening to their conversation so Mother told us to go away quickly and we went upstairs to our bedrooms. However, Grandma was muttering as she came close to me that she was going to tell Father about my not obeying her. I was wondering what she would say to Father and what he would do to me. I found my way to Sister's room where I could hear her reciting her lessons. I told her about Grandma and said I was dying to hear what the grown-ups were talking about, so that I could know what they were going to do to me. We went and asked Brother to come with us and the three of us tip-toed downstairs, carefully opened the door into the garden, crept out and found a place below the sitting room window.

We could hear what they were saying perfectly clearly and we got there just as Grandma was finishing her complaint about me, but Father made a non-committal reply and went on to talk about going away in a few days' time on a long business trip. That meant I had nothing to worry about, so I whispered to Brother and Sister that I wanted to learn my way about the garden. They took me all round and showed me the way in and out of the house; we were all thrilled to have a garden.

When I was sure we could not possibly be overheard, I asked Brother and Sister if they had ever heard how Father and Mother addressed each other. They said they would give anything to find this out. Oddly enough, only two weeks later we did find out. That day when we came home from school, Sister said there was a letter in the mailbox and she could recognise Father's handwriting. We took the letter to Mother and as she opened it, we asked her how Father addressed her. She did not answer the question, but on impulse Sister went up behind her and quickly glanced at the letter, then she pulled me aside and burst out laughing as she told me that Father addressed Mother as "My Little Sister" and he signed it "Your Big Brother." We were helpless with laughter until Mother came over and said, "You're a pair of rascals. I don't know what I'm going to do with you." This time her tone of voice was smiling so we knew she was not angry with us.

Later I found out that this form of address between married people was common up to my parents' generation, but is now regarded as terribly old-fashioned—though one still finds it in literature and on the stage.

But coming back to that first night at our big house—after exploring the garden, we children went back to our rooms and I knew I was late in getting my work done so I tried to work as fast as I could. I do not know how long I worked, but Ah Wor came and brought me a few biscuits and said everyone was in bed and as it was my first night in the strange house, she would come and sleep in my room until I got used to it. I asked where she could sleep and she said she would be all right on the floor. It was winter time and I thought she would be terribly cold on the floor. Anyway, I felt I knew the place well enough and proved to her that I could find my way to the bathroom and back. I managed to convince her, so she left me and went back to her own room.

Somewhere a clock struck two. I was very tired and decided to go to bed. I was on my way to the bathroom to brush my teeth when I suddenly wondered how I was going to stay behind after school for my readers, since Mother said I was to come home with Brother and Sister in the car. I was thinking about this while cleaning my teeth and washing my face and as I went back to my room I lost count of the doors. I opened what I thought was my door and to my dismay heard snoring. Recognising that it was Grandma, I closed the door very gently, with my heart in my mouth, for if I woke her up I would be in endless trouble. By then I knew I had lost my bearings and was not sure where my own room was. I stood still to try to get my sense of direction but that did not work. Then I realised I could hear the toilet cistern filling up, so guided by the sound I made my way back to the bathroom and started out again, counting carefully this time, and to my relief got back safely and felt the raised-dot papers on my table.

I found it very strange at first to have a room to myself. No Sister sharing the table—and no Sister to pick up what I dropped on the floor and could not find. Many a time, on my own, I did not even know I had dropped a sock or a handkerchief or even a piece of paper until I noticed something was not where it ought to be. When I missed something I would start searching on the floor on my hands and knees. This taught me to be very careful not to drop things and to remember exactly where I left everything. Gradually I realised that I could train myself to put everything in a definite place. When I shared the room with Sister I could not very well do this as she would move things when they were in her way and it would not occur to her to tell me about it. But now things would not be moved accidentally and it was up to me to organise my things the way I wanted them.

Early next morning, as soon as I saw Ah Wor, I told her I was worried about staying behind after school and she said she had been thinking about the same thing. She said I had better wait for a suitable moment to ask Father and Mother and that meanwhile the best thing for me to do was to tell the driver he would not have to pick me up after school. Then I could stay behind with my readers and she would come and pick me up at seven-thirty as usual. I asked her how we could get back to the house, as it was right out on the outskirts of the town. She said she didn't know but she thought we would manage somehow.

So, I stayed behind with my readers. At seven-thirty Ah Wor arrived to pick me up. Because neither of us could read the street signs or bus routes, we had to ask people in the street, but we got no help; people just shook their heads. Finally, after many enquiries, we found out where to go and what number bus we had to catch. It turned out in the end that we had to change buses twice on the way, asking questions each time. I asked Ah Wor how she had managed to find her way to the school. She said she had started out from home at five o'clock and had made enquiries until she got there, but then she was unable to find her way back as it was a different route. After almost two hours of travelling we finally found our way back to the house. I realised I must talk to Father and Mother about this, but Father was away and I did not want to broach the subject with Mother alone. We did this awful journey for at least a week, but Ah Wor said we could not go on like this—it was taking too much time from my work (and hers) and also it was winter and very cold, which made it worse. She decided that instead of taking several buses and having to walk quite a long way between bus stops, we would take a taxi. This certainly meant that we were home much more quickly but it was very expensive and I knew Ah Wor could not afford to do this every day even if she used up all her month's wages on it.

When Father returned home from his business trip I waited for an opportunity when he and Mother were both in the house together, explained the difficulty and asked them what to do. They did not say anything for quite a while and I sensed that yet again I had irritated them by causing a problem. Apprehensively, I asked what they thought. Finally Father said I could ask the readers to come with me to our house and we would pay for a taxi to take them home. I had a nasty feeling that this was not going to work.

However, next day I duly asked them, only to be told, as I had feared, that they could not spare the extra time to do this. So, in the end, it was decided that Ah Wor would pick me up at seven-thirty and she and I would come home by taxi. I asked Ah Wor if she could possibly show me the way so that in due course I could do the journey by myself, but she was worried about kidnappers who would take a blind girl to sell for a few dollars to a slave mistress in another city. She said very firmly that as I was only nine years old I was not to travel alone.

CHAPTER 14 ●●●●●●●●●●●●●●●●●●●●●●●●●●●●●●●●●●●

As TIME WENT on I was able to catch up with the rest of the class in school work, but I found that compared with my classmates I knew very little and was in fact very ignorant in many ways. I heard them discussing world and local affairs which they read about in the newspapers—things I knew nothing about. Sometimes I would ask what they were talking about, but they were either too busy to explain or they were all talking so hard that they really did not hear me. It was tantalising to know that all sorts of important things were happening in the world—a world of which I was, after all, a small part—and at the same time to lack any way of finding out about them. Well-meaning friends would sympathise with me about being limited to my textbooks; many a time I found myself wishing they would spend the time reading items to me from the newspapers instead of lamenting kindly but uselessly about my handicap. I used to wonder how, in a better world, things could be arranged so that blind people need not be deprived of access to news of current affairs.

In our Chinese language lesson Teacher Lee told us we must read more books in addition to our textbooks if we were ever to increase our vocabulary and improve our writing style. There was a rush to the school library for books, but it was useless for me to go with them. Even with my two readers reading to me every day I could not put all my textbooks into dots. Then, one day Teacher Lee told us to read a book of our own choice and do a critical review of it. She said I could be excused from this. However, I felt that as I was at the school I ought to try to do all the work, so I made up my mind to do this particular assignment somehow. I realised that I would never have the time to get a whole novel down in dots; but I thought that if I could listen to the book once and form a general picture of the story I would be able to manage well enough. Of course I would very much prefer to be able to read the book again and again and refer back to particular parts, but this just was not possible. I remembered Teacher Lee talking in class about a book called *Pride and Prejudice*, and I had a faint idea of the story, so I decided to try to borrow it from the library (in Chinese translation, of course).

I had never been to the library before. I asked where it was and found my way there by myself and went in. I was immediately aware of the strong smell of books and of the curiously deadening effect they had on the sound of the closing door. I walked forward slowly until I felt myself up against a desk. There was a dead silence and I felt very nervous. Finally I said, "May I speak to the Librarian, please?" I heard footsteps coming towards me, then they stopped and I could feel she was looking at me. I did not need to be able to see her face. When I said what I wanted she came round the desk and stood close to me and I could feel her breath as she stared at me. She asked how I was going to read the book if I took it. I think she was watching me intently to satisfy herself that I really could not see. Finally she sighed loudly and walked away, muttering about the trouble it must be to read to me and that she certainly would not want to do it. Still grumbling, she evidently went to a bookshelf because I could hear her moving the books and at the same time remarking to her colleague that she could not understand what good it would do for a blind girl to be studying with the seeing ones. She went on to say that if I remained uneducated, I probably would not realise how different I was from the normal youngsters, but now, the more education I had the more I would be able to think for myself and the more miserable I would feel about my fate. The other woman replied that perhaps it was a progressive step in education. But the first woman said finally that she was certain this was not the case, for if it were, the institutions for the blind and the Education Department would have done something about it before. She said she thought it was both wrong and crazy. After all, what could a blind person do even if she obtained all the knowledge in the world?

I was glad to take my book and make my escape from the library. I was upset: I just did not know how I could arrange for the book to be read in time to do my review of it, and listening to the two women in the library discussing me did nothing to increase my confidence.

Several days went by and not a page of the book had been read. There were only two weeks left before we had to hand in our reviews. Then one evening at supper I heard that the family was going to the cinema to see the film *Pride and Prejudice*. Apparently the driver, who was sent to buy the tickets, bought an extra one by mistake and Mother had been looking for someone among her friends to use it, but without success. Ah Wor knew that I was desperately trying to have this story read to me and I had said to her that if only I could go to the film, it would help me enormously, so she bravely asked my parents to take me with them. As might be expected, my parents were displeased and said no, it would be too much trouble.

That night I felt miserable and confused beyond anything I had felt before. I did not want Ah Wor to see this; she suffered enough on my behalf as it was. She came and said good night to me and then I collected a bunch of handkerchiefs and crawled into bed and let all my tension go in a flood of weeping.

I had been working since September without any relaxation or break, always worried about getting work done, and now the business of the book was making it worse; I remembered the conversation between the two women in the library and suddenly I began to have awful doubts as to whether I had really done the right thing in persuading the school to have me. Perhaps the library woman was right about the Education Department's attitude to blind people and about my meagre chances of finding a job even if I knew everything there was to know. One thing was certain; all my efforts had failed to persuade my parents to accept me as equal to my brothers and sisters. And then there was Ah Wor—poor dear, loyal, devoted Ah Wor—who gave up so much for me and was alone in defending me. Other amahs ridiculed her and said she was a fool because she had missed so many things in life through staying with me, including the chance to fly to Hong Kong for the summer holiday.

When I had had a good cry out and there were wet handkerchiefs everywhere, a thought suddenly came to me; I slipped out of
bed and knelt on the floor and told God all about it and asked
what I ought to do. Perhaps He made me remember what Ah Wor
said on that evening when she put the gold coins in my hand—that
if it was important for my brothers and sisters to go to school, then
it must be important for me to go to school too. Thinking about
this I felt comforted, especially as I remembered again the solemn
promise I had given to my blind beggar friend and to God. At last
I went to sleep.

All my life, ever since I became a Christian, whenever I have
been in any sort of difficulty my habit and practice has always
been to pray. In this way I have received practical help and, sometimes, I have been given strength, courage and peace of mind. The
problems may have been trivial or serious, ranging from being lost
on the landing the first night in our new house or feeling nervous
before playing the piano in a music festival to the graver matters of
pleading with schools to accept me or despairing of finding a place
to live in for the few weeks before I left Hong Kong for America.
The wonderful thing is that whenever I prayed, help came. I might
not receive the kind of help I wished for, the situation might not
change for the better, but I was given, in the words of the Bible
used in the Blessing, "the peace of God, which passeth all understanding." The Bible tells us that God's grace is sufficient for us
and that He would not ask us to endure more than, with His help,
we are able to endure. Sometimes I might not understand exactly
what was happening, or why, but I could always have the assurance that if God permitted this to happen, it must be right for me.

I shall never forget the time in 1964 when, as a scholarship student of the Royal Commonwealth Society for the Blind in England,
Sir John Wilson, Director of the Society, who is blind himself, hearing that I was going to church asked me if I was just a Sunday-
church-going Christian or if my faith went deeper than that. I told
him how my practice of prayer had formed an essential and vital
part of my life. He sighed with relief and said that as a pioneer in
my studies and in my field of work in my part of the world, I
would probably have more than my share of problems and difficul-

ties. These were likely to be far greater than those of a blind person in the Western world and as a human being I would be disappointed, crushed and depressed. However, these problems and difficulties, he said, no matter how great they were, would not break my spirit because of my practice and habit of prayer. Through all these years I have found that what he said has proved to be true.

Next morning when I woke up I felt that my eyes were hurting. I carefully touched them and realised they were swollen. In order to avoid other people noticing, especially Ah Wor, I put my dark glasses on before I came out of my room and also held my head down. I was glad Ah Wor did not ask me anything. After breakfast she came to my room and said she had had an idea. She wanted me to invite Lai-ying and Yin-hing to see the film which my family had been to see the previous evening and after that I could treat them to supper at the kind of restaurant that they would normally go to. I tried to argue that I really did not want to see the film all that badly now and anyway I had too much work to do, but she insisted that it was time I had an afternoon off to enjoy myself, adding that I would probably work all the better if I had a little break. She then firmly gave me some money—her money—and I was so overwhelmed that I did not know what to say, so I just rushed out of the house to the front gate and got into the car.

The next day was Saturday so Lai-ying, Yin-hing and I went to the cinema and had a lovely afternoon. It was my first visit to a cinema and I was impressed by the atmosphere, so different from the Cantonese opera. It was much quieter and people talked in whispers or in very low voices which made it much easier for me to listen. I already had some idea of the story, so I was able to follow the dialogue, which was in Chinese. My friends gave me whispered descriptions of the settings and the costumes and told me the names of the actors and of the characters on the screen. I was soon able to recognise the characters' voices and to follow the story with great excitement and interest.

After the film we went to a restaurant for supper. Yin-hing said it was the one her parents usually took her to when they went out for a meal and I knew from the name that it was the one my parents took my brothers and sisters to. Again, the atmosphere was quite different from the one we had gone to with Ah Wor's sister after the opera. In this better-class one, people talked quietly and the waiters were courteous and attentive. Even the chairs were more comfortable. I asked my friends to look round and see what other people were having, to help us to order, but they said there was no need to do this as there was a menu and we could choose what we liked. I felt happy and proud; it was the first time I had ever been able to invite my friends for a meal. When we were ready to pay the bill I gave the money to Lai-ying, but she insisted that as I was treating them I should the pay the bill myself. The waiters were whispering that they had never seen a blind girl come to a decent restaurant like that, still less pay the bill. For the first time ever, the overheard comments were surprised but faintly admiring—not contemptuous.

That evening did a great deal to restore my confidence in myself. I felt reassured once again that I could do and enjoy almost anything which seeing people did and enjoyed, if only they would let me do it. And what sixth sense guided Ah Wor to do what she did, at that psychological moment, I shall never know. Her instinct and her intuition never failed her and she knew me better than I knew myself.

The film of *Pride and Prejudice* saved the day for me over the book review. I only ever managed to have a small part of the book itself read to me, but I did the best I could from the film and wrote it out in dots and handed it in—or rather, I read it to Teacher Lee who wrote it down. I always had to do this with written work. A few days later the work was returned to us and to my delight I had been given a B for it. Teacher Lee even read mine out to the class and told them all that I managed to do it well in spite of not being able to read the book.

After class she asked me to stay behind for a moment. I waited, wondering if I had done something wrong while I listened to her putting things away in the cupboard. Finally the cupboard door clicked shut and she came to where I was standing. To my surprise she said my Chinese writing had improved considerably and suggested I should write an article for a youth magazine. This was an exciting and slightly alarming idea; I asked her what she thought I could write about. She said I could tell the story of my brother and the ham radio and the doctor in the Philippines and how I began to learn my raised dots. It had never occurred to me that this was something people would be interested in. Anyway, I said I would love to try.

I wrote the article during the weekend and Wai-wan, who had been my "tutor," in Arithmetic, wrote it down for me so that I could give it to Teacher Lee. Teacher Lee read it and suggested a few corrections and then said she would address an envelope for me to the editor of the magazine, which was in Hong Kong. I said I wished there was some way I could write and address the envelope myself. She thought for a moment and then said that perhaps a bit later on I could learn to use a typewriter to write English. I was amazed and asked how a blind person could type without being able to see what she was doing. Teacher Lee explained how typewriters are arranged, with the letters and signs in a standard order, and said that many people become "touch typists" even though they can see and type without looking at their hands or the keys. It sounded ideal to me; I felt sure that I would be able to memorise the positions of the keys, and this started me thinking about English and whether, if I could learn it really well, it would widen my horizon. I remembered the old radio programme, two or three years earlier, where I had heard about books and magazines in dots in England and America—some of them even free of charge to blind people. Secretly, hardly even daring to admit it to myself, I began to dream of going to an English school once I had a good grounding in Chinese.

Several weeks went by and I had almost forgotten about the article. One afternoon during the last recess of the day, a messenger came to our classroom and said there was a letter for me. Someone looked at the stamp and said it was from Hong Kong. I opened it quickly—then realised that of course it was not in dots and I could not read. The next class was just beginning so I had to wait impatiently till school finished and then ask my reader to read it to me. To my joy, the magazine had accepted my article for publication, and as a token of appreciation I would receive a year's free subscription to the magazine. At first I was delighted, but it soon dawned on me that with so much reading of school work I would probably not be able to have any of the magazines read. However, to have an article published did a great deal for my morale. The magazine asked for a photograph of me. That evening I told Ah Wor all this and she was as overjoyed as if she had won a thousand dollars. That weekend she took me to a photographer's shop and for the first time in my life I had a professional photograph taken.

As a result of the publication of the article I received several letters, mostly from people in Hong Kong, who wanted to be penfriends. There were seven or eight in all. Two or three of them were girls in Canton, but the one that particularly attracted me was from a girl named Cheung Yau-lan. She said she was seventeen and had become deaf about two years before through illness. She desperately wanted to stay at school but her family was hard up and made her go to work at a factory. She wrote that she envied me going to an ordinary school. I asked one of my classmates to write her a note suggesting a meeting.

I was eager to meet her for the first time. I thought that as she could not hear I would have to shout in her ear as loudly as I could, but I was surprised to notice that the cousin who came with her repeated to her what I said in a low voice, almost a whisper, and Yau-lan heard every word. I asked them to explain this and found that she could understand what people said to her by lip reading. From then on we became very good friends and went out together from time to time. She learned to read my lips very well so that we were able to talk quite easily. She read me the Chinese translation of *The Story of My Life* by Helen Keller, a wonderful and encouraging book.

Our move to the new house in the suburbs took place in the autumn. I remember asking what the slippery things underfoot on the pavement were and being told they were leaves from the trees. There had been so few trees near our old flat that I had never known about leaves falling off in autumn. The weeks were going by and the weather grew colder. This brought another problem. My life seemed to be a succession of problems; we solved one and another cropped up to take its place. I began to find it more and

more difficult to read my raised dots with my fingertips when they
were cold and this slowed down my work. Previous winters had
been just as cold but as I had not been at school I had not had the
same difficulty.

One morning Teacher Lee asked me to read in class. It was bitterly cold and my fingertips were almost numb; this affected my
reading speed. I struggled with the dots but could not read any
faster. Teacher Lee was surprised and asked whether I was not
feeling well or whether I had not had time to do my preparation. I
was afraid to tell the truth; goodness knows why. It should have
been enough to explain that I could not feel the dots because my
hands were cold, but with typical childish irrationality I suppose I
was afraid of being laughed at or scolded. As it was, I heard whis-
perings that I was either lazy or stupid. I made a mess of the whole
thing and sat down feeling ashamed and embarrassed.

When I told Ah Wor about this she said I should wear gloves to
try to keep my hands warm. I tried it the next day, but it was no
good. With my hands in gloves I could not feel anything properly
and even found it difficult to open the car door. My hands are my
substitute eyes and for me to wear gloves is like a sighted person
being blindfolded. I put the gloves away and decided cold hands
were the lesser evil. However, one thing worried me: I was wearing out my raised dot papers more quickly. I used old newspapers
for all my work and they could not stand much rubbing at the best
of times. I had to read my lessons over and over again and the dots
began to get rubbed flat quite soon, and because my hands were
insensitive with cold I rubbed the dots harder in an effort to feel
them and found that I was making them unreadable.

Yet again it was Ah Wor who came up with the solution. She
said we might ask around for old English magazines which were
printed on thicker, better quality paper. We did not know anyone
who read English magazines and Seventh Auntie lived too far
away, so Ah Wor decided to buy what we needed from the paper-
sellers who bought and sold used papers. I tried this new paper
and it made a wonderful difference; the dots were firmer and easier
to read and they kept in reasonably good condition for much
longer. Also my classmates told me my hands did not get covered

in black printer's ink as they did when I used newspaper. With the first term exams looming ahead, I was thankful for anything that would help my work.

My two main difficulties were, of course, reading the textbooks and finding out what notes the teachers had written on the blackboard.

My readers read to me for four hours daily, but even so I could not put all the work into dots and then there was no time left to study what I had managed to take down. The hours of reading after school and then the long journey home meant that by the time I had had some supper it was already late in the evening and I was too tired to work properly. I usually studied from about nine-thirty to midnight and struggled to stay awake; I tried to cut down my sleep to two hours but it was no use—at around two in the morning I just fell asleep. I got up again at six or six-thirty, but even so I only managed to read through most of my text once or twice before the exams. I used to think how wonderful it would be to have the whole text in dots.

The difficulty over the notes in class was a less clear-cut issue. It was all mixed up with the problems all blind people have of making contact. I knew there were notes on the blackboard—the teachers would refer to them and I could hear the sound of chalk—and it ought to have been a simple matter to ask my classmates to read them to me. But it was not as easy as that. Only a few girls were willing to read aloud; most of the class, though friendly with me, said they did not enjoy reading out loud. Some of them avoided me and I gradually realised that blindness makes it very difficult to take the initiative in making friends. I could not make eye-contact with people and did not know when someone was looking at me and might perhaps smile if I smiled at them. Someone might even be smiling at me already, but a smile does not make any sound and I depend so much on sound. I had to wait for people to talk to me first, and if they did not, there was no contact. I could recognise some of the girls by listening to their footsteps, but I often noticed that they walked quickly past me and I was afraid to risk making the first move and getting a rebuff. I was equally reluctant to keep on asking my two or three friends, who had their own work to do, to spare time to help me. However, even though I did not get all the class notes from the blackboard, I managed to make my own notes by listening to the teachers, as constant practice had made me very fast at doing the dots. I know the notes I made were not as detailed as those on the blackboard, but they were better than nothing.

The dreaded day came at last. We were assigned to different classrooms for the exams and we did not have our own teachers as proctors. I was afraid the unfamiliar teachers might not know about my particular situation and about the need to read the questions to me. In fact, circumstances varied from exam to exam. Sometimes, when the papers had been given out, the proctor would come and read to me without being asked; at other times they evidently had not been told, or had forgotten, and then I had to raise my hand and stand up and wait till I was asked what I wanted. The questions would then be read to me, but all this meant I had much less time than the other pupils to write the answers. At the end of the time I had to read out what I had written to the proctor, who would take it down. I soon found I could not finish the papers in the time allowed, because even when I worked at top speed my dots still took longer than ordinary writing. Greatly daring, I asked if I could give oral answers to the questions I had not had time to put down on paper, and to my relief was given permission. So what happened was that the unfortunate proctor had to give up her own recess time to write down all my answers, whether from my dots or given on the spur of the moment, so that they could be given to my own teachers. The teachers were amazingly kind and patient about this and surprised me, when I apologised for the trouble I gave them, by saying they were glad to do it for me.

I awaited the results with dread and could hardly believe it when I found I had passed in everything. My highest marks were in Chinese, English and History; my worst (though still a Pass) in Arithmetic. Relieved and thankful though I was to have passed, I felt frustrated by the knowledge that if only I could have had more of the textbook material available for study, I could have done better. This tantalising awareness dogged me throughout my eight years at school. On average I reckon I had access to one third of the texts used by my schoolmates. However, I never failed an exam.

With exams safely over everyone relaxed. We suddenly found time to think about Chinese New Year, which was the next landmark ahead of us, and about all sorts of other things that had nothing to do with school work.

I remember one story which fascinated us all. It went on for days in the newspaper; the others told me about it and we followed it eagerly. It was about the workers at a particular company who said they saw ghosts, all sorts of ghosts, even in broad daylight. I began to have nightmares about ghosts who followed me around with horrible screams, so that I woke up feeling frightened. I told the other girls about this—we always told each other about our dreams—and Mei-ling said she had dreamt of a terrible ghost with a dragon's head on the body of a fish. I knew what a fish was like because I had examined one Ah Wor bought, but I had no concept of a dragon. When I asked the girls to describe a dragon, Yin-hing said she had noticed that I only talked about sounds and voices in my dreams, never shapes or colours or anything visual, and wanted to know why. I had never thought about this before and had to work it out. In the end I told them I thought that dreams must be based on impressions of things we have experienced and as I had never experienced anything visual—and no dragons—I could not see them in my dreams. I could not even imagine them properly when I was awake. My dreams were, and are, full of sounds and voices and sometimes the feel of things, because those are the things that make up my world, conscious and subconscious.

I asked them to try to explain to me about happy faces and cross faces. They tried hard but it was very difficult and I did not really get much idea of what they meant. I asked them not to avoid talking about the colour of their clothes or the scenery when I was with them. I wanted to know more about the seeing world and how they saw things. I loved reading descriptive words and when Yin-hing said, "Here comes Pui-ping in a bright red dress," it caught my attention and I began to associate red with brightness. I asked them to tell me what white meant. They said it meant there

is no colour in it. Thinking that everything had a colour, I asked
what colour wind is, and they said wind does not have a colour. I
therefore asked if the wind is white. They said that perhaps one
could put it like that but they sounded very doubtful about it.

Now, after all these years, I can remember so well trying to understand about colour. I have since learned much from people's descriptions and from reading, but as I have never seen, I shall never
really know what colour means. I have to accept the suggestions of
Ah Wor and people whose judgement I value as to the colours of
clothes that suit me. It is easier in some ways for people who lose
their sight later in life, because they know about colours and what
the world looks like, so they can make their own decisions about
clothes and so on from memory. I have no choice but to accept
what people tell me and take it on trust.

Chinese New Year was drawing near; we all looked forward to
it. On New Year's Eve my family followed the usual practice of
putting out brown sugar as a thank-offering to the Stove God, who
is also called the Kitchen God. There is a traditional belief that it is
the job of this God to report to the Head God in Heaven on the behaviour during the past few years of the family in the house where
he is in charge. By stuffing his mouth with sugar he would be
forced to make a kind and benevolent report on them and not be
able to say anything sour or bitter.

Brother and Sister talked about putting on their new clothes to
go with Father and Mother to visit relatives and friends. New
clothes at Chinese New Year always include something red: red is
the colour of good luck and even I associate it with a feeling of fes-
tivity. Brothers and Sisters would be given the red packets of *lai
see* (lucky money), and although I knew I would not be taken
along with them, I looked forward to the good food and special
sweets that go with Chinese New Year. I would get some *lai see*
too, from the grown-ups in the family and from relatives and
friends visiting our home. We children were told that on New
Year's Day we must remember only to say good words and not to
say anything bad; we must not wash our hair or take a bath or
sweep the floor as that would wash out our good luck or sweep the
wealth away.

On New Year's Day we said *"Kung hei fat choy"* to Grandma, Father and Mother. I went to the kitchen and said it to Ah Wor and the other amahs and the gardener, and they all gave me *lai see* packets in return. Then, before breakfast, my brothers, my sisters and I went into the garden where we could not be heard and said every bad thing we could think of to each other, such as getting bad marks in exams and having all the *lai see* packets stolen. We wanted to find out whether bad things would really come true if we said them.

Fire crackers are a traditional part of Chinese New Year. When I was younger I used to be frightened by their noise but as time went on I learned how to light them and run away quickly as they started to go off. It was fun but I only did it when the grown-ups were not around as they would certainly have forbidden me to play with dangerous things. Ah Wor did not stop me—she only said I must run as quickly as I could after lighting one and try not to burn my hands.

Another thing I especially enjoyed at Chinese New Year was the smell of flowers in the sitting room. Father and Mother usually went out to buy flowers on New Year's Eve. They tried to choose flowers that would bloom on the right day because that was a sign of good business and good fortune. I can still remember how upset they were one year when the flowers they bought did not bloom properly. The year was 1949.

CHAPTER 15 •••••••••••••••••••••••••••••••••••••

AFTER THE CHINESE New Year holiday we went back to school where everything was now directed towards the final examinations of the year, which took place in June. At home the family was already making plans for the summer vacation. Once again, Father and Mother were taking my brothers and sisters and Ah Luk by air to Hong Kong and once again I would be left behind, but I did not feel as bad about it this year as I had last year. I just felt sorry for Ah Wor who again missed the chance of flying to Hong Kong. I told her this, but she laughed and said we would enjoy ourselves on our own.

The term wore on. The weather grew hotter and we eventually did the all-important end-of-year exams in sticky discomfort. The teachers and I followed the same procedure as we had for the first-term exams and I was again allowed to give some oral answers when I ran out of time.

I passed in all the subjects, doing much better in English, Chinese and History than in Geography and Arithmetic. One funny thing happened. The morning we had our English paper I met the school cook as I was on the way to the exam room. He was sneezing hard and every time he sneezed he said, "Oh, good, may everything turn out well today!" (Many older people say this to avert a superstitious belief that sneezing is unlucky.) I soon forgot about this, but on the last day of the exams we met Teacher Leung in the playground and asked how we had got on in our English exams. She said that I was the best one in the class and would probably get 94 marks. The older girls gave a cheer and at that moment the cook came by and asked what was going on. We told him and he said that without doubt he had achieved this by saying good luck each time he sneezed that day, and that his good luck had spilled over on to me because I was passing at the time. I did not believe this, but I was delighted by what he said.

When we received the results I was indeed top in English with 94 marks and I was among the top four or five in Chinese. I thought wistfully of the approval given to my brothers and sisters for doing well—and they did not have my problems. But Ah Wor was proud of me and that meant everything to me.

It was Ah Wor who suggested that perhaps I could spend the summer with my readers, taking down the textbooks for the next year, so that I could have more time for studying. This certainly sounded a good idea. I asked Father for money to pay my readers and I asked the girls in Form II to lend me their books. I asked Wai-wan whether the books were changed from one year to another. She said that for the past three years the book list had been the same, so when the holidays came I spent six hours a day putting the books into dots, and in my spare time Ah Wor taught me ironing and other household jobs.

During that summer holiday of 1947 Ah Wor and I went over to the Mo Kwong Home to visit my former teacher. Through her I had become friendly with some of the residents of the Home. Although they were much older than I, we still had a great deal in common. They were interested in all I learned at school and I shared as much as I could with them. One thing they wondered about—only having their own experience of ill-treatment and prejudice, before they came to the Home, to judge by—was how I kept my end up, one blind girl in a school among hundreds of sighted ones. They found it amazing that I had real friends among the sighted girls.

Little by little I learned more about the Home. It was supported by a group of Baptist ladies in Blue Mountain, Mississippi. The practical concern and generosity of these ladies, so far away, who would never visit China or see any of the blind women, impressed me very much and reinforced my own conviction of the power and lasting value of the love of Christ.

The only thing the residents could do towards their own support was hand knitting. The ablest of the residents, like my teacher, had been sent to the Ming Sum School for the Blind to learn braille (or, as they called it, the raised system); they then came back and taught the rest of the residents what they had learnt. We met Miss Dodson, an American lady who lived there as representative of the Baptist Missionary Society. She was impressed that I had managed to get into an ordinary school. She said she hoped that one day perhaps I could teach the women in the Home. I was encouraged and cheered as this was the first time anyone had ever suggested I could do a proper job.

I was thrilled to discover that the residents had put some portions of the Bible into Cantonese braille, using handframes. The Home paid a sighted staff member to read the Bible to the transcribers. I borrowed some of the transcriptions and made copies for myself. They told me that what they had done so far—which was a fair amount of both the Old and New Testaments—took up so much room that some of them literally had to move out of their rooms to make space for the storage of the volumes. They used sheets of paper from old magazines, several at a time, as this was all that was available. It seemed so sad that they had spent an enormous amount of time, care and effort on this transcription, only to find that because the paper was so poor and unsuitable the dots were easily flattened, and that when they stored the volumes in stacks the ones at the bottom were ruined and made unreadable. Constant reading of the most popular volumes also rubbed the dots flat and meant that the volumes had to be regularly re-brailled.

We often said we wished someone would discover something for braille that would retain the dots. Of course none of us had ever even handled a sheet of normal thick braille paper, let alone heard of plastic sheets and thermoforming.

One day that summer I went through the old original packet of raised-dots cards and papers to see if I could read some more of them. I found a card with the name of the John Milton Society and its address in New York. I had learnt in school how to write a letter in English, and I decided to write to the John Milton Society in dots, thanking them for the things they had sent me, which had enabled me to study English and go to school. I spent days and days working out my thank-you letter, reading and re-reading it until at last I felt that it was as good as I could make it. Then Ah Wor took

me to the post office in the centre of town. She described the
different counters and let me feel them with my hands, and showed
me the line of long holes the letters went in. We asked the clerk to
address the envelope for me, which he kindly did. He said it would
be quickest to send the letter by airmail. It was quite expensive,
but we decided to do it this way. We pushed it into the right hole
and went home and other things soon put it right out of my mind.

As I had heard about the Ming Sum School for the Blind from
people in the Mo Kwong Home, I asked Ah Wor to take me there.
It was a long way on the other side of the city and we had to cross
a river (not the Pearl River) by sampan. I was delighted to find
blind women of all ages, as I badly wanted to meet some of my
own age. After that Ah Wor and I went there almost every Sunday
during the summer.

At the time I visited the school the superintendent was Miss
Schaeffer. She told me that the school was founded before 1900 by
an American missionary, Dr. Mary Niles, who was a doctor of medicine. She had seen blind girls begging and singing in the streets
and, thinking of the blind women in her country who received all
kinds of education and training, she decided to help blind people
in China. She appealed for funds from the United States and set up
this school. We were talking in Cantonese, but at one point Miss
Schaeffer used a word I had never heard before—braille. She told
me this was the word for what I and all the people at the Mo
Kwong Home called "raised dots" and that Dr. Niles (who died in
California in 1933) had pioneered a Cantonese braille system. Dr.
Niles had been fluent in Cantonese and, after a lot of research and
hard work, had worked out the initial and final symbols and tone
marks to create Cantonese braille, based on the phonetic system
she had used when she learned the language. Her basic system was
revised and adapted and eventually came to be accepted as standard Cantonese braille and is used all over the southern part of
China. It was, of course, her system that my teacher had learnt and
had taught me.

The school was supported by generous friends in America, including the John Milton Society which made a large, regular grant
to the school. The teachers and pupils were all blind; only the su-

perintendent and the domestic staff were sighted. Most of the people there had been abandoned by their families on river banks or hilltops or in remote parts of the city, or were begging either on their own or for the slave managers to whom they had been sold. The missionaries had rescued them and brought them to the school. In recent years the Government had begun to take an interest in the welfare of the blind, and in an effort to reduce the number of beggars on the streets the police took them to the school, where their maintenance was paid for by the Government. For the rest, the school tried to establish contact with the families of girls who came to them, and to obtain some contribution towards their upkeep. Unfortunately, families were either unwilling to pay or could not be found, so the destitute girls had to be maintained out of the school's grant and gifts. To help with the situation the missionaries tried to find someone—usually a non-Chinese lady—willing to act as a friend and sponsor for each resident. As I came to know the girls better, they all said how lucky I was to have parents who not only did not abandon me but even paid my school fees.

The school itself was large with classes in English and Cantonese braille, music and handicrafts. I was surprised that some of the girls played the piano, and I asked them to teach me the braille music code. When I was first told about it, I thought it sounded terribly difficult, and I later found this to be all too true. The music and mathematics codes must be the most difficult forms of braille. Braille music notation is complicated by the fact that there is no clef as used in staff notation. The naming of notes does not follow the literary braille alphabet. There are seven pitch signs, each indicating to which octave a note belongs. For instance, lower C would be called first octave C and each successive C, with its correct pitch sign, begins a new octave.

For their part, the girls in the school wanted to know what I learned at school, so I passed on to them all I could of History, Maths and Geography and hand-brailled some of my textbook material for them. As I worked at this, my thoughts kept returning to Tse Tse.

The remark which Teacher Lee had made about touch-typing was never far from my mind. I asked Miss Schaeffer about this and she told me that blind people in America and England learn typing and are able to write their own letters and address envelopes quite independently. I asked if I could see a typewriter and she showed me hers. I put my hands on the keys and I just knew, without any shadow of doubt, that I could memorise the positions and learn to type. Unfortunately, she could not teach typing to her pupils because they knew only a very little English—not enough to enable them to communicate in English. I was exhilarated by her encouragement, especially when she said that her school would be glad to have me as a teacher. This was wonderful—another promise of a job, despite all the gloomy predictions—and, moreover, a job which I would dearly love to do and which would be the fulfillment of my cherished dream.

I asked Miss Schaeffer how blind people in America and England studied in schools that provided a curriculum—how they managed about textbooks. She told me that their braille textbooks were transcribed and duplicated partly by the Government, partly by voluntary societies, and partly by many sighted people who learn braille in order to become volunteer transcribers to prepare textbooks and other reading material for blind people. Upon hearing this I really envied blind pupils in America and England and began dreaming of the time when I could express myself in English. It was so obvious that English was much more use than Chinese as a medium of communication for a blind person. That day I made up my mind to try to go to an English school after I had finished Form III. Then, when my English was better, I would write to the John Milton Society and ask them to tell me more about the way blind people live and the things they could do in America.

I remember one other incident about that summer. Soon after the family returned from Hong Kong, Sixth Uncle came to see us and brought a dog, a cat and a "tiger" as gifts for Father and Mother. They all called it a "tiger," and to this day Ah Wor sticks to it that it was a tiger, but I think it was probably some smaller, though doubtless rare and expensive, type of wild cat. My parents were pleased with these gifts. The dog would be a watch-dog while the cat would live indoors as a pet. As for the tiger, the idea was (I am sorry to say) to keep it until it was big enough to be killed and made into a special wine, as tiger wine (*po lai*) was believed to be very nourishing and good for the health. He was young and Brother and Sister said he looked like a kitten.

I asked Brother and Sister to let me see the animals so that I could feel them, but Brother and Sister said they might hurt me and would not show them to me. I realised that I would never know about these animals unless I could examine them with my hands, so I waited until the rest of the family had gone to bed and then asked Ah Wor to take me to see them. She said it would be all right for me to feel the cat and even the little tiger, as he was harmless, being so young, but we had to be careful with the dog which was quite big and was not used to us yet. While Ah Sung, the gardener, held him I put my hand out. Fortunately he was very quiet and still and did not even bark. I sensed he was friendly, so I put my arms round him and examined him very carefully. The little tiger was quiet too, and I walked about the garden with him for a while. The gardener said that after a few months, when he grew bigger, he might get fierce and attack me if I fooled around with him. Next I put my hand out to the cat and stroked her. She was lovely; her fur was soft and warm and she stayed in my arms and curled round and went to sleep until at last I had to put her gently on the floor. That evening I felt that all these animals were alive to me and when I thought about them I could imagine them properly.

I enjoyed playing with the dog in the garden. Whenever I called Kau-jai (little dog) he came running to me and wagged his tail against my legs as if he wanted to tell me he was there. The cat also became my good friend. She spent a great deal of time in my room, and whenever she came in she would give a little miaow so that I would hold my hand out to her and she would come and rub against it. I called her Little Ah Wor and Ah Wor called her the same. Many a time when I called Ah Wor the cat would come running too. One day Grandma heard me call the cat in Ah Wor's name and told me I should never call any animal by a person's name as it might bring bad luck or even illness to the person. Ah Wor said that, on the contrary, ever since I called the cat by her name her headaches had stopped. Grandma thought for a minute and then said that in that case I could go on doing it. I had a job not to laugh; I knew Ah Wor had only made up the tale about the headaches on the spur of the moment to save me from getting into trouble, but Grandma actually believed it.

The summer vacation came to an end and I was happy and confident about starting school again in Form II, knowing that I already had a lot of my textbook material in braille. The first class of the first day was History. I found what I felt sure was the right lesson, thinking I would join in with the rest of the class in reading. To my dismay, what the class was reading was not what I had in braille. During recess I asked a girl to check her book with mine and found that although the subject matter was much the same, the text was different. The books had been changed. I was horrified, and knew that I had to face brailling all the books all over again. And, moreover, now that I was in a higher class the lessons were longer, which meant even more time spent in brailling and therefore less time than ever for studying. It was not only the History books which had been changed—it was all of them. None of what I had taken down during the long summer vacation was of any use to me. I had been so full of confidence, having it all brailled ready. . . . I think this was one of the blackest, most defeating moments of my life. It was several days before I could either attend properly in class or face starting brailling all over again.

We had been back at school for about two months when a roll of papers tied with a piece of string arrived for me by post. I was afraid to open it for when I slipped my finger inside the roll I could feel it was braille and I did not want to risk damaging the dots, so Ah Wor opened it for me. I could not wait to read it. There were some new words in the letter but I could understand most of them. It was from the John Milton Society for the Blind in New York.

They said they were delighted that I had managed to learn braille in this way and promised to send me an extra slate and stylus, as spares. They also said they were sending me a book so that I could learn English braille in a shorter form that would save me time in putting my lessons into braille. I was unable to understand all the things they said, but I had a general idea. There was also a piece of paper with no dots which Ah Wor said had typing on it. I telephoned Seventh Auntie and told her that I had received a letter from America. She was very pleased and came and read the letter to me. It turned out to be exactly the same as the braille letter and she explained all the new words to me. Soon afterwards I received the box of braille material. This time there were no loose cards—all the papers were bound together between hard covers, like a book. There was a small printed book in the box too, so Seventh Auntie came over again to read it to me and helped me to learn the braille contractions. These contractions meant that instead of writing out words letter by letter, groups of letters or even some whole words could be represented by short signs. I memorised them as quickly as I could and before long was able to use them in brailling my English lessons.

I passed on this information to the Ming Sum girls, who made what use they could of them, with their limited English. I am afraid I passed on a lot of mistakes about the rules for using the contractions too—mistakes which I had to unlearn years later when I went to Perkins and was at last taught braille properly. At least the contractions I memorised were some slight consolation during my days and weeks of labour brailling the changed textbooks. I was able to take them down just a little bit quicker, which was something.

Although I realised I really had no time for anything except my school work, one thing stayed obstinately in my mind and would not go—the desire to play the piano. When I went to Pooi To School some of the girls were taking private piano lessons. When I asked the piano teacher, who was another Teacher Leung, the sister of the Teacher Leung who taught us English, to give me piano lessons, she said she would be glad to but had no idea how to set about teaching a blind pupil. For this reason she did not feel able to undertake to do it unless I had some idea myself, or could get someone to show her. That seemed to be that—but then I thought back to my visits to the girls at the Ming Sum school. They had taught me how to read braille music, and they played the piano themselves. I reckoned that music braille lessons from the girls and a trial period with Teacher Leung might be enough to enable me to follow a sighted teacher. I knew money would not be a problem, as my father's business was flourishing and he could afford it.

I asked for an appointment with Teacher Leung and told her about my plan. At first she was doubtful whether it would work and we did not come to any conclusion. But the more I thought about it, the more I felt sure it would work. Teacher Leung was worried whether I could follow her in things like correct hand position, timing, and fingering, but I said that if she would let me feel her hand, and take my hands and place them correctly, I was sure I could follow her. Finally, in an effort to convince her, I asked Miss Schaeffer if she thought this would work or whether it would be better for me to go to have lessons at her school.

She said Ming Sum was too far from where I lived for regular visits to be practicable, especially as I needed so much time for my school work, and it would be far better for me to learn from a sighted teacher. She told me that in the United States there are plenty of sighted piano teachers teaching both blind and sighted pupils, adding that there are also many blind teachers teaching both blind and sighted pupils. I asked how a blind teacher would go about teaching sighted pupils. Miss Schaeffer explained that teaching the piano is a profession where an accurate ear and deft, sensitive hands can really substitute for sight. When he teaches he uses ordinary staff notation books in raised form so that both he and the sighted pupil can read at the same time. He shows the pupil the correct fingering and hand movements and can detect errors by listening; if he is really in doubt, he can "see" their hands with his and make corrections.

She went on to tell me that she had been struggling for years to improve the standard of piano playing among the girls, but they were stubbornly opposed to going to a sighted teacher for lessons. She had tried to persuade the more able ones either to go and have lessons or have a sighted teacher come and teach them at Ming Sum, but they would not do it. When she tried to insist, they went on hunger strike. Now she hoped that if the girls heard that I was learning satisfactorily from a sighted teacher it might change their outlook.

I borrowed some of the braille piano lessons and made copies for myself, and the girls and Miss Schaeffer helped me with explanations. Then Teacher Leung found the same pieces, and this worked beautifully—I got on well and Teacher Leung said I was easy to teach. There was only one snag—the piano at home was quite close to Grandma's room and she often complained that it disturbed her. I was afraid she would complain to my parents who might stop me practising. Then Ah Wor had a good idea—that I should ask Younger Brother to put on his radio or play records whenever I wanted to practise, so that his noise would drown mine. As Grandma held her grandsons in traditionally high regard, as bearers of the family name, she would not complain about them even if she did not like the noise. This did the trick and I practised in peace.

Not that I dared allow myself much time to practise. The very fact that I enjoyed it so much made me feel guilty since I took time from the never-ending reading and brailling, brailling and reading. But on the whole I kept up with the other girls, doing better than many of them in Languages and History and less well in subjects with a more visual element, like Geography with maps and Arithmetic and Chemistry with signs and symbols and figures. In the exams at the end of the year I finished in the upper half of the list. Our results were sent to our parents by post. One day Mother told me mine had come. I knew they were quite good and waited expectantly for some slight hint of approval. Neither she nor Father said a word.

And so we all moved up into Form III and 1948 became 1949. As Chinese New Year and its festivities faded into memory, the storm clouds were already gathering.

CHAPTER 16 ••••••••••••••••••••••••••••••••••

UNABLE TO READ newspapers and dependent for information on what people told me or on what I happened to hear, I had only the most sketchy idea of all the tremendous events that had been taking place in China since 1945. Of course I had by then heard of Mao Tse-tung and of the Communists, but even then, in May 1949, I was not very clear about what Communists were exactly or what they did. I knew only that in some way they threatened us and that we might have to go away. People said Shanghai and many other cities had fallen to them and that they were coming towards Canton. Everyone was nervous and unsettled and there was an atmosphere of uncertainty and fear.

The Government—which at that time meant Chiang Kai-shek and the Nationalists (the Kuomintang, or KMT)—was apparently running away from the Communists. They were rumoured to be heading towards Canton.

In school, where we were supposed to be working for our Form III final exams, none of us was able to concentrate. There were empty seats in every classroom. In our class alone the numbers had dwindled from forty-two to twelve. "I am going to stay," I boasted. "I'm not afraid of the Communists. Why should I be? They're Chinese, aren't they?" But when we heard that Chiang Kai-shek and his ministers were planning to leave China completely and go to Taiwan, I began to have doubts about staying.

At home, Father and Mother were very worried. They no longer talked about it in private, as they had always done before when important things were happening. Now their discussions were quite open. They tried to decide what was best to do—whether we should stay in Canton or go away, and if we went away, where should we go?

They did not want to leave. Leaving would mean losing Father's thriving business and our home and everything. Father was the director of his own firm and he had worked very hard to build it up. He had had help in this from Third Uncle, whose official position with the KMT made him influential, and this was what especially worried my parents—the fact that one of Father's brothers was actually a member of the group of Nationalist government officials who were planning to leave for Taiwan. Father felt sure that if he stayed in Canton, this connection with the KMT would make things very difficult for him when the Communists came.

We heard them talk about going to Hong Kong. They said rich people from Shanghai had gone there, taking much of their wealth with them in gold bars. Father knew he could not do this and he worried whether he could even find a job in Hong Kong to keep the family going. So many people were going there and there would be no Third Uncle to help him. He had no influential connections. Also he knew no English, which would be a further handicap. When he was young, learning English had not been regarded as important, and in recent years he had employed an English-speaking secretary to overcome this problem.

Despite all these difficulties, he finally decided that we would all go to Hong Kong. He said that maybe we might have to go on to Macau, but we would try Hong Kong first. We were to leave in two weeks' time.

When I went to school I told the teachers I had to leave the school the next week. I felt uneasy, remembering my confident statement about staying, but no one threw my words in my teeth; they only felt sad that we had to part, as none of us knew when we would see each other again. A few days later it was the turn of Lai-ying and Yin-hing to tell us that they had to leave for Taiwan very soon. We certainly did not want to lose touch as we were good friends.

We promised to write to each other. "But how will you read our letters and write to us?" Yin-hing asked. I said I would have to ask someone to read their letters to me and write a reply at my dictation, but this did not satisfy Yin-hing, who pointed out that we might want to say things to each other which we did not want anyone else to know about. This was tricky. We wondered if they could learn the English braille alphabet, but soon realised that this would not really be of any use as none of us knew enough English to say what we wanted to in it. In the end we decided it would be of some help if they knew the English alphabet in braille so that they could write their names on the corner of the envelope to let me know who the letter was from. I gave them my spare frame and stylus to take with them to Taiwan. In fact, this worked. I had several letters from them with their names brailled on the envelope. Warned by this I was able to avoid giving the letter to someone who knew us all and who might gossip about our affairs.

Now that the decision to leave had finally been taken, there was no time to lose. The family's whole life in Canton had to be packed up and brought to an end in two weeks. School exams were forgotten—we children did not even go to school for the last few days. The house was in chaos as everyone sorted and packed and argued about what to take. The most important thing to me was my precious braille papers. There were masses of them, but I pleaded and said that they meant more to me than anything else. Ah Wor backed me up and finally said she would rather leave her trunk of clothes than my braille, so in the end we took them.

I have rather confused recollections of some of the time. Everyone was packing. My parents were continually going out on errands and coming back to the house. They were often huddled together, talking quietly and anxiously. We children did not know all the details but we knew enough to be upset at leaving home and a feeling of dread of the future hung over us all—so unlike the excitement of the days of preparation for going on holidays.

At last, we had only a few days left. We were going to Hong Kong by boat. Father had bought the tickets for all of us. I was excited about going on a boat. Ah Wor said I had been on one twice before—on the fateful visit to the village where the herbalist blinded me and on the subsequent journey to Hong Kong—but as I was only six months old then it meant nothing to me. I could not remember ever having travelled on anything more exciting than a car or a bus. However this excitement was somewhat marred by the wretchedness we all felt about leaving Canton. This journey to

Hong Kong was not a happy holiday; we were refugees. Like thousands of our people we had to leave our home, not knowing whether we would ever return.

What worried me most was what was to happen to the animals. I specially loved Little Ah Wor, the cat, but I was terribly anxious about the dog and the tiger too. Ah Wor's two sisters were soon leaving for their home village so we could not ask them to keep any of the animals. The tiger was a real problem. Since he had grown bigger, I had prayed every day that my parents would not remember about turning him into wine. Ah Wor knew how this horrible idea haunted me and suggested we talk with Ah Sung, the gardener, about it. He was sympathetic and decided to move the cage away to the end of the garden, out of sight of the house, to a place my parents seldom went to. We all hoped that somehow the wine business would be forgotten.

But it was not just the wine; what was going to happen to the poor tiger when we went? Ah Wor said that probably we would not be able to find a home for him. He was much bigger now, about twelve months old, and though he was still gentle and affectionate he ate a great deal of meat and we did not know anyone who could give him a cage in a garden, as we had done. One evening, when the rest of the family were out, I went down the garden to see the tiger. The cat and the dog came too and I talked to them all and told them my worries about their future. I felt so wretched that I sat down on the ground and cried. Ah Sung was there listening and he said I was silly to treat them as human beings—how could they understand what I said and how I felt? But later he said that he and the amahs who were watching too were surprised that the animals seemed to understand me and to want to comfort me.

The next day Ah Sung told me that the dog and the tiger refused their food and Ah Wor said Little Ah Wor did the same. She and the other amahs were convinced that the animals really did understand and were sad. On an impulse I begged Ah Sung to take the dog and Little Ah Wor to live with him as he was planning to stay in Canton. At first he was hesitant, saying that if he and his family did not have enough food, it would be difficult to feed the animals. However, I pleaded with him and Ah Wor helped by saying that as many of us believe in the cycle of life—that after we die we come back to earth as another human being or, if we have led a bad life, as an animal—how could we be sure that these three animals were not our relatives, even members of our own families in the past? This touched Ah Sung's heart, and I offered to give him my New Year money to help feed them. Ah Wor then offered to give him some of her money too. In the end Ah Sung agreed to have them. He said he would give them whatever food he had but he would not take our money. However, we insisted, so eventually he did take it. We felt better, because we had done all we could to prevent the animals being a burden to him.

But there was still the tiger. Ah Sung finally suggested that the night before we had to leave, after the rest of the family had gone to bed, we would take the tiger up into the hills, which were not too far away but were quite wild, and leave him there in the hope that he could find food and fend for himself. Although I was afraid that he would be caught again by another hunter, this seemed the only hope that he would not be killed and at least, even if he was, I would not know about it. Neither Father nor Mother ever mentioned the tiger. They had so much on their minds that they completely forgot about him.

It was our last night in Canton. We had to go on board the boat early the next morning. Father and Mother had decided to take three amahs—Ah Wor, Ah Luk and of course Ah Yung—with us, on the understanding that Ah Wor and Ah Luk would be free to find other jobs if they could no longer afford to pay them. That evening the other amahs and the gardener, Ah Sung, were paid off and dismissed. Ah Sung asked if he could stay the night and see us to the boat in the morning. I realised he wanted to keep his promise about the tiger. Luckily the rest of the family went to bed fairly early, as we had to make an early start in the morning. When they were all safely in their rooms, Ah Wor came to tell me it was time to take the tiger.

Ah Sung had arranged for two friends to come with us, carrying sticks and lanterns, because he was afraid we might be attacked by thieves. It was a long walk which took us about one and a half hours, and the road was rough and steep up to the place which Ah

Sung had in mind. We reached it at last and there was nothing to do but take the collar off the tiger's neck and let him go. I said goodbye to him and turned to go home, but he just followed me and licked my feet. I tried to explain to him about staying there but he still followed me and would not go away. This went on for quite a time until in desperation Ah Sung beat him. I begged him not to beat him, as it was bad enough for him to be left alone in the wild when he had always been fed and looked after since he was a cub. Finally, fortunately, he must have seen a bird or something move and chased after it. Ah Wor said he was running away from us, so we quickly ran away too.

We walked home. It was a long way and we were tired. I felt sad about the animals and sad about leaving the house with its garden, which I had come to love. Earlier in the day I had wandered round it, saying goodbye to all the trees whose bark had become friendly and familiar to me, putting my arms around their solid, rough trunks and resting my face against them. I remember kissing one or two of them—and hoping no one was watching me when I did it. Long after midnight that night I crept into bed for the last time in China. Ah Wor whispered cheerfully to me as she said goodnight but she was unhappy too at leaving her country to come with us. She could probably have stayed on quite safely but she chose to come.

She and I were only in bed for about three hours. Very early next morning we all got up and pushed our last odds and ends into our bulging suitcases. The bedding was rolled up and tied in bundles. Personal belongings, clothes and bedding were all that we could take with us. Everything else had to be left behind. Ah Sung, who had been a good and faithful servant and friend to the family, was to have everything in the house which had not already been sold or given away. There was still a good deal of furniture and all the kitchen equipment. I hope it did him some good. We never heard any news of him.

Downstairs in the dining room we found we were having rice for breakfast, which was unheard of—we always had toast. Father and Mother explained that rice would keep us from feeling hungry later in the day, and as food on the boat was sure to be very expensive, they did not want us to ask for anything until we reached Hong Kong.

All the cases and bags and bundles and trunks were collected together in the hall. Father kept on checking and counting the things and every time he seemed to get a different number. Ah Sung was sent off to find a couple of coolies to help and to agree on a price with them for the job. Several *pak pais* (hire cars) had been ordered and all the luggage and the people were loaded in. On the way the coolies recognised Father and immediately demanded a higher price. Ah Sung argued, reminding them that they had fixed on a price before they started, but they flatly denied this. They grew more and more angry and threatened to hit Ah Sung, so at last, in order to avoid more unpleasantness, Father paid up. It did not help us to feel any more cheerful.

At last everything was on board. The boat was crowded with people and their luggage; all were doing what we were doing. We said goodbye sadly to Ah Sung. Sister told me that he stood on the quay for a long time, waiting to see the ship sail.

I heard shouts and goodbyes and the rhythm and noise of the engines changed. We were leaving Canton: Grandma, Father, Mother, my two brothers, three sisters, me, Ah Wor, Ah Luk and Ah Yung. That was in June 1949. Four months later—on October 13, 1949—the Communists occupied the city. As I write this, Grandma, Father and one sister are dead; Mother, one brother and two sisters are in the United States; one brother is in Taiwan; Ah Wor, Ah Luk and I are in Hong Kong; and Ah Yung is in Macau. Not one of us has ever been back to China.

CHAPTER 17 ●●●●●●●●●●●●●●●●●●●●●●●●●●●●●●●●●●●

BEING YOUNG AND on a boat for the first time and going on a journey were exciting, and pretty soon we began to cheer up and look
forward a little more hopefully to the future. The deck was packed
with people and luggage and we sat in a huddled group in canvas
chairs. I kept quiet. I was tired and felt nervous. There were long
silences, and I could sense that my parents were depressed and apprehensive.

Suddenly Father broke the silence. He had just remembered the
tiger and asked if anything had been done about it. Ah Wor and I
were the only people who knew and we kept quiet. After a pause
Ah Wor said that as no one seemed to have any use for the tiger,
Ah Sung had taken him up into the hills and set him free. Father's
immediate reaction was to be angry, but Ah Wor said calmly that
everyone had waited for Father to give an instruction, and when
he had not done so, she and Ah Sung decided that setting the
caged tiger free might bring good luck to the family (which we
could certainly do with), so they did it on their own responsibility.
As this was in line with traditional Chinese belief, my parents
could not be angry and that was the end of the matter. I have often
thought that Ah Wor would have made a good diplomat. It was
marvellous how often she managed, quietly and apparently by instinct, to take the heat out of a situation.

After about seven hours on the boat we reached Hong Kong late
in the afternoon. Some of Father's friends met us on the wharf with
some taxis and helped to carry our luggage. I was in a taxi with Ah
Wor, my two brothers and Mother. I began to feel almost at once
that the atmosphere in Hong Kong was quite different from that of
Canton. I could hear many more vehicles on the road and Brother
told me that there were more tall buildings and the shops were bet-

ter decorated. I asked what Hong Kong money felt like—remembering the amah who said that one dollar in Hong Kong was not the same as one in Canton. Ah Wor whispered to me not to ask so many things and promised she would take me to a money changer as soon as possible so that she could show me some Hong Kong money and work out how to identify the new coins and paper notes. As Ah Wor said this, I realised that Mother had not said a word since we arrived, and in fact had said very little during the entire trip. I felt that if only I could see the anxiety and strain on her face I would be more conscious of our situation and less curious about the things outside.

We reached a small flat which Mr. Leung, Father's former secretary, had rented on our behalf. It was in Kowloon City. Everything was carried inside and put on the floor but we could not unpack our cases or make our beds as the flat had no furniture in it. Mr. Leung and Father and Mother went out immediately to look for second-hand furniture and we children and Grandma and the amahs were left in the flat. I wandered round and realised that it was very small, even compared with our old one in Canton, and tiny compared with the house we had just left. Ah Wor helped me to explore everything I could, but she said it was not much use my learning the place until there was some furniture in it as that would change everything and give me different landmarks.

It was strange sharing a room with all my brothers and sisters—six of us sleeping in three pairs of two-decker wooden bunk beds with only two chairs and all our things still in our suitcases on the floor. Poor Ah Wor, Ah Luk and Ah Yung had to use the small passage as their bedroom, which must have been wretchedly uncomfortable for them. In Canton, when they had finished their day's work, they used to sit in the nice roomy kitchen talking and laughing, but now they were very, very quiet. Perhaps they did not want to intrude on us, or perhaps they were worried and frightened about their future.

It was June and very hot and humid; the tiny flat was like an oven. Penned in it with nothing to do, we children squabbled and fought and got on Father's and Mother's nerves. In desperation they decided to take the whole lot of us, me included, to the beach to get some fresh air and be out of the flat for a few hours. A friend of Mr. Leung owned a small beach hut and had said that we could use it, so we all set out, taking Ah Wor with us to cook lunch. It was quite a long way by bus but when we got there it was worth every minute of it.

The sand was soft as we walked around barefoot; I loved the feeling as it pushed between my toes. It was fun except for the times when I stepped on sharp shells or stubbed my toes on rocks. It smelt damp and salty and made me feel good. The up-and-down sound of the waves was tempting and I wanted to go into the water, but I felt nervous. My brothers and sisters were already in, splashing and shouting, and I was determined to go in too and find out what it was like. Ah Wor took me into some shallow water and showed me how to float on my back and how to move my hands and feet. Just as I was starting to float a big wave came and I felt I was being rolled over; I got water and sand in my mouth, ears and nose and swallowed some. For a moment I panicked and did not realise that the water was barely deep enough to drown me and I could easily stand up in it. I struggled to my feet and at the same moment felt Ah Wor's comfortable arm round me. To my horror I realised that she was in her ordinary clothes and did not have a swim suit. I started to gasp out apologies, but she just laughed and said it was all right because her clothes would soon dry in the sun.

I asked her how she knew how to float. She said she used to enjoy swimming in the river in her childhood village, and also she could just look at other people and see what they did.

After a while I learned to float on my back and to swim a little on my front. The waves did not bother me any more and it was fun. Before long Ah Wor said she had to go back to the hut to cook our lunch, but I did not want to get out of the water. Although she was reluctant to leave me, Ah Wor said that my sister was not far away and if I called out to her, she would hear me, and I was to stay close to her so that I did not go the wrong way. I called to Sister and she was surprised to see that I could float and even knew a few strokes.

Ah Wor called us from the edge of the water. She said she had some lunch ready for us, so we scrambled out onto the sand and dried ourselves. With our dripping hair and sandy hands, lunch was a bit salty and gritty but delicious, as we were all hungry.

After lunch my sister and I decided to make a sand castle. While we were working we were joined by someone who stood and watched us. I guessed it was an old person because even on the sand I could hear the tell-tale sound of a stick as well as footsteps. The person spoke at last—it was a woman and her voice sounded most peculiar. She was evidently watching me because she asked me in a mumbling, indistinct voice if I could see a little. I said no, not at all. She sounded surprised and said the bus journey to come to the beach must be difficult for me. I said it was fun and I enjoyed it. Then she said that in seventy-four years she had never seen a blind person on the beach or a blind girl playing with sighted girls. Sister explained that we were sisters, and I could tell from the direction of her voice that she was looking up at our visitor, who was standing close to us as we knelt on the sand. Then Sister whispered to me that she had no teeth. I thought about trying to eat without teeth and, not very tactfully, asked her straight out why she did not go to a dentist and get some dentures, as it must be awkward for her. Sister dug me in the ribs to shut me up, but the woman did not seem to mind.

To our amazement, she explained that some years previously her son's business had been losing money. A fortune-teller had declared that her teeth were to blame for the misfortune. She therefore had all her teeth extracted as she did not want to eat the wealth of her descendant. Ah Wor told us later that this is a common belief among elderly people, but I do not expect that many people actually go to the length of having all their teeth out. I asked her if her children became any richer after she got rid of her teeth and she said quite seriously that her son prospered for three years afterwards. She did not tell us how long ago that was or what happened at the end of the three years. She watched us for a bit longer and remarked that my castle was bigger than Sister's, then she wandered away and we never saw her again.

For two blissful weeks we went to the beach nearly every day. It was somewhere near Castle Peak and took about forty minutes by bus. Then one evening Father said we could not go any more; he could not find a job and soon all his money would be used up. He dared not spend the money on bus fares.

We knew he was going out every day to look for a job. He could not work at his old profession as an architect because his Chinese qualifications were not acceptable in Hong Kong, so he tried to find work as a salesman in a big shop. But the shops wanted people who could speak English and Father knew none at all. And it was no good asking the smaller shop keepers as they mostly employed their own friends and relatives.

The sense of strain and anxiety became more marked as the days passed. Unable to go to the beach, we children hung around the tiny flat, bored and edgy. My brothers and sisters went out for aimless walks round neighbouring streets but I mostly stayed in with the amahs, who did not have much to do since the flat was so small and limited. Mother was moody and irritable and Grandma spent her time sitting in the one armchair in the cramped living-room, grumbling steadily, whether anyone was listening or not.

After a week or so of this depressing state of affairs, a letter came from Third Uncle in Taiwan saying that he planned to resign his political office with the Kuomintang and come to Hong Kong to start a small business. This sounded a good idea as he and Father would be able to work together and this might solve Father's problem.

Father and Mother were never absolutely sure, but it seemed probable that Third Uncle decided to do this because of the complex series of overlapping relationships between his original and legal wife, my Third Auntie, and two concubines.

To get the story clear we must go back about fifteen years, to before the Sino-Japanese War. At that time Third Uncle and Auntie had a son (their only child), who was in his twenties and was at the Ling Nam University in Canton. They owned a farm in the country outside Canton and one fateful day the son, my cousin, drove into and killed a cow belonging to a farmer.

Uncle's immediate impulse was to offer compensation, but the young man was against it. He maintained that the cow had behaved in a crazy, unpredictable way and that the accident had not been his fault, so why should his father pay? The matter eventually came up in court and this was the court's decision, on the evidence. Uncle and Auntie still wanted to pay, but as the court had ruled that my cousin was not responsible, he was strongly opposed to payment.

Only a short time afterwards the young man was taken ill with a high fever. His father arranged for the best doctor in Hong Kong to examine him, but the illness was never diagnosed and after five or six days he died. Inevitably everyone said it was a judgement on him and that the cow's aggrieved ghost had taken vengeance.

Poor Third Auntie never got over the shock and grief of his death. She never touched beef again and she remained a sad, dispirited person until her own early death from cancer, for which she came to Hong Kong for treatment. Father and Mother always said she had lost the will to live and no treatment could have saved her. She died during the Second World War.

Third Uncle grieved for his son for some months, but he was a more resilient person. He believed in the Good Life and had taken a concubine even while his legal wife was still alive. Third Auntie mustered enough strength to resist the intrusion of her rival into the household, so Uncle had to install her in lodgings somewhere else, where he visited her. However, before Third Auntie died Uncle took the concubine to the house and Auntie was charmed by her warm and pleasing personality and she came to be recognised by the family, who called her "Little" Auntie or "Little" Sister-in-Law. Everyone liked her. Uncle had sent her to a private tutoring school in Canton (she was in her early thirties) and with the additional polish this education gave her, coupled with her naturally attractive personality, she was a welcome newcomer in the family. For some reason she seemed to dislike being called Little This and Little That—the accepted and quite respectable indication of her status as a concubine—and suggested that she be known as "Miss Six" instead. Why "Miss Six" I have no idea; it evidently meant something to her.

The obvious thing would have been for Third Uncle to promote Miss Six to the status of first wife. All he had to do was to notify the family of Miss Six's new position and then the family would have had to recognise her as enjoying the same status as legal

Third Auntie. It would not be necessary to have a formal marriage as they were regarded as being the equivalent of married. There would not be any official marriage document, but this is quite acceptable in Chinese society. However, one thing stopped Third Uncle doing this. Before she died, Third Auntie said she did not mind how many concubines Third Uncle took but she made him promise not to let any of his concubines succeed to her legal status.

Third Uncle was not the only one who had a roving eye. My Father, before he was matched with my Mother by the marriage broker, had intended to marry a woman he loved. Unfortunately she was at that time a well-known professional prostitute, and Grandma would not allow this. She felt that the respectable status of the Ching family would be damaged if her son took a prostitute to be his first wife. She insisted that Father must marry a respectable virgin as his first, or legal, wife. Then he could take the prostitute home to be his concubine.

I think it must have been very hard on Mother, who knew perfectly well that my Father had had this lover before she married him. However, I never heard her complain about "Little Mother," who did not live with us but came to see us from time to time. I remember that she addressed my mother as "Mistress," which was considered to be proper. She and Mother were courteous to one another, and I can still remember that "Little Mother" used to pick me up and carry me about when she came to see us. I must have been about four or five years old at the time.

Third Uncle arrived from Taiwan and moved in with Miss Six. Father asked them both to supper. There was a great deal of discussion of everybody's problems and Uncle surprised Father by saying he thought it might be better to start a business in Macau, as everything was so difficult and becoming more expensive in Hong Kong. Also, in Macau Father's lack of English would be far less of a disadvantage. Uncle pressed this so hard that Father was alerted to look for the real reason—and he and Mother came to the conclusion that Uncle wanted to ship the whole family off to Macau, thereby leaving the field clear for himself to live as openly as he liked with concubine Number Two.

Concubine Number Two dated back to the war years in Hong

Kong. Uncle had kept her secret from the family for a long time, but Father found out about her and he and Mother suspected (correctly, as soon became apparent) that she was putting pressure on Uncle to get her accepted by the family as Miss Six had been. The fact that Miss Six was to be included in the mass exodus to Macau lent weight to the theory that his main motive was to free himself from surveillance of his private life.

There was talk of Miss Six and Grandma setting up a flat together in Macau. Grandma, however, effectively scuttled this plan by forming an unforeseen attachment to Number Two after Uncle had carefully arranged for them to meet. Armed with Grandma's approval of her, which was the real purpose of bringing them together, Number Two set about trying to induce some members of the family to call her "Aunt" or "Sister-in-Law." She was only partially successful; no one liked doing it. Father, Mother, Seventh Uncle and Auntie refused outright and avoided ever using any form of address to her. Undaunted, she embarked on a campaign to try to get herself accepted as Uncle's legal wife and doubtless the exaggerated attentiveness she showed to Grandma was part of a well-calculated plan to consolidate her position.

At some stage Uncle suggested that Miss Six and Number Two, who had of course met by now, might set up house together. This, however, was altogether too much for Miss Six, whose patience had been tried to the limit, and she refused. Number Two next made it known quite openly that she wanted full family recognition and said publicly that she did not want to be called "Little" Anything. This was the last straw for Miss Six, who certainly had prior claim. Unable to stand the humiliation, she told Uncle they must part and she left the family. I think this must have been a source of real regret to Uncle—though not sufficiently so to make him mend his ways. Number Two departed triumphantly for Macau, with Grandma, to find a flat and set up a base for Uncle.

A few days later Father went as well to look for a flat for all of us. After a couple of days he came back with the good news that he had found a small flat, so once again we were all busy packing. The furniture, bought less than three months ago, had to be sold. A young couple just setting up house came to see it and said they would like to buy it all but did not want to pay the costs of moving it from our flat to theirs. It looked as if the deal would fall through when Father figured it out and found that the expense of hiring a van and coolies to move it would be almost exactly the same amount as he would get from the sale. However, he had reckoned without Ah Wor and her determination to get round difficulties. She said there were the three amahs with practically nothing to do —they would carry the stuff on foot. And they did—from Kowloon City to Tsim Sha Tsui, probably the best part of three miles. It took them two days, making several trips a day. How many hot, dusty, exhausting miles they walked, goodness knows. They carried, amongst other things, beds, chairs, a table, and a chest of drawers through the streets.

The buyers were so impressed by the loyalty and devotion these amahs showed in doing this that they offered Ah Wor and Ah Luk jobs with them, holding out promises of much more money than their present employer was able to give them. (Had they but known, the amahs were receiving no pay at all at that time.) Ah Wor and Ah Luk refused, saying they had formed bonds of affection with the family of their employer and had every intention of staying with them.

Boat tickets were bought. We were to leave the following day. The furniture had gone, the flat was bare and we all slept on the floor. Late that night there was a knock on the door and we all felt apprehensive. We called out in a chorus to know who it was. It was Third Uncle. We let him in and he immediately launched into a long monologue about ensuring the continuity of the Ching family name. All this sudden anxiety had been triggered off by the anniversary a few days previously of the death of his son. He had no other children and as his legal wife was dead he could never produce another son who could fully represent the family lineage. Seventh Uncle and Auntie had only daughters, so this meant that the continuation of the line depended solely on my two brothers. There were, in fact, two other boys—sons of Second Uncle—but as they were descended from Little Grandmother, a concubine in the previous generation, they did not count as full family members from the point of view of the lineage. So Third Uncle had become terribly anxious to make sure that all the family graves at Chung San, the family village in southwest Kwangtung, were in good order and propitiously sited. It did not take very long to convince Father that this was a matter of vital importance and urgency and must at all costs be dealt with before the Communists reached the area.

I listened, fascinated and amazed, to this discussion. Privacy was impossible—the grown-ups were talking in the middle of the group of half-asleep figures lying on the floor. Next Uncle produced a package, apparently something wrapped in paper, which I could hear rustle. He gave it to Father and it became clear that it was money which Father was to use to hire the best geomancer available and to carry out whatever recommendations were made about changing the graves.

He then raised the matter of schooling for all of us children. He said specially—and I'll never forget this—that if Little Girl wanted to go to school and could find one willing to have her, she should be allowed to go. Father was inclined to argue that school was more important for the boys and that for me it was just something to keep me occupied, but Uncle said this was not necessarily true. He actually said I was bright and one never knew what the future might hold. Amazingly, he had once read a Chinese translation of the story of Helen Keller and had realised that even blind people might have unsuspected talents and abilities.

I can recall vividly the emotions I felt, lying there pretending to be asleep and listening avidly to everything that was said. Ever since leaving Canton and the school that had, after much pleading, agreed to have me, I had been terribly worried that I would never find another willing to take me. It was not as if I could depend on the family for support. Even in the good times my parents had been at best indifferent and in general opposed to my efforts to get education. My only true and unfailing supporter was Ah Wor, whose opinions would have received little attention at parental or school principal level. I had come forlornly to the conclusion that our retreat before the advancing Communists could well mean a retreat for me back into the frustrating, circumscribed life of being almost a prisoner in a little flat.

Also there was the question of money. Our present financial situation was so poor that we might not have enough even for food, so I knew there was little chance of fees being paid for me. My parents might struggle to pay for my brothers and sisters, but I could hardly plead with them to pay for me when they did not regard my education as anything but a form of indulgence to keep me happy. I suspected that by this time Ah Wor had spent most of her savings on my education, paying for my Arithmetic tutor, for readers, for taxis, for English magazines to use as braille paper and so on, so I could not expect more help from her.

But now, like an answer to prayer, Uncle had come unexpectedly in the middle of the night and proved to be my champion, taking my side and arguing my case with my uncomprehending parents. Their respect for Uncle, despite his philanderings, made them listen. I could not have wished for a more persuasive advocate—they accepted what he said and agreed that, if possible, my schooling should go on. I may feel critical, looking back, of some aspects of my Uncle's behaviour, but my gratitude and indebtedness to him for this miraculous support makes me hold him in high regard to this day, though he has now been dead for some years.

I fell asleep, reassured and happy and much more confident about our uncertain future.

CHAPTER 18 ●●●●●●●●●●●●●●●●●●●●●●●●●●●●●●●●●●●●●

EARLY NEXT MORNING we set off to get the boat to Macau. This meant crossing Hong Kong harbour as the boat left from Hong Kong Island. The children and the luggage, with the three amahs, were loaded as tightly as possible into two taxis and Father and Mother went by bus. We all met at the Star Ferry where we had to pick up and drag all our belongings down the long entrance passage and the ramp onto the ferry. When we reached the Hong Kong side we carried everything from the Star Ferry to the Macau Ferry Pier. The distance is not very great but it felt endless that day. There were plenty of coolies clamouring to help, but we refused to hire them because of the expense and struggled on unaided. The coolies cursed us for our meanness and shouted that they hoped we would never be prosperous—which in the circumstances was ironical. We were cross and jaded by the time we finally loaded ourselves and the luggage onto the boat, which felt nearly as big as the one we had come on from Canton. We travelled in silence. No one spoke except when Father or Mother told us or the amahs what to do.

Ashore in Macau, I felt that the atmosphere was different from anything I had known. We were taken to our new home by several strange little vehicles which were new to us. They were called three-wheel cabs or pedicabs and were not pulled by coolies like rickshaws, but seemed to me to be something like a bicycle. The flat Father had found for us was quite pleasant, on the ground floor of a two-storey stone house.

Father said they must go and find some second-hand furniture. Mother and the amahs were to go with him to help bring back what they bought. However, Ah Wor suddenly said she must show me the toilet before they left the house. I said if she would take me to the door of the toilet once, I would be able to find it again, but

Ah Wor insisted that this toilet was different from any I had come across before. She took me and explained that it was one without a pedestal and seat and that I had to find the right place to put my feet, by the edge of the hole in the floor.

The following day Father told us children that we must be good and not get into mischief because he and Mother were going to the village to see to the family graves and were leaving us in the care of the amahs.

During the next two or three weeks we were free to do pretty much as we liked. We gradually forgot about being hard up and about the uncertainties ahead as we enjoyed the fun and interest of exploring Macau. I said to my younger brother that we must find a church to go to. We discovered a Baptist church not too far away from home—about twenty minutes' walk. The first Sunday we went to church together and my brother met several of his former classmates from his school in Canton, both boys and girls, whose families, like ours, had left China. We soon became friends and they all joined in calling me Third Big Sister, which I liked. We went around as a group and this made me very happy as I was accepted into equal companionship. Two members of this group were Daniel Tse and Jachin Chan, now President and Vice-President of Hong Kong's Baptist College.

One thing that happened each night at supper aroused my curiosity and suspicions and I made up my mind to find out about it. In an earlier chapter I described what normally happened at mealtimes—all the food was put on the table in the dining room and when the family had eaten what they wanted, the amahs ate the left-overs in the kitchen for their meal. When Father and Mother went to the village I noticed that the amahs were doing things differently. They said they had kept some food back in the kitchen and that we could finish up all that was on the table. I told my older brother and sister that I did not believe this, but we did as we were told and ate up all they gave us. Food was certainly less plentiful than we were used to and there was less meat in it, but we had enough.

But I was still suspicious and one evening, when we had finished and we knew the amahs were eating in the kitchen, I took Second

Sister's hand and asked her to come with me and look. We went to the kitchen and Sister at once exclaimed that they were just having plain rice, without any of the vegetables and meat we had just had. I was so moved that I cried. The amahs told me not to be upset; they said they were grown-up and did not need the food as much as we children did while we were still growing. Sister and I went back to the others and we decided we must do something about this. Finally we all insisted that the amahs must eat with us. The next day we asked them to come and join us at table. They refused and said that such a thing could not be done. We told them that since they treated us as if we were their own children and since they were in charge of us in our parents' absence, they must eat with us or we would not eat our meal. In the end, seeing that the food was getting cold, they reluctantly agreed to eat with us and the others promised me that they would make sure that they had their share of the food.

I came to love Macau. There was a calmness and peace in the streets. The main means of transport were rickshaws and pedicabs. The only motor vehicles were the cars of a few wealthy people and of government officials. Nowadays Macau has developed into a tourist resort and is noisier and more sophisticated than it was in the early 1950s (though still much quieter than Hong Kong). But at that time it was lovely to walk around the quiet streets, feeling the fresh air and smelling the scents of all the trees and flowers. I loved to feel the tree branches which reminded me of the friendly branches in the garden in Canton.

After about three weeks Father and Mother came home from the village. They were pleased with what they had done about the ancestral graves. The geomancer assured them that the changes made would ensure that my two brothers would be able to have sons to continue the family name. In fact, Father and Mother left the village only shortly before the Communists arrived and occupied it along with all of Kwangtung Province except Canton.* All

* Mao Tse-tung proclaimed the establishment of the People's Republic on October 1, 1949, despite continued resistance in southern China. When Chiang Kai-shek's government fled from Canton to Chungking on October 13 and to Taiwan on December 8, the conquest of mainland China was complete.

this did not make sense to me. How could Father and Mother be sure that the Communists would not interfere with the cemetery and undo all they had done? I dared not ask them about this but I talked to Ah Wor about it. She said she did not really know, but she reckoned that perhaps, no matter what happened, the spirits of the deceased would realise all the efforts the living family had made to please them and gain their blessings, and therefore such blessings as continuing the family name would be granted.

School term had already started about a week before Father and Mother came back. In order that the children should not miss the entire term, Father immediately set about finding schools for them. They were all admitted to the Ling Nam School and the Pooi Ching School. I was alone in the quiet house with no brothers and sisters to keep me company. I was terribly anxious about my education. I did some work on my own, reading through all my old braille notes, and I tried to listen, as in the past, to the others when they were doing their homework, but I knew I would drop behind all too quickly.

Father finally found a job as a cashier in a grocery store, but his salary was hardly enough for us all to live on.

When we had been in Macau for about six weeks I noticed that Ah Yung was unusually quiet. She was absent-minded too, and several times when we were talking she forgot what we were talking about. One day, when there was no one else about, I asked her if something was worrying her. She said no, but I felt sure that there was. I tried hard to persuade her to tell me. Finally she gave in and admitted that there was something, but it was no use talking to anyone about it as it was an insoluble problem. I pointed out that even if I could not help I could at least listen, and that just talking it over with someone might help. So she told me that one day while she was going to the market she had met a man. He had asked her to go out with him, but she had refused. From the way she spoke of him I realised she was attracted by him and wanted to see him again. From what she could gather from other amahs, he was a good man and worked as a tailor.

She had never had a date before, but it was quite obvious that she wanted to meet him again. However, what was worrying her was that she was a slave and was therefore not free to choose friends and make dates. I told her, truthfully, that I had never, in all the years she had been with us, heard any conversation between Father and Mother that suggested that they thought of her as a piece of property or as anything other than a normal human being with normal rights, and I felt reasonably sure that they would not object to her going out with a friend after her work. But Ah Yung was not convinced and said she would not want to run the risk of displeasing her master or mistress. She said that although they had been very good to her she would not want to test their kindness to that extent. I understood what she meant and how she felt and I had to admit that I could not be absolutely sure that they would not mind, so I suggested to Ah Yung that if she could wait for a couple of days I would try to think what to do.

I knew Father and Mother usually went to bed very early and in any case they would seldom ask for Ah Yung once supper was over. If she were to slip out quietly by the back door and not be out for too long, she could have her date and come back in the same way. I suggested this to Ah Yung and Ah Wor. They both thought it very risky, especially Ah Wor who was supposed to be responsible for Ah Yung. But as Ah Yung thought about it and began to get excited at the prospect of seeing her young man, she decided it was a risk worth taking. If she was caught, the worst thing that could happen would be a bad scolding from my parents. As Ah Wor had told her on the day of her arrival, my parents did not beat their children or anyone else. Understandably, Ah Wor took more persuading than Ah Yung, but in the end she agreed to let Ah Yung go ahead with it. After all, it was important for Ah Yung to have some social life. For the next nine or ten weeks Ah Yung met her friend most evenings in this way. She would come back and tell us all about it—how their friendship matured to real love and understanding and, later, how he proposed to her and how she would like to marry him. But had it been left to her I think it might never have got further than that; I do not think she would ever have asked my parents herself. If Father and Mother were ever going to know, I would have to be the one to tell them, so I waited for a good opportunity.

One Saturday afternoon after lunch Father and Mother were talking about their property in Canton, including the house intended to provide for my future. The chances of them ever going back to Canton were remote, but they felt they should still keep the deeds, hoping that perhaps someday, in years to come, some descendants might be able to claim something. Father suddenly asked me what I thought I would do with the house if I ever got it back. He seemed to be in a good humour so I thought this might be my chance. Instead of answering Father's question, and trying to keep my voice calm, I told them about Ah Yung and her boy friend. I was afraid they would ask how and when Ah Yung saw her friend, but they did not, and when I had finished there was silence. I could not tell whether they were pleased or not, so I went on to say that I would much rather know that Ah Yung was happy than have a house of my own. It was Mother who spoke first. She said she was glad Ah Yung had found herself a husband and even said that she had heard of the tailor—neighbours and friends had mentioned him and spoken well of him, saying he was a good and honest man.

Father asked why Ah Yung had not spoken for herself, but Mother said she could understand that Ah Yung would feel unable to broach the subject as she was a slave. Father made one interesting comment. He would never, himself, he said, have bought or owned a slave, and if Sixth Uncle had told him beforehand that he was buying them a slave as a gift, he would never have agreed to it. But by the time Sixth Uncle told him about the girl, he had already paid for her, so he could not refuse.

I told them that Ah Yung had often said that she was happy to be with us and that she believed she was one of the luckiest slaves anywhere as she was so well treated. Father then said that he knew Ah Yung and I got on well together, and he had been wondering whether she would stay with us and be my companion and helper when I grew up. I said that I did not think it would be right to a her to do this just when she was on the point of beginning to live her own life. She and I could always keep in touch, but I would never want to impose on her.

On an impulse I asked Father and Mother whether they would

let Ah Yung go free. Mother said that as far as they were concerned Ah Yung was a free person. Overjoyed, I ran to the kitchen to tell Ah Yung—not that there was really any need to tell her because the kitchen was close to the living-room and she had heard every word. As I went into the kitchen she threw her arms round me, laughing and crying at the same time. Ah Wor told her to control herself, and went into the living-room to thank Master and Mistress for their kindness. Ah Yung and I followed her and Ah Yung knelt down before my parents, but she was crying too much to speak.

"For heaven's sake," Mother exclaimed, "it should be such a happy time for you. Why are you crying as if you were a country girl being forced to marry a man you'd never met?"

Ah Yung laughed, despite her tears, and finally managed to say, "Master and Mistress, I could never thank you enough. I don't know what to say."

"You don't have to say anything," Father said. "Go and tell your friend that you have our blessing."

"I will go and tell him immediately and I know he'll want to come and see you and thank you himself." And she ran back to the kitchen to get her shoes and hurried out.

Later however she came back alone. She told Ah Wor and me that her friend was afraid to be presented to her master and mistress. She explained that for some time he had been saving money to be offered as a gift to the parents of his wife-to-be, but now that he was going to marry Ah Yung, a "freed slave," he was afraid that her master and mistress, generous though they had been in freeing her, would certainly expect a larger sum of money from him than he could offer them. I said I did not think they would expect a large sum of money from him. They had not said anything about expecting money at all. I asked Ah Wor what this was all about and she said that in any marriage, when the man proposed to the girl, the girl's parents or guardians would certainly expect money as a condition of allowing the girl to marry him. In many cases a young man had to borrow money in order to meet the demand, and therefore started married life in debt to money-lenders. In the case of a slave, the master and mistress would be likely to demand more than usual to recoup what they had spent on feeding her and keeping her. Many people bought a slave as an investment, later to be sold as a concubine at a high price. Very seldom would a slave be allowed to marry the man of her choice unless the man could offer a large sum of money to her owners.

Having heard all this I began to understand why Ah Yung and her tailor were worried. Knowing how Ah Yung was treated in the family, I could not believe that my parents had any intention of exploiting her in this way. Ah Wor agreed. However, it was clear that we must find out how much they would be expecting, because until the tailor knew it was a sum he could pay he would not dare to come and see them. I asked Ah Wor if she thought I could ask Father and Mother about this and then tell Ah Yung, but Ah Wor said it would probably be better for Ah Yung to speak to them herself. They had proved themselves kind and generous in freeing her and agreeing to her marriage, so she need not be frightened to ask them this question herself. But Ah Yung did not like it; she said she could not go and bargain with her master and mistress about the price of her freedom. Next minute she was in tears, saying she would rather tell the tailor she would not marry him.

There was only one way to settle it. I ran to Mother, took her hand and dragged her from the living-room to the kitchen, saying I had something important to ask her. She was a bit irritated and said I was always making trouble, but she came to the kitchen with me. There, I blurted out that Ah Yung's boy friend was worried about paying money to Father and her. Mother sounded cross and snapped at Ah Yung that she should know better by now than to think they intended to make money out of her. I begged Mother to ask Father, to make sure. She said she was sure, but to satisfy us she went back to the living-room and asked Father in a loud voice if he was expecting to get money from Ah Yung's marriage. Father just laughed and said, "Perish the thought!" We all sighed with relief and Ah Wor urged Ah Yung to go to the living-room and thank them. Ah Yung walked slowly and nervously into the living-room and Mother said, "Why are you hanging your head like that as if you are ashamed of yourself? Go and tell your silly boy friend that we are not expecting money from him."

Ah Yung's boy friend was overjoyed. He told everyone about his good fortune and in no time the matter was a subject of gossip all over the neighbourhood. A number of women either called on Mother or stopped her in the street, urging her to change her mind and demand some money, even if it was not much. They said they had never heard of anyone letting a slave be married off without receiving at least something for all the money they had spent to feed her, and pointed out that if you bought property you did not let it go for nothing—especially when you were refugees, as we were. But I am glad to say Mother and Father took no notice of all these. They evidently did not regard Ah Yung as a piece of real estate.

They had little enough money to spare but they managed somehow to give her some new clothes, a few presents to start her household and even a small gift of money.

Her wedding had to be simple but we were all happy for her. She lives in Macau with her children and grandchildren to this day.

CHAPTER 19 ●●●●●●●●●●●●●●●●●●●●●●●●●●●●●●●●●●●●●

SOON AFTER AH YUNG left us I heard Father and Mother say that they must let the other two amahs go. Although they were so devoted and were willing to stay with us whatever happened, the fact that they were two more mouths to feed was too much at this time. The thought of losing Ah Wor appalled me. I was fond of Ah Luk, but Ah Wor meant more to me than anyone else in the world. She was not only dear to me; she was my lifeline. I spent sleepless nights wondering whether or not I could talk to Ah Wor about this. With a little flicker of hope I remembered her promise never to leave me.

The next day I asked her to take me with her to the market and told her all this on the way. In fact, I had already heard Ah Luk say confidentially that the way things were, Father and Mother would not be able to keep her for long and she had been looking round for a job. I was terrified Ah Wor would feel that she had to do the same. To my intense relief she said she would plead with my parents to let her stay. She had been finding out about small factories which gave outwork to people to do at home, and hoped to find something that would contribute to her own keep and allow her to stay at home with me. It was lucky she had made these enquiries because the moment I dreaded came all too soon. Father asked Ah Wor and Ah Luk to come to him and he told them he could not keep them any longer. I could hear by his voice that he was very sad. Ah Luk said that although she would have to work for another family, she would come back and see us as often as she could and would always regard our home as her home. Ah Wor told Father of her plan to get outwork from a factory and asked him to let her stay. So she stayed and Ah Luk left us to get another job.

It took Ah Wor a while to find any suitable outwork, but she found some in the end. She was to string beads for decorating bedroom slippers and sweaters. She handed over all her earnings to Father and this not only paid for her own food but in addition made a useful contribution to the family finances. A curious little ceremony took place every time she contributed money over and above her keep—Father gave her an IOU for the extra money and told her to keep all these notes safely. He was realistic enough to know that he might never be able to repay her himself but he was confident that his sons and daughters would honour the debt in time to come. It was a regrettable fact that my mother found it very difficult to adapt to our new way of life. She occasionally gave Ah Wor a hand—she even cooked a meal now and then—but on the whole she was probably the person who was least ready to admit the need to alter her way of life, and found it very distasteful to have to curtail her social activities. She preferred to preserve the polite fiction of gracious living, complete with an amah to ensure her leisure. And she went on playing mahjong.

Ah Wor gave as much time as she could spare to take me round all the schools to see whether one of them would accept me. The interviews always followed the same pattern: I tried to convince the school people that I could study like other children, showing them my reports from Pooi To School and my exercise books containing my corrected written work. Of course I always had to explain about braille and about someone having to write my work down for me so that it could be read and corrected. This was where trouble always started. People might be fairly easily convinced that I could do the work but as soon as they began to realise that I needed test questions and exam papers read to me so that I could put them into braille, and that I then had to have someone to take down my answers in writing so that they could be marked, the reaction was always the same; they said they were sorry, but they were sure no teachers could give that much time and attention to me. It looked as if my hope of continuing my schooling was doomed to disappointment. I felt very depressed.

I asked our friends at church to pray with me that I could again be helped to go to school. Although at the moment things looked hopeless, I had a feeling that Pooi To's acceptance of me might show that I was meant to go to school and that perhaps, if I kept trying, I would get there in the end. I asked everyone I met to tell me the names and addresses of schools and I soon realised that I had tried practically every one in Macau. One principal said he would let me listen in class but made it clear that I should never try to take part fully in the work as the teachers just could not afford the time.

By now I had become friendly with some of the young people at the church. Two girls who lived quite near us offered to take me to church with them. One Saturday afternoon we were on our way to a meeting at the church when I overheard two unknown girls who were walking near us discussing a lesson from a Chinese Language book which I had studied at Pooi To. They were worried because they could not understand the lesson and as they walked along talking about it, they became quite agitated. I said to my friends that I thought I could help them. My friends spoke to the girls and as a result we arranged to meet in the park when our church meeting was over. My friends told me that the two girls looked at me curiously. I guessed they must have been wondering why I was wearing dark glasses and had to hold the arm of a friend.

When we met in the park, before we began talking about the Chinese lesson, I told them I was totally blind. I thought they would ask a lot of questions, but they did not, asking only my name. I told them and asked theirs. One of them was Annie Lau and the other Lydia Wong. These names puzzled me—they were different from any I had heard before. They did not sound like Chinese names. Lau and Wong, which surely were their surnames, were placed after what sounded like their given names. I asked them to explain this. They explained that Annie and Lydia are English names which are placed in the opposite order from Chinese ones. I asked them which school they went to, and they said they were at the Sacred Heart Convent English School for Girls. An English school! I could hardly suppress my excitement. For so long I had dreamt of going to an English school. Could it be . . . ?

It was soon clear that Annie and Lydia wanted help with several of their Chinese lessons, so I suggested to my friends that it might be better if they went on home and did not wait for me. I had an umbrella with me which I could use as a stick and I had a pretty good idea of how to find my way home from the park, which was not far away. However, the two Sacred Heart girls said they would see me home. I was delighted to find myself accepted by two more seeing girls and we set to work.

While we were working a Portuguese lady whom I knew came and spoke to me. I had met her during our stay in Hong Kong. In fact, she had been staying in the same building we were in, on the floor above. She had been very kind to me, letting me go up to her flat and talk to her. It happened that she came across the park that afternoon and recognised me. It was a happy surprise for us to meet like that, made even happier by her promise to call in for Ah Wor and me the next afternoon to take us to her flat. After that, she added, we would know the way and could go and see her whenever we wanted to.

That evening I could not think of anything else except the Sacred Heart English School. From what Annie and Lydia said, I could work out where it was—not right in our immediate district but not very far away, probably about fifteen minutes' walk.

Next day the Portuguese lady, whom I called Auntie Mica, kept her promise and took us to her house. While she was in the kitchen making some tea, Ah Wor suggested that I might ask her if she could help me make some contacts with the school. This sounded a very good idea. We knew that she was a Macau-born Portuguese and a Catholic, and that her late father had held a high position in the Macau Government. Her brothers were influential people, so it was quite possible that she might be able to establish a contact for me, or she might even know some of the Catholic Sisters at the school.

While we were having our tea, I told Auntie Mica about my wish and asked if she could help me in any way. I did not have to convince her, as I did the school people, about being able to study with seeing girls as I had already told her all about my time at Pooi To School. She was most sympathetic and understanding. She said that she did not actually know anyone at Sacred Heart but she would be glad to take me to the school to see the headmistress.

I knew there would be a big difficulty with this school—language. I had asked the two girls if the teachers spoke Cantonese and they had said that most of the teachers were Catholic Sisters from abroad who spoke no Chinese at all. But Auntie Mica said that there must be some Chinese Sisters who could interpret for me. She thought that although it was something which no one in Macau had ever thought of doing before, there was nothing to lose by trying, and it might work.

On the following day Auntie Mica, Ah Wor and I went together to the school. I had not told my parents we were going. Once we were inside the school gate I heard nothing but English being spoken all around me. I tried hard to understand it but could only pick up a few words here and there. We were taken to the headmistress's office. The headmistress at that time was Sister Margaret, an Italian. Auntie Mica told her about my desire to go to an English school. Knowing that I had been in a Chinese school, Sister Margaret spoke very slowly and clearly. I knew she was doing this for my sake. I was able more or less to understand what she said but was unable to say what I wanted to in reply to her. A Chinese Sister was called to come and interpret for me. I found I could understand a great deal of what she said when she translated my Chinese into English. How I admired her excellent command of both languages! My Pooi To school reports were interpreted for Sister Margaret who said, without hesitation, that although none of the English schools in this part of the world had any experience of this kind, she would be glad to give me a trial period. She made an appointment for me to see her again during the following week, by which time she would have had time to talk to the other Sisters. She would then let me know definitely one way or the other.

That week of waiting was a dreadful mixture of hopes and fears. I wanted so much to go to the English school, but I had a mass of worries and misgivings, especially about the textbooks. I realised that having books read to me in English would be much more difficult than in Chinese—and the Chinese had been bad enough. In Cantonese braille, as all words are based on the phonetic system, I could put into braille whatever was read to me, sentence by sentence, phrase by phrase, rather like shorthand. But with English books I would be in trouble as English braille is based on spelling, not phonetics, and my readers would inevitably have to spell out many of the words to me before I could take them down. Then, unlike my former school, all the subjects would be in English, not just one language subject, and there were so many words whose meaning I did not know and yet I had no way of looking them up in the dictionary. The more I thought about it, the more anxious I became.

On the day of my appointment with Sister Margaret, Auntie Mica came to take me to the school. Ah Wor, of course, came too. We went in and the Chinese Sister who had interpreted before was there. She took me to a chair which was close to the table. There were several English-speaking Sisters present. Sister Margaret asked me to use my handframe and write down the twenty-six letters of the alphabet and then read them out. She then read me a few sentences to take down in braille. There were some words I could not spell so I asked her to spell them for me, which she did, and when I had taken it all down Sister Margaret asked me to read it back to them. Apart from a few errors of spelling, most of it was right. The Sisters talked together for a short while. I tried desperately to keep calm but my hands were damp and clammy and I dared not think what I would feel if in the end they said no.

At last Sister Margaret spoke to me. She said they loved me very much and wanted to give me a chance. However, as I probably would not be able to follow in class they suggested that I should have a tutor to help me two or three times a week. I asked if they would let me try for a couple of weeks before deciding whether this would be necessary. I knew we could not possibly afford a private tutor. Ah Wor whispered to me that I might as well agree to have a tutor as I would certainly need to have a reader, and even though there might be no time left for tutoring, someone competent to be a tutor would undoubtedly be a much better, clearer reader and would be more help to me all round. However, the Chinese Sister heard only what I said; she did not hear Ah Wor's whisper. She translated what I said to Sister Margaret who, in the end, agreed to let me try for a couple of weeks before any decision was taken about a tutor.

Sister Margaret said she would help me to fill in my school registration form and asked me my name. When I told her it was Ching Man-fai she suggested that it would be better for me to have an English name as it was easier for those teachers who did not speak Chinese. I said I could not choose an English name for myself as I did not know any. I asked her if she would tell me some so that I could choose one. She read out a long list of names. It was difficult to pick one as they were all strange to me. Some were difficult to pronounce and some were long, made up of several syllables. I asked her to tell me some which were short and easy, so she gave me another list. Still nothing sounded right and I felt at a loss. Then I heard her say "Lucy." It sounded good and it was easy to pronounce. I asked how it was spelt and found that there were only four letters. I said I would like to have Lucy as my English name. She asked if I knew what this name meant. I said I did not, but I just knew I liked it. She patted me on the shoulder and said that the name meant "light" and that I would carry God's light wherever I went. She added kindly that the girls would learn a lot from me and that I had much to give them. I asked what I, a blind girl, could give to seeing girls. The Chinese Sister translated this and Sister Margaret said that perhaps the girls would complain less about all the work they had to do when they saw how much harder it was for me and how hard I had to work to keep up. She said she was glad that God had given her the opportunity of helping me and that as a result of my coming to the school as a sort of pathfinder, they would know better how to help other blind girls coming after me. All this made me feel very humble, but at the same time gave me strength to face the difficulties ahead.

There were indeed difficulties—plenty of them—but I can never put into words my gratitude for the kindness and real Christian love with which I was treated at that school, for the help I was given and the warmth with which I was received. They did have other blind girls after me, so I was like the tool of Providence, guiding the school to find out how to give help and education to those in very special need.

I asked which class I would be in and was told I would go to the Special Class. I argued and said I did not want to go to a Special

Class; I said I would try to do my best if they would let me go to an ordinary class with the seeing girls. They all laughed at my instant protest and explained that the Special Class was for girls who, like me, had previously been at a Chinese school and needed to improve their English. The form mistress could speak some Cantonese. Most people had one year in the Special Class during which they gradually got used to listening and speaking in English. At the end of the year the teachers would recommend which of the regular classes they should go into.

As Ah Wor and I walked home I whispered my English name in time with my footsteps—Lucy, Lucy, Lucy, Lucy—hoping that I would recognise it when someone called me by it at school. I told Ah Wor how to say it and asked her to call me Lucy from now on, but she said she could not possibly—as an amah she must go on addressing me as Miss Three. I argued, saying that she was much more than an amah to me. However, she stuck to it that it was something she could never do, and she never has.

As we entered the flat we heard voices. There were two strangers talking to my parents. I dawdled so that I could listen and quickly realised that the two men were bargaining with my parents about Mother's fur coat. It was the only good, warm coat Mother had managed to bring with her when we fled from Canton. I knew she loved it very much and she and Father had said they would not part with it in any circumstances. I felt sad to think that after these few months they had to sell it in order to feed us.

What made it worse was that I realised with dismay that I had to break the news to them about going to an English school and had to ask for money to pay the fees. I heard the men leave. The flat was suddenly quiet; I could not even hear my parents' voices. Ah Wor had gone to the kitchen. I was in a quandary. It was Friday evening and I was supposed to start school on Monday. What ought I to do? This hardly seemed the moment to tell them of yet another expense. Then, cutting across my indecision, I heard Father say to Mother that they might as well give the money to my brothers and sisters to pay their school fees for the whole term, instead of giving it to them month by month, so that no matter what happened, whether or not we had enough to eat, they would be able to continue school.

This made up my mind for me. I must tell them now, hoping they would include my fees with the others. Gathering up all my courage, I went into the room where Father and Mother were still talking together, and sat down on a chair. I sat there for a long time but no words came. It was as if something inside me was stopping me from speaking. All the excitement and elation I had felt so recently had faded and only fear and anxiety remained. I knew it would be no use going into details about all that had happened, and how, and about my English name—they would not have been interested at the best of times and now, with so much else on their minds, they would not even listen. But somehow I had to get the fact over to them that I needed ten dollars for a month's school fees and that I needed it on Monday.

At last I steeled myself to speak. I heard my voice sounding tight and high-pitched, telling them very fast that the headmistress of Sacred Heart had agreed to take me and that I was to start on Monday. "And please could I have ten dollars . . ."

I said all this in one breath and they did not understand. I made myself repeat it slowly. Father and Mother did not say a word. I tried to think what I could say. Now that I had taken the plunge, I must go on—I might not get another chance. Suddenly I remembered Sister Margaret saying that perhaps if I could study more English I might be able to give conversational English lessons as a private tutor. As soon as I said this, Father brightened up; his voice sounded pleased and he said that he was glad to hear of this possibility. Now, when he could no longer be sure of providing me with a home or putting money in the bank for my future, anything I could do to contribute towards my own keep would be a help and a relief to him. This cheered me enormously. At last Father had taken my education seriously and accepted that it could be useful. I felt sure now that he would pay my fees. He even asked about uniforms and told me to go back and ask Sister Margaret where I could have it made.

Sister Margaret told Ah Wor and me about a tailor where the

uniform could be made. The uniform (it was now the end of September) was a woollen dress and a short coat. We asked one or two other tailors but found they were all much more expensive than the one Sister Margaret recommended. The coat cost forty dollars including the material, and Ah Wor paid half of this to help Father and to make sure I got it. I found out later that she worked late at night doing extra bead-threading to get the money. It would be a week before I could have the dress, so I had to go for the first week in ordinary clothes.

The following Monday a new phase of my life began. Conscious for once that what I was doing had the approval of my parents as well as Ah Wor's blessing, I walked with Ah Wor to the school. It was early and the girls were in the playground. I did not know where to go or who to ask. Ah Wor told me the girls were mostly in little groups and I could hear some of them talking in Chinese and some in half-English, half-Chinese. I really did not know what to do; then I remembered about the Special Class. I asked Ah Wor to walk round with me and take me close to as many groups as possible till I heard Chinese being spoken. We did this but group after group was speaking English. Then the bell rang. Not knowing where I should go, I asked Ah Wor to find me a place to stand where the teachers could see me. Before long I heard brisk footsteps, far away at first but coming nearer. Ah Wor said it was the headmistress and that she had seen me, so I told her I would be all right now and she could go home. Sister Margaret greeted me kindly and told me the school was all lined up for prayers in the playground. She took me to join the line of Special Class girls and spoke to those near to me, asking the one on my left to let me take her arm and walk with her to the classroom. Then she went away and I soon heard her voice leading the prayers.

When prayers were finished I was immediately surrounded by running feet as everyone dashed past me. I thought of trying to catch the arm of one of the girls and asking her to take me, but I could not be sure of who was going to the Special Class. I tried to ask but no one heard me, or if they did they did not grasp what I wanted. Maybe it was because I was not in school uniform. Finally I was alone. I did not know what to do. I was holding my umbrella, which I used now to find my way in the direction from which I could hear voices. I went up some steps and walked on until I could hear a voice talking quite close to me. I knew I was outside a room. I listened but could only make out a few words in English—of course, it was an English school! The only thing I could do, I thought, was to knock on the door and ask the way to the Special Class. But I had to try to ask in English. What I wanted to say was, "Could you please show me the way to the Special Class?" I knew all these words in English but putting them in the right order to make a sentence defeated me. I worked on it for some minutes but all I arrived at was, "I go Special Class." Finally, very nervously, I knocked on the door, found the doorknob, opened it and said breathlessly, "I go Special Class." The teacher came to me. I did not catch what she said so I repeated my phrase several times. The teacher was evidently at a loss and must have beckoned to someone in the class for, a moment later, a girl came and asked me in Cantonese what I wanted to say. She immediately told the teacher, whom I now knew from the form of address to be one of the Sisters, that I was lost and wanted to be taken to the Special Class. I could understand each word she said. It sounded so easy, the way she switched from Cantonese and back again. How I wished I could do it.

The Sister took my hand and I realised she was taking me to my classroom. I wanted to apologise for interrupting her class and to thank her but all I could say was "thank you." It was frustrating, not being able to say such simple things. We came to a flight of stairs; I heard footsteps and recognised Sister Margaret's voice as she spoke to the other Sister. It was all in English and they talked fast so that I could pick up only a word here and there. Then Sister Margaret spoke to me. She spoke slowly and clearly but she used some words which were new to me. I grasped that she had been looking for me. We went along some passages and came to a classroom where I was greatly relieved to hear the teacher speaking Cantonese. She spoke with an accent but I could understand her fairly well.

Sister Margaret introduced me to her—she was Sister Christina, the form mistress—and to the class and said she hoped they would make me welcome. Sister Christina took me to a desk, gave me a chair and went back to the lesson. Cautiously, I took stock. I was sitting at the side of another girl's desk. I had of course brought all my braille things with me so I put my hand out to see if there was any room on the side of the desk nearest to me. There was not—it was all taken up with books, pencils etc. As I was trying to arrange my things on my lap, the girl whispered to me that she would move some of hers so that I could use half the desk. I whispered "thank you" and was glad she had spoken to me first. I listened attentively and took down some notes and began to feel more cheerful. Sister Christina was reading very slowly, pronouncing every word clearly and carefully and spelling them out when necessary. My anxiety began to fade.

The bell rang. Not wanting to be left stranded again by everyone running off, I quickly put my hand on my friendly neighbour's shoulder and asked if she would take me with her. Together we went to the playground. I asked her to tell me something about herself and also to help me meet some of the other girls. Soon there were six of us. They all came from Chinese schools, mostly in Canton, and like me were refugees. One of them was from Pooi To School, several classes my senior. This group of girls became my friends and they helped me to learn my way at the school.

Our class only had half-day lessons so I had the afternoons and evenings to braille and study my textbooks. This meant I did not have to work late into the night as I had done at Pooi To. With the help of the girls who read to me I managed to braille most of my textbooks. At first when I asked them to read, they were very hesitant, especially as they had to read in English. I told them not to worry about pronunciation but just to spell the words out, so finally nine girls agreed to take turns to read. Naturally during the reading sessions we sometimes discussed the lessons and they soon found that I could remember more of the meanings and pronunciation of English words than they could. This saved them looking things up in the dictionary (which did not give pronunciation anyway). After my first few days, Sister Margaret decided I did not need a private tutor, because Sister Christina told her I was doing well in spelling and general grammar.

After two weeks we had our first written test. I did as I had done before, back in Canton—as soon as I could hear that Sister Christina had stopped writing on the blackboard I asked her to read the questions to me. When I read my answers back she was surprised and pleased to find that I could do written work in this way and said that I could have a desk to myself. I was delighted, as this made me the same as the rest of the class, quite apart from giving me more room.

The first weekend, I asked Ah Wor to show me the way from home to school and back. We could not do this on weekdays as I had to hurry to school in the mornings, and when school finished at midday I had to rush home to lunch so that Ah Wor could begin taking me to a series of different houses for my friends to read to me. Ah Wor would go home in between to get some work done and then come back to take me on to the next place, just as she had done in Canton. This time it was a little easier for her, because Macau is much smaller than Canton, and so she did not have such great distances to travel. Father had asked all my brothers and sisters to read to me, but as they seemed to have difficulty managing their own work, I did not have the heart to bother them except in real emergencies.

One surprising and heart-warming thing happened: Father told Ah Wor that she was not to worry if for any reason to do with my readers she could not be back in time to cook the evening meal. He said that he finished work at around six o'clock, and if Ah Wor had bought food in the morning, as she usually did, he could prepare supper for all of us. Ah Wor of course felt strongly that it was her job, as an amah, to cook the meals and she seldom let Father do it unless she was very rushed, but she did accept his offer to wash the dishes so that she could take me to a reader's house as soon as possible after supper. I was encouraged and cheered that Father really seemed to be taking an interest in my school work. After all that had happened in the past, it was wonderful that at last he evidently regarded it as important. I almost felt a full member of the family.

One day I found out that several girls were boarders at the school and were in the habit of spending an hour in the playground from five to six P.M. I asked one girl, who said she often used the time to work, if she could read to me for a little during that hour. I was delighted when she agreed, since Ah Wor had by now taught me how to find my way to school and back on my own, with an umbrella as a stick. I only had to cross one road. Although Ah Wor fretted about the possibility of a kidnapping, she let me travel alone after watching me a few times to make sure I was all right.

On the afternoon when I first asked a boarder to read to me, I started doing my braille and pretty soon there was quite a crowd round us, watching and asking questions about the braille. I tried to demonstrate both Cantonese and English braille until all of a sudden, to my horror, I realised that half an hour had slipped by and I had only asked the girl to read for half an hour. My disappointment must have been apparent in my voice when I said I must let her go back to her own work, because an older girl who spoke Cantonese with an odd accent said she would be glad to read to me for half an hour until she had to go back to her room. I was relieved and grateful.

Her English was very clear and distinct. Instead of spelling most of the words out to me, as the girls in my class did, she just read them. As I had to ask her to spell most of them for me she soon realised how limited my English was and adapted her method of reading accordingly, speaking the words very slowly and clearly at first to give me the pronunciation and then spelling the difficult ones. It was a great help, as I was able to learn both spelling and correct pronunciation at the same time and I began to catch up on what I had missed in class. The girl offered to do this with me for half an hour every day, and of course I gladly accepted. I found out that she was a Form V pupil and, judging from her excellent English and the accent with which she spoke Cantonese, I realised that she must be an English-speaking girl. I asked her name and she gave a surname which was not Chinese. She said I could just call her by her Christian name, which was Norma, so I called her "Big Sister Norma" to conform with Chinese custom in addressing an older person. However, she told me that now I was in an English school, that did not apply and that it was really perfectly all right for me to call her "Norma," so I did. I believe one of her parents was Portuguese and the family spoke English at home. Her English was not quite perfect and she had a slight accent, but I was unaware of such minor flaws at the time. It was wonderful to have a fluent reader who made such good sense of what she read.

CHAPTER 20 ●●●●●●●●●●●●●●●●●●●●●●●●●●●●●●●●●●●

QUITE LATE ONE evening while I was working in the bedroom I shared with my sisters (as I did not need the light, I could work till all hours without disturbing them), my attention was caught by a familiar sound: it was Grandma's voice. She was talking to my parents and she was crying as she talked. Her voice was so muffled and indistinct that I could not make out what she was saying. I tiptoed to the door and listened carefully.

Grandma was going to leave Third Uncle and Number Two—or "Third Aunt," as we now grudgingly called her. Third Uncle was good to her but he was seldom at home, so she was left to the tender mercies of Third Aunt, who had treated her badly ever since the move to Macau. Bit by bit, Grandma came out with a list of the humiliations and unkindnesses she had to put up with. Third Aunt would not let her have the types of food she liked; she only spoke to her occasionally; she refused her requests for simple things like face cream, saying they were extravagant. All this was when they were alone together; when Third Uncle was around she was as sweet as could be. She had searched Grandma's belongings, looking for money and valuables, and that afternoon things had come to a head when she had decided to take Grandma's gold and jade bracelet. She tried to take it by force. Grandma, not wanting either the bracelet or her wrist damaged, said she would give it to her if she could soap her wrist so that it would slip off. She finally removed it and handed it to Third Aunt. This bracelet was Grandma's most treasured possession. Third Uncle had given it to her for her birthday some years previously, in Canton, and it had cost thousands of dollars. Birthday presents are not usually given to younger people, but as people grow older their relatives of the immediately younger generation may give them quite valuable gifts as a token of respect and esteem. My Uncle had given Grandma the bracelet in this way.

This episode had been the last straw for Grandma, so when Third Aunt went out later in the evening Grandma had packed her clothes and asked an amah to bring her to us. I heard Father say she was welcome to be with us if she wanted to, but she would not find our small, crowded flat as comfortable as Third Uncle's much roomier one. Grandma pleaded to come. Hardly able to believe my ears, I heard her say she would rather sleep on the floor with us than go back to Third Aunt. I had never known her so upset.

Later that night, when everyone had at last gone to bed and the flat was quiet, I heard a curious sound. At first I did not know where it came from, but I went to the door of the room and listened and then I could tell that it came from the little room—it was a box-room really—where Ah Wor usually slept and which Grandma was now in. Ah Wor had gone to sleep in the little kitchen. The sound was unmistakable—Grandma was crying. Apart from snores from my parents' room, there was no other sound, so I knew I was the only one awake and aware of what was happening.

I was confused. Grandma had always been the autocratic head of the Ching household. It was strange that she should be reduced to this state. It was the first time she had had a taste of her own medicine. I felt sorry for her, but then I remembered how highhanded and demanding she had always been with everyone and, as far as I was concerned, how unkind she had been, and I found myself thinking it served her right. A glow of malicious triumph that she was getting paid back for some of her unkindness and injustice stole over me. Then I felt shocked and ashamed at my reactions. I claimed to be a Christian and Christians were taught to love and forgive. The Old Testament said we must love and respect our parents, then we would be blessed—the only Commandment with a promise. "Dear God," I thought, "How can I love Grandma? But as this is Your Commandment, help me to do it."

I found I was crying too. I went and sat on the edge of my bed for a long time, thinking. Suddenly it seemed as if an electric current ran through me, leaving me with a calm and peaceful feeling. I knew what to do.

I tiptoed to the living-room, found the flask of tea which I knew was always left there, carefully poured out a cup, making sure it was not too full so that I would not spill it, and crept towards Grandma's bed with it and whispered to her. She did not respond at first. She was weeping with a muffled sound. I could not tell whether she had heard me or not or whether she did not want anything to do with me. Hesitantly, I reached out to touch her and found that her face was covered by the blanket. I gently patted her and whispered "Grandma" again. She pulled the blanket off and stopped sobbing, but did not say anything for what felt like a very long time. It must have been only a few moments really. I suppose that she must have been staring at me in surprise. I heard her sit up and she took the cup of tea from me and drank it. I tried to say something to comfort her, but I just could not get any words out. Tears ran down my cheeks and Grandma began to cry again. Finally Grandma said something which startled me: "Dear child, forgive me, please, forgive me." Impulsively I put my arms around her neck. At that moment I felt I could really love her. "Go to bed now Little Girl, I'm all right. You have warmed my heart."

"Good night, Grandma. Sleep well," I whispered. With a full heart I went back to bed.

Not very long after Grandma came to live with us, Father said he could no longer manage to pay the rent of the flat we were in, and we must move to somewhere cheaper. He found a place which had a very low rent, which was hardly surprising as it was barely habitable. It was on the first floor of a wooden building, and Second Sister told me in a whisper that termites had eaten great big holes in the wooden walls. I asked Ah Wor if anyone lived on the ground floor. She replied that there were stacks of wood and piles of buckets and crates and jerricans, which made it look like a store. There was a strong smell of petrol and kerosene and we hoped it would not catch fire. But there was nothing we could do about it if it was the only place that Father could afford.

My school work was going quite well; I could manage the learning and note-taking part all right, but I could not solve the problem of how to present my homework to Sister Christina. The exercises were not difficult, but they consisted of many repetitions of grammar patterns and sentence constructions—too many to read to her during our short fifteen-minute recess time, which was all we had each day. Sister Christina decided she would just pick out part of the exercises for me to answer orally, but as I had brailled the whole exercise each time it was disappointing not to have it all corrected.

One Sunday afternoon I was at Auntie Mica's flat and she introduced me to her sister, Miss Nora. They were asking about my school work and I was telling them about the difficulty over the exercises when I suddenly remembered Teacher Lee at Pooi To saying that it should not be too difficult for me to learn to type. Miss Schaeffer at Ming Sum had confirmed this, saying that blind pupils in ordinary schools in America and England used typewriters to type their work for their sighted teachers. I told Auntie and her sister about this, and asked if they thought they could possibly find out for me how much it would cost to have typing lessons. Miss Nora at once said that she was an office worker and had just recently retired and if I could rent a typewriter, perhaps she could teach me. She said she did not think it would be too difficult, as touch typists do not look at the keys anyway. I was thrilled beyond words—though I realised that even this unexpected solution involved the problem of money, which always dogged us. Ah Wor, as usual, read my thoughts. She said she would see to it that money to rent a typewriter was found.

We said goodbye to Auntie Mica and Miss Nora and went to look for a typewriter shop to find out the cost of renting a machine. The cheapest was fifteen dollars a month. On the way home I said to Ah Wor that I must ask Father first to see whether he could help. I realised it was not the time to ask him for more money, but I thought it was only fair to Ah Wor to see if he could manage before letting her do extra beading work to pay for it. However Ah Wor insisted that I really must not ask him. She pointed out that although Third Uncle was sending a monthly contribution to help with the family expenses, Father's salary from the grocery store was so little that, with school fees and all the other inevitable expenses, he could barely make ends meet. Therefore, she said firmly, she would look after the typewriter for the time being.

The following day we rented a typewriter and took it to Auntie Mica's flat. Miss Nora had told us that she would be glad to teach me free of charge. I was so anxious to learn that I found it really was not difficult at all. After a few days I had memorised the positions and decided to take the machine home. Everyone in the family was surprised that I could actually type and do my homework on it. Father asked how all this happened. When I explained, he was so pleased that I had another means of communication besides braille that he said he would pay the rent of the typewriter.

I asked Sister Christina to let me type my test and exam papers. I knew that if I was very, very careful, I could do it without making too many mistakes, and if I did make mistakes, as Miss Nora said, I could back space and put x on them. Of course I knew it would be more difficult for me than brailling because in braille I could always read back what I had written and cross out wrong words. I could not do this with type. Once typed, my contact with the words was lost. I knew that by doing this I was, in a way, adding to my handicap. But on the other hand it was better than making do with the limited amount the teacher could write down at my dictation.

For just a little while things seemed to be going well. Life at school improved and the days passed smoothly and peacefully. But before long another trouble loomed. My Second Sister, the one who was so close to me, was in some sort of trouble or difficulty which I could not understand. She complained that she was always tired. She did not eat much and yet everyone said she was getting fat. She had to struggle to keep up with her school work and would sit until late at night repeating one or two sentences of a subject over and over, like an automaton, and yet she did not remember them. She slaved at it for long hours, received almost no marks for her work and was terribly worried.

One night while she was working, the lights went off. She lit a candle so that she could carry on, but she was so tired she fell asleep. I thought she was reading silently to herself until I smelled burning hair. I woke her up but she said she could not move. In alarm, I felt for the candle and ran with it to the kitchen sink, then poured a bucket of water over her head. This drenched her clothes and everything but at least it roused her properly. She discovered that her book was soaked and she wept with anxiety and misery. All this commotion woke Ah Wor who was sleeping in the passage. She came to see what was going on. It was lucky, she said, that I had rescued Second Sister in time. The hair on her forehead was badly burnt but at least her skin was untouched. As for the book, Ah Wor gave her money to buy a new one.

Father was furious with her for doing so badly in her exams, and blamed her for being lazy and not caring about her work. I knew how unfair this was, but could do nothing. I knew, too, that Sister was constantly in pain and she showed me where the pain was, at the left back of her waist. This meant nothing to me then but I knew intuitively that there was something seriously wrong. I urged her to tell Father but she said that if she did, it would only cost money. He could not afford to take her to the doctor, so she said nothing and struggled on.

By this time Seventh Uncle and Auntie had moved to Macau with their family of girls. The political changes in China had made great difficulties in their lives, as they had in ours. Seventh Uncle had had a good education and for some years had held a post with the Kuomintang. Now he, like Third Uncle, was finding life hard and was having problems getting a job. They went to Macau because it was possible to live there much more economically than in Hong Kong.

Worried and unhappy as I was about Second Sister, there was some consolation in having Seventh Auntie near and being able to see her quite often. She encouraged her daughters to take me around with them and she herself took me to church every week until, to my great regret, they moved back to Hong Kong.

I told Auntie privately about Second Sister. She looked at Sister very closely; she pressed a finger into Sister's arm and noticed that it left a dent which did not immediately disappear. She told Father and Mother that Sister was not fat but was puffed up with illness and fluid and offered to take her to see a doctor. Tests were done and the diagnosis was that Sister had a kidney infection which was already at an advanced stage. The doctor said she must go into hospital. But the hospital treatment did no good. She became more and more ill.

The doctor asked to see my parents and told them she was dying. I was shattered. I loved her so much and she had always been my close companion, even though she was three years older. When I went to see her I just wanted to cry though I tried hard not to. I also realised she was terribly weak and tired and Ah Wor said she did not want to open her eyes or talk to anyone. However, when I went she would make an effort to open her eyes and smile and even talk to me, though her voice was very weak. One day she asked why I cried every time I went to see her. I did not know what to say. She begged me to tell her the truth. She said she knew, inside herself, that she did not have long to live but she was not afraid. Finally I told her the truth.

Instead of giving way to fear for herself, she comforted me and told me not to be so sad because we would see each other in Heaven. With a great effort she sat up, and the nurse put some pillows behind her back to make her a little more comfortable. She asked me to start a prayer, saying she would finish it. I wanted to pray but no words came, so in the end she started to whisper one. She asked God to continue to help me with my studies so that one day I could really help other blind people. She also asked Him to give Ah Wor good health so that she could be with me for many years to come. Finally she asked God to give me a pair of eyes so that I could see. She said the prayers quite calmly, without crying. Her courage is something I shall always remember.

Before I left I made her promise that she would not tell Father and Mother or anyone else that I had told her the truth, as Father had told me that I must not let her know. She promised, and she said that after she died I must tell Father and Mother not to waste money on priests or nuns chanting prayers or burning incense for her, or on finding a husband, living or dead, for her. I promised.

One day Sister said she was feeling much better. She was still all puffed up and in pain, but she wanted to talk and she wanted me to be with her all the time. This the hospital agreed to, as she was so ill, and luckily the two beds on either side of her were empty so we would not be disturbing other patients—though of course we kept our voices down as much as we could. Fortunately the other patients in the ward were not too sick, so they did not mind having me there. Sister was on an intravenous drip, so they let me have her meals. I learned my way to the washroom and felt quite at home.

Sister kept wanting to talk about what would happen in the family after she died. At first I could not bear this, but after a while, because she was so calm and matter-of-fact about it, and perhaps because my emotions had had such a battering that they had become a bit numb, I was gradually able to bring myself to talk about it with her as if we were just talking about fairy land. Sister was concerned that although she had gone to church with me many times she had never made her profession of faith. She felt much better when I asked the pastor of our church to come and see her.

One thing that worried her very much was the thought that Father and Mother would spend money on a ghost medium to talk to her. I said I thought they would probably do this and certainly Grandma would insist, as she firmly believed that it must be done. Then curiosity got the better of me. The Christian part of me did not believe in all this but the traditional Chinese part of me was not so sure, and I suddenly thought that perhaps there would be a chance now to prove it, one way or the other. So I said to Sister that if our family really paid the ghost medium to talk to her I would want to have some evidence whether it was really she who spoke or just the medium making it up. Sister suggested that we should decide now on some points that she would ask me about, so that if the question was not asked, I could be sure that it was not she who spoke. After thinking for a while, Sister said that if she was really talking through the ghost medium, she would ask whether I had all the books I needed at school and whether I had been able to catch up with the lessons I had missed during the days I had spent with her in hospital. I then asked Sister if she really believed in the existence of ghosts of dead people. She said she believed it could be true because the Bible talked about the devil and evil spirits.

While we were talking about all this a new patient arrived and was given the bed next to Sister. Like Sister, she was a girl in her teens, and as she was settling in, her mother was scolding her all the time, saying that she had caused the family to spend a great deal of money on her and now there was not much left. The mother rambled on, talking about what the fortune-teller had said when the poor girl was born. Apparently he had said that as her father owed her (the girl) a lot of money in a previous incarnation, she was sure to get it back from the family somehow and this was what was happening. She went on and on, blaming the poor girl. I could not bear this and cried. Sister said that if I cried, it would make her cry too. She did and I think the sight of us both in tears perhaps startled the woman and she quickly went away. Soon after she had gone the girl came over and sat on Sister's bed and she cried too. I felt I was crying for both of them but most of all for the heartbreak of losing my dear Sister. But now, realising guiltily that I had made both her and the new girl cry, I tried to control myself. We all stopped crying but none of us said a word.

Another patient in the room came over and asked what was wrong with the new girl. She was the same age as my Sister and apparently had the same illness. She told us that when she first became ill her mother took her to the temple to get some ashes of incense to put in the herbal tea which was prescribed for her by the medicine man. However, her condition became worse and worse, so her parents looked for a specially good medicine man who would cure her. In the end they found one who assured them he could make her well, but they had to pay a fee of two hundred dollars before he would start. Then, he said, he would give her treatment for as long as she needed until she was well. At that time this was quite a common practice and I know from my acquaintances that it still goes on, although it is gradually dying out. Anyway, the parents drew out all their savings, which were just over a hundred dollars, and had to borrow money at a very high rate of interest from private money-lenders to make up the balance. All this was more than eight months before and although the medicine man said the girl was recovering, everyone knew it was not the truth. As she was telling us all this she suddenly felt dizzy and the other patients helped her back to bed.

I have never found out how her parents were persuaded to bring her to a proper hospital. I believe it may have been through the intervention of neighbours. I know she was already very ill when she got there. In fact, I overheard one nurse whispering to another, "Oh dear, it's much too late." I do not know for certain that she died but I think she was far too ill to have recovered.

During the next few days Sister got worse and worse, and so did the other girl. Knowing that I was missing many days of school, Sister insisted that I must go back and only visit her after I had done my brailling with my readers. I was so anxious to be with Sister that I hurried through the work, leaving parts unfinished, and when the other patients in the room told me that Sister asked for me every time she woke up and cried when I was not there, I decided to take my work to the hospital so that whenever she woke up I would be beside her.

One day she became unconscious and did not know anyone, not even Father and Mother. Then, late one afternoon, she was conscious again and gathered all her strength and tried to talk to me. After a while, knowing she was exhausted, I told her to try to sleep. She still tried to talk; it seemed as if there were things she wanted to tell me. Her voice grew weaker and weaker and more and more difficult to understand. All of a sudden she stopped in the middle of a sentence. I thought she had drifted off to sleep so I stayed quiet, not wanting to disturb her, but a nurse came and saw that she was dying. Several doctors were called to come and do what they could and a messenger was sent to tell my family. As it happened, my parents were already on their way to the hospital. They rushed to the room but found her quite unconscious. A little later she died peacefully.

CHAPTER 21 •••••••••••••••••••••••••••••••••

THERE WAS NOTHING we could do—we just had to live with our sorrow. For a whole long day none of us said a word. The house was still and silent. Late at night Grandma, Father and Mother at last began to talk about the burial. They said that none of them could go to the burial; according to Chinese custom, it is regarded as inappropriate for older members of a family to go to the burial of one of the younger generation. It was just not done. Third Uncle and Auntie did not attend the funeral of their son although he was their beloved only child.

My parents therefore decided to accept the offer of Uncle Leung, who was a close friend of the family but not a relation at all, to take us children to Sister's funeral. Once they had settled that point they went on to talk about arranging a place for Sister's photograph in the temple so that prayers and incense would be offered for her by Buddhist nuns. I heard them say they would have to borrow money to pay for this. I longed to tell them that Sister did not want this done or money spent on her in this way, but remembering that she had mentioned it to Father and Mother a few weeks back and had been scolded for saying it, I knew very well it was useless to say anything.

During the days that followed I was desolate without Sister. I missed her terribly and found little comfort in remembering how we had agreed that we would see each other again in Heaven.

It is hard to believe that anyone could be so unfeeling, but at this time, while we were all absorbed in our first acute grief, some neighbours actually wanted me to try to get Sister to help them forecast what horse they should bet on at the Hong Kong races. The scheme was to put some small numbered bamboo sticks into a container and then shake it while I prayed to Sister to help them.

Every time a stick fell out they would use that number as one to put their money on. I was angry and outraged that they should have asked me to take part in such a charade, but I just said as politely as I could that to do this would be against my principles and Sister's. They were furious and called me names and said that since I was deliberately preventing them from making money they would never forgive me, and furthermore would pray to heaven that no one would be kind to a blind girl like me. This did not bother me as they had often said life could not mean anything to me as I was blind. I knew better by this time than to let them upset me for long.

Father was conscientious about customary observances. Also, he had loved his eldest daughter and it grieved him that he could not afford to pay for prayers and ceremonies for her soul as he would like to have done. He even had to sell some of his remaining possessions to obtain enough money to pay the hospital bill. He often said that ideally, if he could have afforded it, he would have paid Buddhist priests or nuns to chant prayers every day. At the very least he would have wanted to have it done once a week. As she died on a Friday, every Friday should have included a special ceremony for her spirit, with prayers and offerings of delicious food and burning of paper models—of money, cars, houses and other luxuries—to make life good for her in the place she had gone to. This would have been done every Friday for several weeks. On the seventh Friday, the end of the period called "seven times seven" there should have been a special ceremony marking the climax. At this ceremony the whole family would join in, making it a big occasion for Sister.

But, sad to say, poor Father could do none of this and he felt very guilty about it. The climactic seventh Friday was reached and it was a very wet, stormy day with all the signs of an approaching typhoon.

For some time the termites had been eating bigger and bigger holes in the wooden walls of our house. Father was worried that it was becoming dangerous, and he repaired the holes with cement whenever he had time to work at it. On this particular day the rain came down in torrents and there was water everywhere in the house. We were all busy trying to mop up but the rain came so fast that we could not keep up.

The storm grew stronger by the minute and we had an anxious, alarming night, almost literally trying to hold the house together round us. As Saturday dawned black, threatening and tempestuous, the full fury of the typhoon struck.

The kitchen was separated from the rest of the house by a sort of bridge, open to the sky, and the kitchen itself was a flimsy structure—a later addition to the original house—supported on wooden poles. The open bridge was deep in water and Father told Ah Wor that she should not go to the kitchen to prepare the midday meal. She said it was only a short distance and she would be all right, but I was very worried about her out there and prayed desperately for her safety. While she was out in the rickety little kitchen Grandma and Mother were saying that it might be Second Sister's spirit, offended by lack of observances, which was causing the storm. Father said he did not believe this, but he did feel bad that he had not been able to offer her the ceremony which was her due on the previous day. At that point I was relieved to hear Ah Wor coming back into the house. At the very moment she put the rice on the table there was a splintering noise followed by a loud crash and the entire house rocked violently, as if it was about to collapse. We all screamed with terror and I shouted that the sound came from the kitchen. Father rushed out to look and we all followed. The supports of the kitchen had collapsed and the entire kitchen had disintegrated and was lying in ruins on the ground below us.

Grandma said that it must be Sister who had saved Ah Wor. I could not keep silent at that; forgetting all the rules and traditions about children never contradicting their elders, I said loudly and firmly that I had been praying for Ah Wor's safety and that I knew God had sent a guardian angel to watch over her. As soon as I had said this I realised what I had done and felt frightened. Father began to speak and I could tell he was angry with me but, amazingly, Grandma broke in saying, "You are right, Little Girl. It must be that your God and Sister worked together to protect Ah Wor." I believed only God could perform such a miracle, but Grandma had saved me from a bad telling-off and I was relieved.

The storm blew itself out as it moved inland and the next day was bright and sunny. Father went out early in the morning, just before my younger brother and I were ready to go to church. When we came home I could hear the noise of a saw cutting wood and my brother said that there were piles of wood, cement, tools, nails and all sorts of things which Father must have bought. Father himself was hard at work in the ruins of the kitchen. My brothers did what they could to help, and after lunch Ah Wor joined in. Lunch was a simple affair anyway, with no kitchen and no stove.

I asked Father about the possibility of contacting the owner of the house. He said that the owner lived in Hong Kong and left it to a relative living in Macau to collect the rent. Father did not know where this man lived, and he said that even if he could get in touch with him, the man would probably say he could not do anything without the owner's agreement.

We all worked at the rebuilding. Father even managed to find me a job—sorting out different sized pieces of wood for the boys to stack so that he could pick up what he wanted quickly and easily. It took more than a week to rebuild the kitchen and to repair the damaged windows and doors and the termite holes in the walls. Secretly, I felt proud of Father; with his experience he was able to tackle all these jobs and he not only rebuilt and repaired our house, but he helped some of our neighbours too. At the end of the month, when the man came to collect the rent, Father told him what had happened. The man said he would inform the owner who would certainly come over from Hong Kong and see for himself.

The owner did come, and was full of praise for all that Father had done. He said he had not realised Father had rented the house to live in—he had assumed it was being used as a store. He was both surprised and grateful that Father had made the place truly habitable, admitting that it had not really been fit to live in before. After some thought he put a proposition to Father: as the house was now in such good condition, he wondered if Father would mind if he put it up for sale. He told us he was going to emigrate to Canada soon and this would solve the problem of what to do with the property. He said that if the house fetched a good price, he would repay Father for all the materials he had bought for the repairs and would, in addition, give him some money in compensation for his labour and for having to find somewhere else to live.

As soon as the advertisement about selling the house appeared in the local paper, people began ringing the bell asking to see it. Father was worried that so many strangers were being let into the house with no man around, so he decided to work half days only for a week and be at home to show prospective buyers round. Before long a couple decided to buy the house and offered a very handsome price for it. The owner accepted and the deal was completed. The buyers were considerate and allowed us time to look for another place. After a search, we found a flat in a stone house only two blocks from the wooden house. We had the ground floor and I felt much safer there than I had on the first floor of the old wooden place, which always shook and trembled every time anyone moved or coughed. The size was about the same so we were still as crowded as ever, but we were used to that by this time.

The owner kept his word and offered Father a handsome sum in compensation as well as paying him back for all the labour and building costs. Father thanked him for his generosity, but the owner said he was really very grateful to Father as he would have had to pay a contractor much more.

This unexpected windfall was a relief and a godsend to Father. He immediately put aside what was needed for our school fees for the next year. He also offered to pay Ah Wor back some of what she had spent, but Ah Wor had made up her mind not to take any. So in the end Father found himself with some money in hand and decided to do something nice for Sister, to make up for the poor treatment she had had since she died. The first thing he was anxious to do was to find a husband for her, so that she would not be lonely in the spirit world. I tried to explain that Sister did not want anything like this—that she would be with God in Heaven where, as Jesus said, there would be no marriage or giving in marriage. Father said Sister was too young to know what she was talking about and that by now she must have regretted what she had said and be wishing that her family on earth would arrange something for her. Grandma thought the best way would be to ask Sister herself what she would like so that whatever we did would be in ac-

cordance with her wishes. Mother found a woman who worked as a
medium, and a day was fixed to invite Sister's spirit to make contact with the family.

Although I had been expecting this to happen, I was not sure
what to do now that I was faced with the situation. I was convinced
in my own mind that it was all superstitious nonsense and a waste
of money, but nothing I could say would make my elders change
their minds. I talked it over with friends at school. One girl—Polly
—who always had good ideas, said that I should get my parents to
let me join the séance and I should ask something known only to
Sister and me to find out if it was true. Thinking about this, I
remembered what we had arranged when she was still in hospital
—that if it was really she, she would prove it by talking about a
pre-arranged subject. I felt a sudden excitement that perhaps it
would turn out to be Sister: I missed her terribly and was misera-
bly lonely without her. But next minute I felt shocked and
ashamed. How could I even remotely consider believing in all this
when it went right against my Christian beliefs and against Bible
teaching? On the other hand, it occurred to me that if, by some
means, I could help to convince the family that there was nothing
in it, I might be able to stop them from spending any more money
on such deceptions, so in the end I decided to try. But there was a
snag. I realised that Father and Mother, knowing what I thought
about it, would not let me take part, and I could not ask Ah Wor to
help persuade them because she had been in trouble so many times
for taking my part and pleading for me. Then I thought of
Grandma. Ever since the night when she had returned to us she
had been very good to me. Next day when I returned from school I
managed to find her alone and told her about this. At first she was
hesitant but in the end she agreed that I ought to attend the
séance. She said Sister and I had been so close that Sister might
tell me things which she would not say so easily to other members
of the family.

Thanks to Grandma's efforts, my parents finally agreed to let me
join them. Ah Wor came too, to be with me. I was excited and
wondered what I would find out. However, as soon as we reached
the house of the medium woman, she firmly told them I could not

be allowed to stay because I was a Christian. She said if I was there, Sister's spirit would refuse to come. I wanted to argue and tell them all that Sister herself had really been a Christian at heart, but I knew it was no use. I dared not risk irritating my elders any more, so Ah Wor and I left quickly.

Once we were out in the street I asked Ah Wor if she believed that my Sister's spirit could have let the ghost medium woman know that I was not a Buddhist. Ah Wor said no, it was a lot simpler than that; the woman was a rubbish collector in our area and she must have seen me and my brother going to church so she would know perfectly well that I was a Christian and not a Buddhist.

At home I waited impatiently for the grown-ups to come back. It seemed like hours but in fact Ah Wor said that it was only just under one hour. They reported that Sister had said she was very lonely down there and wanted to be married to another ghost whose surname must be Tam. She also wanted to have a big wedding feast so that she could invite her friends and the friends of her husband to celebrate the occasion, and that she would like to have furniture, cars and plenty of money to start their new home. As I listened to all this I grew more and more upset and furious. The last thing Sister would ever have wanted was that our parents should spend money on her in this way. I remembered back to when she was ill and in constant pain before she went into hospital and how, when I urged her to tell Father and Mother, she said she did not want to give them the additional burden of finding money to take her to the doctor, as she knew they could not afford it. I told Grandma and my parents about this. Ah Wor, who had heard Sister say it at the time, confirmed what I said. But it was no use. The instructions "Sister" had given through the ghost medium must be carried out.

So the search for a suitable husband started. Months went by. After enquiries through relatives, neighbours, friends and marriage brokers, my family finally found a Tam family whose son had also died young, at the same age as Sister. This boy had said through the medium that he wanted to have a wife and that he wanted his family on earth to arrange a marriage for him. Through the marriage broker, my parents and the mother of this dead young man met and exchanged photographs of their dead children. Both families found that they were happy and satisfied with the match, so arrangements for the wedding were put in hand. According to custom the first thing to do was to consult a fortune-teller or geomancer to find out whether all the details of their births and their horoscopes accorded well.

This was done and it was found that they matched perfectly, so they decided to go ahead with the arrangements. Father decided to make this a big occasion for Sister, to make up for all she had been deprived of since she died. There was nothing I could do to prevent it, although I knew how completely it conflicted with Sister's own wishes. If I said anything, I only got into trouble, so I gave up trying.

The worst thing was that Father agreed to give the boy's mother a lump sum of money—much more than he could afford. She was a widow and not very well off. She said Sister would become a member of her family, and the burning of incense and the offering of food for two instead of one would cost her more so she would be glad of the money Father would give her. It was discovered that their family is actually distantly related to my family and of course they welcomed the whole arrangement, which was a stroke of good fortune for them. My Father gave a generous dowry for Sister, consisting of all sorts of gold things—bracelets, necklaces, etc.—all of which, of course, went to the husband's family. This was intended to ensure that Sister would get all the respect and rituals and ceremonies due to her.

The wedding feast took place near Chinese New Year the following year—1951—about nine months after Sister's death. We all took part and so, of course, did all the members of the boy's family —brothers, sisters and all the in-laws. The finest food was offered to the couple and was placed on the ceremonial table where their photographs in silver frames were surrounded by incense and joss sticks and by a paper house, furniture, car, clothes and millions of dollars in "hell money" to enable them to start a comfortable home in the spirit world.

We children were told that all the paper things would be burned and Sister would receive them, but the food must not be touched until the next day, so that she and her husband could come at any time and enjoy it. We were told that we could have the food the next day, but that the dead couple would have taken all the taste out of it.

That night after everyone had gone to bed I tiptoed to Ah Wor's bed and said I wanted to feel the paper things which had not been burnt. She tried to talk me out of it but I persisted, so together we crept into the living-room. She helped me to feel the paper things, which were well back on a large table, near the food and the photographs. They were fascinating. Ah Wor guided my hand to the food and all of a sudden I was overcome by the delicious smell. To her horror, before she could stop me, I had grabbed a chicken leg and several pieces of meat and some peanuts and stuffed them in my mouth. They tasted lovely—lots of flavour!

Poor Ah Wor was in a panic and said I would be beaten for committing such a crime. I was frightened too but I prayed to Sister to help me and save me from being punished. I do not think I really believed she was there, but in the moment of crisis I acted without thinking.

When the chicken leg and the pieces of meat were found to be missing there was great alarm, but Grandma insisted that Sister must have come and taken them because nobody else would have dared to. Ah Wor and I kept quiet and said nothing and, thank goodness, it was accepted as a miracle and all blew over—although I thought Grandma had her suspicions about me. I wondered if Father might have guessed but as Grandma said firmly that it must have been Sister, he did not pursue it. Grandma had evidently made up her mind to save me from punishment.

Years later, when I was grown-up, I mentioned this incident to my parents. We all laughed over it and they told me they knew perfectly well I was the culprit. Grandma had even heard Ah Wor and me creeping past and whispering, but they realised that if the whole thing came out into the open they would have had to discipline me and dismiss Ah Wor, so the "miracle" was seized on as a welcome way out of the difficulty.

It might be supposed that ghost marriages are a thing of the past, but I am sorry to have to say that this is not so. As late as 1977 a friend of mine had to attend just such a ghost marriage in the New Territories (the rural northern part of Hong Kong). Such practices still prevail and, sad to say, money—often large sums—is still squandered on them.

CHAPTER 22 ●●●●●●●●●●●●●●●●●●●●●●●●●●●●●●●●●●●●

BUT WE HAVE jumped ahead; we must go back to 1950.

It was May, and the yearly exams were drawing near. Despite having missed nearly two weeks of school when I stayed in the hospital with Sister, I had caught up with most of my class-work, but I had not spent as much time brailling texts with my readers as I should have done and therefore parts of the books were missing. However, when the time came, I did well enough to merit a fairly good report. With regard to reports, we worked out an unorthodox system for signing mine. Throughout the year I had weekly reports and my parents were supposed to sign to show that they had seen them, together with the marks of my weekly tests. However, as Father was unable to sign his name in English, my younger sister always signed the reports for him. Sacred Heart certainly never knew that all those signatures were written by my ten-year-old sister. As a result she often teased me and said she was my parent.

Anyway, at the end of the year in the Special Class I was one of the top three pupils and therefore eligible for promotion to Form II. Sister Christina enclosed a note in my report asking me to go and see her at school. I could not think why she should want to see me, since my results were not bad, but I loved going to see her so I went along cheerfully. During the past three months she had tried to speak to me more in English and I tried to do the same when talking to her.

That morning she said all the Sisters were pleased with my work and I should be promoted to Form II. During the year in Special Class both my understanding and use of English had improved, and she thought that although neither the form mistress in Form II nor most of the subject teachers spoke Cantonese, I would be able to keep up with my lessons without too much difficulty. What she was worried about was that in the regular forms, unlike the Special Class, there would be a full day of school, not just a half day, and on top of that the lessons would be longer, covering more material, and there would be many more difficult words. Also, all the subjects—History, Geography, Science, Arithmetic, etc.—would be in English, not just English Language. She was afraid that I would find it impossible to get them brailled and still have time left for study. She asked me to think it over and decide whether I thought it best to go into Form II, to which I was entitled, or into Form I where things would be a little easier for me. I promised I would let her know the next day.

I thought of almost nothing else all day. To have achieved the grade to enter Form II was more than I had dared to hope for, but I had to keep my head. I knew that Sister Christina's anxieties were only too well founded, the thought of what lay ahead worried me too. Back in Pooi To, although I had never had the whole text of a book in braille, I could at least listen to it, even if it was only read in full just once, and make my own notes because everything there was in Chinese. But now it was different. I probably would not be able to take in much by listening to lessons just once or twice because the actual subject matter would be more complex and there would be many new words which I would have to learn to spell. It would certainly be easier if I agreed to go into Form I. But, as always, money complicated the problem, because Father might not be able to continue paying for my schooling. Certainly there was not the remotest chance of another lump sum of money, like the one for repairing the house, most of which had now been spent on Sister's ghost wedding. I hated to bother Ah Wor with all these never-ending problems but she was the only person I could talk to. Late that evening when she had finished her work, I went to talk it over with her.

She was quite definite; she thought that if I was up to Form II, then I should go into Form II as it would enable me to finish school a year earlier. She said that if my grades were good enough for Form II, I would probably be able to keep up with the work somehow, but the problem now was to find paid readers. I could not always depend on the girls at school; their times were too uncertain.

Usually they could spare me half an hour or even an hour, but sometimes the sessions lasted for only a few minutes. I knew from experience at Pooi To that paid readers were much more reliable. But it was not just finding the readers—it was finding the money to pay them.

It was out of the question to ask Father. Ah Wor said she would take care of this; even if she could not manage four hours, she would see to it that I had one or two hours a day. I did not argue —how could I? I needed it and it seemed the only way, but I knew she could not possibly do more handwork than she was doing already. Suddenly, I remembered the day in Canton when Third Uncle asked me to read to him, and asked how I managed to make a braille text from print, and his promise to pay for readers. I also remembered his saying to Father, that last night in Hong Kong, that it was important for me to continue my schooling. Now that I could use a typewriter, why shouldn't I work out a letter to him to ask if he could possibly help me pay for readers? I had some misgivings in case Father heard about it, but decided to take a chance on it—write to Third Uncle, keep my fingers crossed and hope for the best.

The idea of writing the letter cheered me up and cleared my mind. I decided to ask Sister Christina to put me in Form II, since my marks justified it; I could at least try. When I told her this, she wished me good luck, adding that she realised it would not be easy because of the difficulty of finding readers, but that as I had overcome apparently insoluble problems before, perhaps this would work out all right too. She also said that she knew Chinese people generally felt it to be a disgrace to fail an exam or to repeat a class, but she did not think I ought to feel that way as no one can be expected to do more than their best.

I asked her if she would let me have the book list for Form II so that I could braille as much as possible during the summer vacation. She said she could give me the previous year's list but she could not be sure if there would be any changes. She explained that the list was drawn up by the Education Department in Hong Kong, and next year's list would not be available until nearer the beginning of term. I asked if there had been changes in recent years. She said that usually some titles were changed, but not all.

I took the old list home. I really did not know what to do. The experience I had had in Canton of brailling a whole lot of textbooks and then finding them to be useless was a recent and painful memory. What if it should happen again? That evening, I found myself deciding to go ahead and braille as much as I could manage; my previous experience had shown me that even if the books were changed, the content would be similar. It meant that even if I had to braille again when school started, what I had done during the vacation would stand me in good stead. For a reason I cannot explain I had a strong feeling that the books would not be greatly changed.

I told my younger brother and sister what I wanted to do, and asked them if they would read to me for about an hour a day. They said they would. (My elder brother had by this time left school and gone to Hong Kong to find a job.) I did not want to risk buying the books in case they were changed, so I managed to borrow them from girls who already had them. My brother and sister read, as promised, but it was hard for them because there were so many difficult words in each lesson which they had to spell out. It needed a great deal of concentration on their part as well as mine, and we must have made many mistakes. With time spent on spelling and many repetitions, we achieved very little in an hour. I did not want them to get bored and fed up with it, so I did not ask them to do more than their hour each. I tried to contact some of my classmates to see if they could help, but many of them had gone away on holiday and in any case, as most of them would be going in to Primary 6 or Form I, they would find my Form II books tiresome. Ah Wor suggested that they might be more willing to help if I could pay them a little, but even this did not tempt them, especially as what I wanted read was English, not Chinese.

I worked hard to compose a letter to Third Uncle. I wrote and rewrote, and tried to make it sound as much like English as possible. I know now that it was full of terrible mistakes, but I did the best I could and hoped Uncle would not only forgive the bad grammar but be able to understand what I was asking. When I had finally typed it, I realised with dismay that I did not know his address. I wanted to send it to his office in Hong Kong, as I dared not take the chance of Third Aunt reading it. It was too risky to ask my brothers and sisters in case they talked and my parents found out.

Then Ah Wor went through the rubbish in the wastepaper baskets and even the bin in the yard and fished out every envelope she could find, even ones that had been torn up. We cleaned and dried them as best we could and took them along to a street letter-writer. With our hearts in our mouths we heard him reading out all the printed headings and return addresses, as well as people's names. Luck was with us—one of them was from Uncle and his office address was printed on the corner. We paid the letter-writer to address a new envelope for us, and took our slightly smelly bundle back to the waste bin. An hour later my precious letter was in the letter box and I began the long wait for a reply.

Days and days went by and still no reply came. I began to worry whether I had displeased Uncle by writing directly to him. Then, almost three weeks later, at four o'clock one afternoon, which was the time the postman usually came, the school amah appeared and said that there was a letter for me, sent care of the school and written in English, and then it dawned on me that it must be from Third Uncle. Excitedly I hurried with the letter to school and asked one of the Sisters to read it to me. Yes, it was from Uncle. He said that he had been delighted to receive my letter—he had been to Taipei, which explained the delay—and that he was proud of me for having learnt to type and for typing the letter to him by myself. He said he would gladly pay for my readers, just as he had done in Canton, and would write to Father and send him the money every month. He would send enough to enable me to pay for four hours of reading a day. As the Sister read these words, my eyes filled with tears—tears of relief and gratitude.

From then on I grew to love the English language even more. It not only helped me to talk to people but it meant that I could write my own letters and address my own envelopes. I realised that I could really do these things independently in spite of my handicap. Admittedly I would always have to ask someone to read me my mail, but this was much easier than having to ask someone to write a letter at my dictation.

Now that I was able to pay properly for my readers, some of the girls agreed to read to me. I had four hours of paid reading and two hours from my brother and sister. Thus, when September came I started the new school year in Form II with enough braille texts for about four or five weeks. And only two of the books—both Science ones—were changed. However, the start of term meant that neither the other girls nor my brother and sister had time to read to me any more. I would be all right until my existing texts ran out but I did not know what would happen after that if I could not find anyone else to read, even for pay.

A few housewives, contacted here and there via neighbours, agreed to read to me, but they knew only a few words of English—primary school English which they had mostly forgotten. For them to read English textbooks was a dreadfully slow and laborious process as they had to spell almost every word to me, letter by letter. It was better than nothing, but only just. I was getting desperate when help came again, from church this time. One Sunday after service, when I was asking round for readers, a Mrs. Check came and offered to help. She said she had been to an English school in northern China and would be glad to read to me for love for four or five hours a week. We became and have remained good friends. I used to go regularly to her home, as it was a better and quieter place in which to work than our crowded little flat, and thus her son and daughter, who were roughly my age, also became my friends. As we were all Christians, we enjoyed Bible reading and prayers together.

With my reading organised, some anxiety was removed, but it did not solve all the problems. In the Special Class Sister Christina had always been careful to speak slowly and clearly. In Form II the nuns and other teachers were mostly Italian, Chinese or Portuguese who spoke English all the time, much faster than Sister Christina and with a variety of accents. Most of the girls were Chinese and I know they all had dictionaries on their desks and constantly looked up words. This, of course, I could not do. I soon realised that meanings of words could often be worked out from the context, especially when they recurred regularly, but there was still much that I could not understand. Sometimes I asked the other girls but I did not want to pester them too much. For the most part I tried to find out from my more knowledgeable readers or made guesses at the meanings.

Once I was in Form II my life settled down to a routine. The months passed without any outstanding events. Apart from Sister's ghost marriage in early 1951 and the few seasonal landmarks like Chinese New Year and the other main Chinese festivals, there was an unvarying sameness about my life. During term-time I worked hard to keep up with the rest of the class; in holidays I worked just as hard to braille books for the new term ahead.

Exams were a problem because of the time factor. Brailling the questions and answers and then reading the answers took much longer than the time allowed, but I never liked to accept the nuns' offers of extra time as I feared the other girls would regard this as giving me an unfair advantage. Since my school-days, it has become general practice to allow blind candidates in all written examinations extra time at the rate of fifteen or twenty minutes for every hour; but a great deal has happened in the field of blind rehabilitation work in the years since I was at school.

My one real recreation, in the true sense of the word, was my church life and the companionship I had there with people whose friendship meant much to me. Church and school; these were my life. As 1950 became 1951 and then 1952 I could look back on three years at Sacred Heart and find compensation for the relentless pressure of work in the knowledge that my English was steadily improving.

CHAPTER 23 ●●●●●●●●●●●●●●●●●●●●●●●●●●●●●●●●●●

ONE DAY THE church ladies asked me to speak to their group. They wanted to understand blind people so that they could help me or other blind pupils who might later go to ordinary schools. I told them about the code of behaviour which sighted people should observe with blind people—speaking directly to them; offering an arm for guidance; not moving furniture into unexpected positions; not leaving doors half open. I tried to emphasise that a blind person is an ordinary person who cannot see. I also told them what I had heard from Miss Schaeffer and from the radio programme in Canton about sighted people in England and America who learn braille and transcribe books for blind people.

After the meeting four ladies told me they were interested in learning braille. We decided to meet one evening so that I could show them how it worked. I explained the difference between English and Cantonese braille. We all decided that English would be easier than Cantonese for, instead of learning the seventy-two initial and final symbols and tone marks, they could just learn the twenty-six letters of the English alphabet, without bothering about contractions. They agreed to give it a try.

But this offer of help created its own difficulties; I should need more handframes and styluses. The John Milton Society had sent me two sets—the original one and the second one after I wrote them my "thank you" letter. I used one myself and the other was in Taiwan with Lai-ying and Yin-hing. I enquired around Macau, but as far as I could find out I was the only blind person using a handframe and doing braille at that time. How on earth was I going to solve this problem? I remembered that the Mo Kwong Home was supplied by the Ming Sum School, but that was of no help to me now. Then I had an idea. Why not write to the John

Milton Society, asking them to send me at least one more set? As they had already sent me two sets free of charge, I felt that I should offer to pay something towards the cost. I had been taught all my life that I should not accept anything free. I turned this over in my mind for days but could not think of a solution. I had made up my mind that just for once I would not discuss it with Ah Wor. I knew very well what she would do if I told her—more handwork. She already got up very early and went to bed very late, so I was determined not to ask her.

One afternoon, as I was on my way home from school, someone came silently up behind me and put a hand on my shoulder. I nearly jumped out of my shoes. I think my mouth must have been hanging open with fright, for a woman's voice asked why I was so startled just because she put a hand on my shoulder. I told her that as I could not see, I did not know what was happening. She apologised and said she had not thought. She promised she would remember never to do it again. However, she said she would like to walk with me because there was something she wanted to discuss with me. She told me that her two daughters were now in the Special Class at Sacred Heart and were far behind with their lessons. They just about knew the alphabet before going to Sacred Heart and they found they could not understand what was going on in class, either in the books or Sister's teaching in English. She wanted me to help them for a few hours a week.

This sounded like a heaven-sent opportunity to raise the money I needed. I asked the names of the girls, but she gave me their Chinese names, which did not help since we all used English names; I could not work out who they were. However, when I asked for their surname and found it was Wong this rang a bell. They must be Betty and Linda Wong, two girls whom the other girls frequently commented on because they were so completely lost in class. They even ridiculed and teased them, which I thought rather unfair.

At first I was hesitant about doing as Mrs. Wong asked. I told her my English was not good enough and explained that as I had to spend a great deal of time on brailling and reading my work, I might not be able to give the girls as much time as they would like.

However, Mrs. Wong was quite definite; she said her daughters particularly wanted me to work with them as they had heard me talking to the Sisters in English and also they knew that I had just been promoted to Form II. She said Form II was beyond their wildest dreams—they felt that they would be lucky if they even managed to get into Primary 6.

I gave in and promised to try.

From then on, Ah Wor brought my lunch to school for me so that I could work with the two girls during the lunch hour. I enjoyed this and we became friends. I still had most of my Special Class books in braille so I could read with them, and I could remember most of the bits I had not put into braille. Ah Wor took a dim view of these lessons, pointing out—quite rightly—that I never had enough time for my own work. But I insisted that the experience was good for me, so she said I had better do what I thought best.

Betty and Linda told me about themselves and their worries. Their father was at that time the assistant manager of a big department store in Los Angeles. His parents, believing the United States to be paved with gold, had sold most of their property about twenty years earlier in order to buy the birth certificate of a dead man, close to his age, who had been born in America. His name was really Cheung but he took the full name and identity of the dead man and became Wong, the name on the certificate. He had then applied for and obtained an American passport and had gone to America under the sponsorship of a family called Chin, who owned the department store. He worked in the store by day and did another job at night and sent most of his earnings home to his parents, keeping only enough for his bare necessities. The parents arranged for his marriage and his wife went to live in California, but she was not happy there. The couple had a son and two daughters, but after a time she returned with the children to their Cantonese village where her husband visited them every two or three years. When the Communists came they escaped to Macau.

Two years before I came to know Betty and Linda, Mr. Wong's employer and his wife, Mr. and Mrs. Chin, visited Macau on holiday. Mr. Chin had decided to divide his property between his own two sons and the Wongs' son, brother of Betty and Linda. They were anxious to make the links between the two families even stronger, and when they saw Betty and Linda they took a fancy to them and told the grandparents and Mrs. Wong that they would like the two girls to be their daughters-in-law. The grandparents and the parents agreed, honoured by the proposal, and with the prospect of this consolidation of their mutual interests, Mr. Wong was made assistant manager of the store, which enabled him to send more money home to his parents and his wife.

But poor Betty and Linda, the pawns in the game, were frightened and unhappy about what lay ahead. Apart from exchanging pictures, they knew almost nothing about their future husbands. The only thing they knew was that they would be going to America quite soon and their mother wanted them to know some English, which was why they were in an English school, trying to acquire at least a few words of English.

They wept as they told me all this. I said that if they were so much opposed to the marriages, they should try to make their parents understand this before it was too late, but they said there was nothing they could do about it. Every time they tried to talk about it with their mother or grandparents, they were told that one of the virtues of Chinese women is obedience. The Sages taught that the role of a woman was to obey her father when she was at home, to obey her husband after she married and to obey her son when she was elderly. Their grandparents also pointed out that their own marriages and those of their parents, uncles and aunts had all been arranged by marriage brokers and that none of the couples had known each other personally—they had only seen photographs before their weddings—and that despite this they had all got along well enough and there were few reports of broken homes in their generations. I said all this sounded fine but that we knew from books and diaries that in fact many of these marriages were dismal failures and the couples very unhappy. In all too many cases the men took concubines and the wives just suffered in silence and humiliation, never experiencing a full, happy marriage relationship. However, the chances of Betty and Linda escaping their fate were remote.

Their English improved steadily. It was fun working with them. Mrs. Wong paid me fifteen dollars a month, so after two months I had received thirty dollars. Without my knowing, Ah Wor had done extra work and earned fifteen dollars. We kept back about $15 in Macau money for postage and a money-changer gave us $6.50 in American money for the balance. I spent an entire weekend putting a letter into English as well as I could, asking the John Milton Society to send me a couple of frames and styluses as some ladies at our church were interested in learning braille.

Two weeks later I was thrilled and delighted to receive a typewritten letter from a Dr. Nelson Chappel of the Society for the Blind in New York. He was very pleased to hear that I was studying in an English school and that some ladies at my church wanted to learn braille. He said he had ordered four sets of frames and styluses to be sent to me. He also said that in future, whenever I needed anything from America for my braille, I could just let him know without sending any money. He went on to say that the Society was going to send me some of their publications—he mentioned a magazine called *Discovery* for young people and a talking-book magazine (I could not imagine what that was)—and he encouraged me to write to him. He said he could understand my English perfectly. When a friend read the letter to me, she said that Dr. Chappel was described as "General Secretary of the Society." I did not understand those words so I had no idea of his position in the organisation nor of the extent of his duties and responsibilities. Little did I dream at the time that this same Dr. Chappel, who was kind and generous and said he would be glad to correspond with me, but who, nevertheless, seemed as remote as someone on another planet, would one day shape my destiny and open the way to a career for me.

A couple of months passed after Dr. Chappel's letter came. I waited impatiently for the frames and styluses to arrive and whenever I met the ladies at church they asked me when they would come. It was encouraging to know they were so keen. At long last the parcel arrived. I could hardly wait to tell the ladies. But now that I was on the point of beginning to teach them I panicked, realising with horror that I would be trying to teach braille to sighted people who would read with their eyes, not their hands, and that I had not the least idea of how to go about it. I decided to experiment.

I wrote the twenty-six letters of the alphabet in braille and asked a friend at school if she could tell the difference between the sets of dots for the various letters. It only took her a moment to say she could not possibly read the dots as they were on paper that had printing all over it and she could not pick them out. When I got home I found the American cards. I showed them and the braille alphabet I had done to my brother and asked if he could read them. He said he could easily see the dots on the American cards but like my friend at school he could not manage mine. He explained that as mine was on printed paper the dots were all mixed up with the printed words and just disappeared.

I thought back to when Second Sister had helped me, the day the parcel first arrived from America. She had been able to see the dots all right. Then I remembered—I had used her drawing paper and had even checked with Ah Wor that it had no drawings on it. So that was the answer; I must get drawing paper for the ladies. But it was expensive. Luckily there was still some of Mrs. Wong's money left, so I used it to buy some paper and then I was really ready to begin.

The first lesson proved to be a more nerve-racking and demanding experience than I expected. It took place in the small room at the church. My four would-be braillists were there all right, but so was a crowd of curious onlookers, including babies and school children who talked and giggled and fidgeted and made it very difficult to concentrate. But the ladies seemed genuinely interested and we persevered. After an hour and a half we felt we had had enough. I did not feel very encouraged for the future. The general chaos had been exhausting, yet I, as a teen-ager, felt unable to ask adults to be quiet. I was on my own, inexperienced in teaching, and trying to do it in adverse conditions. I thankfully said goodbye and set out for home.

As I was walking home I heard footsteps behind me. They sounded like Mrs. Wu's and I was not sure whether I ought to speak to her or not. She was a friend of Mother's and often came to see her, but she was very unfriendly towards me. Courtesy demanded that I should speak, but it occurred to me that she might not want to be spoken to in public by a blind person. I decided to let her speak first.

She kept behind me and was obviously watching me. I began to feel nervous and hoped I could keep walking straight along the pavement and not slip off into the road. Just as I was thinking this, it happened. I quickly stepped back onto the pavement. I disliked having her behind me, watching me, so in an effort to make her pass me and go ahead I stood still and rummaged among my papers, brushed some imaginary spots off my skirt, and finally took out my comb and combed my hair. However, as long as I stood still, she did the same, so there was nothing for it but to walk on as before. I reached the house and went up the steps to the front door. She came up behind me and stood still as I put my key in the keyhole to open the door. I suddenly turned to her and said, "Hello, Mrs. Wu, are you coming to see Mother?" She gasped at this and then said, "Oh Little Girl, how did you know it was me?" I did not answer but just asked her to come in. I called Mother but Ah Wor came and said Mother was out. Not having any desire to talk to Mrs. Wu, I just told her to make herself at home and went to my room.

I heard her telling Ah Wor how she watched me finding my way home and how I turned to speak to her when we were at the front door. She always talked about me in a loud voice as if I were both deaf and daft. She then went on in honeyed tones: "I love to watch her because she manages so well." To my delight Ah Wor said just what I wanted her to say. "That was exactly what you should never do," she replied. "If a blind person knows she is being watched, it makes her nervous and may affect her concentration on what she is doing, which could be very dangerous when she is in the street." She said that it was an unfriendly and unkind thing to do. I do not think it made the slightest impression on Mrs. Wu, but it was good to hear Ah Wor say it.

As to the braille lessons, we met once a week but the four ladies did not make much progress. They were able to learn the dots for the letters all right but they found the work slow and laborious and were soon bored. Also, they were apparently encountering opposition from their families and friends, who thought they were wasting their time and efforts. "What," they were asked, "is the point of helping blind people to be educated anyway? There is no sense in it." And that was undoubtedly the view of the community as a whole. At first I was disappointed and a bit discouraged, but by this time I was so accustomed to this attitude that it no longer upset me and I was really glad to stop the project as it was wasting my time as well as theirs.

The time I have spent in blind welfare work has taught me that volunteer braillists are nearly all English (or English-speaking Europeans) or Americans. It is a form of voluntary work which for some reason seems to appeal much more to Western women than to Chinese, however good the latter's English may be. Most Chinese women who have the time prefer other forms of voluntary work.

One day Betty and Linda asked me to have supper with them the following evening at a restaurant. I asked if it was a special occasion. They said there was something they wanted to tell me. The next day, soon after school, we went to a restaurant. I knew them well enough by now to sense that all was not well. They were very quiet, but when I asked them what the matter was, they refused to talk about their problems until we had had our supper. Throughout the meal they seemed preoccupied and said almost nothing. There was obviously something seriously wrong. Finally, when we had finished and were having a cup of tea, Linda took my hand, but she was crying and could not get a word out. At last it was Betty who spoke. In a choked voice she said that their mother had recently received a letter from their father telling them that next month they would leave for California. The geomancer of their father's employer's relations in Hong Kong had found a good day for Betty's marriage, which would be held just one week after their arrival in San Francisco. I did not know what to say. In the normal way I would congratulate a friend on her forthcoming marriage, but not this time.

Betty and Linda had to stop school to prepare for their journey and all that lay ahead. First they had to go to Hong Kong for their travel documents. The other girls at school asked about them, but knowing they would not like to have their affairs talked about, I made evasive answers. When they came back to Macau they waited for me one day after school, saying their mother asked whether I would be free on the following Saturday to have supper with them. I asked them for more details and found that it would be a formal banquet for their friends and relatives. They explained that the reason their mother did not send me a formal invitation was that I was still a young girl and would not be expected to take a gift. I felt flattered that Mrs. Wong did not mind that I was blind and evidently was not embarrassed at having me appear before her friends and relations. So I accepted the invitation. But when I got home and thought it over, I began to have butterflies in my stomach. As I had always been left out of all invitations, I had never had a meal out on a formal occasion. It was a frightening thought that I had no experience at all of how to behave in such circumstances and I could easily do something completely contrary to etiquette. But despite this I really did want to go, as it was my very first invitation.

I was afraid to tell Father and Mother about this. I knew they would disapprove and suspected they would try to stop me from going. I had a feeling that they would interpret it as some sort of criticism of them if someone else invited me to do what they had never allowed me to do. Ah Wor agreed with me, but she said that as I had promised Mrs. Wong that I would go, Father and Mother could not very well stop me without offending her. Anyway, Ah Wor said I was going to have to tell them—I could not leave it till the day came—so I had better do it and put up with the consequences.

That evening I awaited my opportunity. The rest of the family were talking about an outing to the cinema on the following Saturday, after which they would all go somewhere for a meal. They seldom went out together (outings were very rare anyway because they cost money). Grandma did not join in because of her age and because her bound feet made it difficult for her to walk. Someone remarked that Grandma and Ah Wor and I would be at home. This gave me my chance; I told them the news of my invitation. For a

minute there was a stunned silence. Finally Father asked if I knew
the occasion of the dinner, and Mother (typically) asked why Mrs.
Wong should bother to invite me. Didn't they know I was blind
and that they would have to put the food in my bowl for me? I
told them that Mrs. Wong and I had met several times and that she
knew perfectly well that I was blind. I explained that her daughters were good friends of mine and that they were going to
America next month because one of them was going to be married.

"In that case, you had no right to say you would go," Father said
sternly. He pointed out that it must be the customary formal dinner
for a wedding at which the Wongs would thank their friends and
relatives for their wedding gifts and this would mean that anyone
invited to attend who had not already given a gift (as in my case)
would certainly take one to the dinner. He said that since he and
Mother could not afford to buy gifts, they had declined several
such dinner invitations. I said that Mrs. Wong had let me know
that the reason she did not send me a formal invitation was because she did not expect me to bring a gift with me. My parents
were adamant and said that I should not take everything people
said so literally, and that Mrs. Wong's reassurance was only given
as a matter of courtesy. It would be a disgrace to go to a formal
dinner of this kind without taking a gift. I wondered how I was expected to know all this, in view of what Mrs. Wong had said.

It was all too obvious that my parents were extremely annoyed
with me. I went to my bedroom and started slowly getting ready
for bed, feeling downcast and sorry for myself. I began to wonder
if Mother was right and that I should have refused the invitation,
knowing that by accepting I was giving people the trouble of helping me. But I had accepted it, so what was I to do? And how could
I get the money for a gift? I lay awake for a long time pondering
all this and at last I got out of bed and went to the bathroom. I
heard footsteps coming towards the door and thought at first that
Father or Mother was coming to scold me for making a distur-
bance, but then I recognised the steps as Ah Wor's. When I opened
the door she whispered to me to go to the back door; she said if we
opened it very carefully and closed it behind us we could talk

without waking anyone up. We did this and sat down on the step outside, and were glad of the slight breeze in the hot stuffy night.

Ah Wor told me not to worry about the gift as she would see to it that I would be able to take something with me. I told her I really regretted accepting the invitation as it had not occurred to me that the Wongs were giving themselves the trouble of helping me at table. She reassured me, saying that I need not feel like that because if people who knew perfectly well that I was blind invited me for a meal, it obviously meant that they did not mind helping me—otherwise they would not have asked me. She reminded me of a talk I gave to the ladies at church, when I tried to emphasise that blind people are just like other people except that they cannot see. I was surprised at her mentioning this and asked why it was that she always reacted and thought differently from everyone else over these things—with the result that most people thought her a fool or just crazy. She laughed and said that through all these years she had tried to act on the advice of the English eye doctor in Hong Kong who had said that a blind person could live as full and as satisfying a life as a sighted person, depending on the attitude of the family in which she grew up.

Hearing this I felt a mixture of humility and strength. I prayed silently, "Dear Heavenly Father, I know You love me because You have shown Your love through Ah Wor. Please help me so that one day some good people will let her know she has been right all the time. Let a friend come to us who will tell her so. And maybe one day You will work a miracle so that she and I can have a chance to enjoy some of what we have both missed, for her sake as she has given up so much for me."

The Saturday of the Wongs' dinner arrived. It was also the day the family were going out together, and though they talked about their plans, for once I was not bothered as I was going out too. Ah Wor had bought me a new sweater, which my sisters admired, and a handbag. There was just the gift to be dealt with, so Ah Wor said we would go together to look for something suitable. Mrs. Wu, Mother's friend who followed me home after the first braille lesson, happened to be in the flat visiting Mother and she heard Ah Wor say this, so she immediately gave her firm opinion that it was unpractical and just causing unnecessary trouble for Ah Wor to take me with her. What was the point, she enquired, of taking me to a crowded shop when Ah Wor could do it more quickly and easily on her own? Ah Wor did not argue but just told me to get ready to go shopping.

Ever since Seventh Auntie and the English people took me to the big store in Canton I had wanted to go again and feel things with my hands and have them described to me. Now at last there was a reason to go again and we had a lovely afternoon. We finally settled on two pairs of pillow slips with embroidered dragons and flowers on them. Ah Wor bought some wrapping paper and said we would wrap them up properly when we got home. I asked why she should spend money on paper—why couldn't I just hand them the pillow cases as they were? She explained that the gift would look better if it was wrapped up and that it was usual to do it this way. This was new to me.

Betty and Linda had said that one of them would come and pick me up at around six o'clock. I was ready and waiting near the door, and when the bell rang I went straight out. Linda said she was glad I was ready as she had two pedicabs waiting. As I took Linda's arm Ah Wor followed us out and said she would come and pick me up after the dinner. When we were in the pedicabs one of the coolies commented to Linda that it was very kind of her to go out with this *mang mui*. Linda immediately said I was not a *mang mui* but her private English teacher. He was amazed that a blind girl could teach English to a sighted girl and he wanted to know if I was paid money for doing it. At first I did not want to speak to him because he had called me a *mang mui*, but as he seemed really interested in how I could give lessons and earn money, I decided to tell him more about it in the hope that it might change his attitude towards blind people. As we talked more, he told me that one of his daughters was blind. I asked him about her and found that they just kept her at home and would not let her go out of the house as they did not want anyone to know they had a blind daughter. I asked him to tell me his address but he would not. Then Linda came to my help and managed to persuade him, saying that I might be able to teach her something so that she could perhaps give lessons and earn some money. This did the trick and he gave me his address.

This led to a lasting friendship between his daughter and me. I called her Po-yuk in memory of Tse Tse and was accepted by her family. I taught her Cantonese braille. Several years later, when the American Foundation for Overseas Blind sponsored a training project in Macau, she took the course. Now she is an efficient housewife. She is happily married to a sighted man and their two children both have normal sight.

The pedicabs pulled up in front of the restaurant and we got out. When we arrived at the part reserved for the dinner, Mrs. Wong greeted us and let me hold her arm. I gave her the gift for Betty. She took it and thanked me and gave me a packet of *lai see*. I said I did not expect it, but she said that it was customary to acknowledge a gift in this way, so in the end I put it in my handbag and thanked her. She led me to my place and put my hand on the back of the chair so that I could sit myself down. I found I was sitting next to her. She introduced me to her friends and relatives as the friend and teacher of her daughters and I had quite a job to explain that we were actually all pupils at the same school. When the tea and melon seed were served, she guided my hand to the cup and the edge of the plate. There was a deafening noise of conversation and mahjong which went on for a long time. I guessed the meal was going to begin when I heard the mahjong tiles being put into boxes. Everything was fine until I heard someone put something on the table. I knew by the delicious smell that the food had arrived, and I began to feel nervous.

At home at family meals, a plate was usually placed near me and something from each of the dishes on the table was put onto it. I was left to help myself from it into my bowl, though often I was not told what was in it; I just had to find out and manage as best I could. It was much nicer when I was alone with Ah Wor as she would tell me what there was and in which positions and let me use a spoon if I wanted to. Inevitably I often dropped things or missed them completely but I did not worry when she and I were on our own.

But now, at a restaurant, in front of so many people, it would be so embarrassing if any of these things should happen. However, Mrs. Wong seemed to understand; she asked me in a whisper if I would like her to tell me what each course was when it arrived, so that I could tell her what I liked and then she would put it in my bowl for me. Of course I agreed gratefully and a moment later I heard her ask a waiter for a pair of chopsticks.

Once or twice through the general noise I overheard comments such as, "Does she like steamed fish?" or "How many brothers and sisters does she have?" Each time Mrs. Wong repeated the question so that I could reply and after a few times people took the hint and spoke to me directly. At one point Mrs. Wong said, "Let's drink!" Just as I was wondering what to do she put my glass against my fingers, so I took it and drank with the rest. From then on, whenever anyone invited guests of the same table to drink, I drank too.

I had a wonderful time and almost forgot I could not see. When it was all over Linda took me downstairs to where Ah Wor was waiting for me. It was not too late so I said I would like to walk home and have some exercise after such a rich meal. On the way I told her all about everything and what we had to eat and how Mrs. Wong helped me. She said she was so glad I had enjoyed it and that what Mrs. Wong had done was probably the best way for me when going out for a meal. I told her about drinking the toasts and she said I had done the proper thing, but she had forgotten to tell me that on those occasions one is supposed to hold the glass in the right hand and at the same time touch the bottom of it with the fingers of the left hand. I realised that I had done this incorrectly and felt anxious in case I had given offence, but she told me not to worry as this was the first time I had had a formal meal out.

After that I received invitations from time to time. I particularly enjoyed going to birthday parties, but I realised this was a Western custom and the girls concerned were Europeans or from Westernised families. It was no good feeling disappointed that we did not do the same in our family because it was just not a Chinese custom to take any notice of children's birthdays. Third Uncle, being a family celebrity, had a birthday feast every year to which all the family (except me) went, and of course we all celebrated

Grandma's birthday with a special meal. Years before, when we had been financially well-off, Father's and Mother's birthdays were made occasions for having a good meal at home. But that was all and for this reason even now I never remember the birthdays of any of my family. Sometimes I remember my own but more often it slips by unnoticed.

The fact that, even when I was growing up and Third Uncle had shown his affection and regard for me in so many ways, I was still omitted from whatever gathering was held to celebrate his birthday seems extraordinary, but it is true. Big feasts were a thing of the past, but usually the available members of the family would meet in a tea house in the morning and have tea and noodles and *dim sum*, but I was never asked to go. Years later I asked him why he always left me out. He was surprised by my question and said it never occurred to him that I would want to go!

As time went on and I grew up, I found myself having to accept invitations to social functions. I was very nervous about them for a long time, but I gradually became more accustomed to coping with the problems. Bit by bit I overcame my fear of making mistakes and spilling things and found myself able to relax more. I tried to do as much as I could for myself but accepted that, when necessary, I must ask friends or neighbours to help. I learned to laugh at my inevitable calamities and blunders and found that not only did other people not mind but that these social contacts were of great value in broadening my horizons and building up my self-confidence.

CHAPTER 24 ●●●●●●●●●●●●●●●●●●●●●●●●●●●●●●●●●

SEPTEMBER 1952—the beginning of my year in Form IV. Every minute of my out-of-school time was needed for my school work, but I found myself having to cope with a new and most unexpected distraction.

After all the years of disliking and despising me and wishing my parents had got rid of me, Grandma now continually sought out my company. Ever since the night she ran away from Third Aunt and came to live with us and I took her tea in the middle of the night, relations between us had changed completely. Now she seemed to want to come and talk to me all the time. It was awkward because I did not want to give her the impression that I was too busy to talk to her—but I was really. And all she did was ask the same questions over and over again: did the girls at school treat me well? Did their parents think that even girls ought to go to school? Did their parents go to a marriage broker to get them married off? I noticed that her voice sounded more and more quavery and Ah Wor said she was very unsteady when she walked and supported herself with her hand on the wall or the furniture. The truth was, she was old; we all knew it. She was ninety, so perhaps she could be forgiven for repeating her questions. When some neighbours said that as I could not see Grandma's wrinkles I must believe she was as young as ever, I thought it a very silly remark. I knew exactly how old and how doddery she had become, so I could hardly fail to realise that she was growing senile.

One evening, when it was time for supper, Grandma did not appear. Most days she took her nap in the afternoon and well before supper time would come tottering into the living-room and sit in what was always called "Grandma's chair." On this evening we waited and waited but there was no sign of her, so Mother decided to wake her. We tried calling her from where we were, quietly at first and then, as nothing happened, more loudly. Father and Mother went to her room. They touched her to rouse her and found that she was stiff and rigid. A doctor came and said she had had a stroke while she was resting and had been unable to call out. She was still breathing but she was half paralysed and could not speak; we did not think she could see or hear either. She just lay there helpless and we knew she was dying.

My ham radio brother was married by now and living in Hong Kong. Seventh Uncle and his family were back in Hong Kong too. Father sent urgent messages to all of them and they all came to Macau as quickly as possible. All the grown-ups took turns watching over Grandma, night and day. Ah Wor told me she really felt sorry for Sister-in-law who had been married to my brother for a few months. She was only in her early twenties, but she still had to take her turn. Grandma could hardly move but from time to time she would grasp someone's hand and would not let it go. This was unnerving for Sister-in-law.

After three days Grandma's condition became worse and she was rushed to hospital. She died that evening. We had all known it was coming but nevertheless we felt very sad.

That night the entire Ching family was gathered together in the funeral parlour. According to traditional custom we all had to sit on the floor through the whole of the first night. We sat in silence on thin rush mats and I found myself thinking about Second Sister more than about Grandma. Grandma had had a long life and, though it had not always been a happy one, she had achieved many of the things people want in life—a big family, respectability, assurance that the family name would go on. Sister had been denied all this. It seemed so cruel and such a waste. I found myself crying, but it was for Sister, not for Grandma.

After sitting for what felt like hours, not daring to move, my feet were so numb that I did not think I could stick it much longer. I whispered to Sister-in-law who sat next to me that I had dreadful pins and needles in my feet. She whispered back that she was stiff and had pins and needles too and suggested that if we were quiet about it, we could go out to the open yard at the back of the room

where we could stand up for a little while. I took her arm and we
moved out quietly and Seventh Auntie and my cousins came out
too. Once we were out in the open courtyard we started whispering
and even giggling a little, not because we were disrespectful to
Grandma but simply because it was a relief from tension. I asked if
anyone knew when we would be able to go home and have some
sleep. Sister-in-law explained that we were not supposed to go
home until the next night, because during the day ahead of us
friends and relatives would come to pay their respects to Grandma.
They would come and bow to the ancestral tablet three times and
we would return the bow just once. I asked whether we would
have to bow in turns, according to seniority. Sister-in-law said no,
we had to bow together as a family. I wondered how I could know
the right moment to bow. Sister-in-law said she would make a
point of standing next to me when we all lined up and when it was
our turn to bow she would touch my hand lightly as a signal.

I heard a movement and recognised Mother's footsteps. We all
stopped talking. She joined the group and, speaking quietly, asked
what was going on. I began to complain about being tired. Seventh
Auntie told me under her breath to be quiet, but I had a headache
and longed to go to bed, so I took no notice of Auntie and told
Mother how I felt. I expected her to be cross, but she was not. In
fact, she sounded gentle and in a good temper. She said that the senior members of the family must stay, but she thought it was too
much for us younger ones, so she told us all to go home and have a
few hours' rest. She asked Seventh Auntie to go with us and see
that we were all back before seven in the morning when the first
people might be expected to come.

Off we went, thankfully, though as it was already well past midnight we had to walk home. We must have had about three hours
in bed before Auntie called us all to get ready to go back at six in
the morning. The day was long, tedious and depressing, but the arrangement Sister-in-law and I had made worked so well that
friends asked me later how I knew when to bow, never too early or
too late, for they knew that in such a solemn ceremony no one was
supposed to speak. They guessed I had some sort of signal but
could not make out what it was.

After that day, the grown-ups took turns to watch Grandma during the two or three days and nights until the funeral.

At the actual funeral Grandma's body had to be taken to the front door of our house where it rested for a few minutes on the way to the cemetery while hell money and paper furniture were offered to her and burnt. This was done so that Grandma could see her home again and be sure of knowing her way to come back. The money and furniture were burnt to ensure that whenever she did come back she would be in a good frame of mind and would bless the family.

When the funeral was over we all went to have a good meal prepared by Ah Wor with the help of Ah Say, Third Uncle's amah. However, before we had our meal there was a curious episode; we were visited by a crowd of beggars. I heard the voices of many people gathering in front of the house, calling out the typical cries of beggars, "Have mercy on me," and "Master, mistress and misses —your ancestor in heaven will bless you." I did not understand what was going on or why, but Mother said she had known this would happen. She said that some of the beggars, or probably even just one, had seen the coffin being taken to the front door during the afternoon. The word had been passed round, so that now nearly every beggar in Macau was outside our house. She called to Ah Say who came quickly from the kitchen. "Go and see what they'll settle for," Mother told her. I wondered what on earth Mother meant. Ah Say opened the front door just wide enough to slip through and closed it behind her, but we could hear all she said as she spoke in a loud voice.

"Be quiet, please," she said very firmly. "The mistress wants to know who your leaders are. Would your leaders come forward." My younger brother was looking through the window and told me that after a pause three men made their way out of the crowd and came up to Ah Say, who was standing on the top step with her back against the front door. I heard Ah Say ask them how many there were altogether, and then she bargained with the three men as to the amount they would accept. This went on for a bit until an acceptable amount was agreed to. Father passed the required money out to Ah Say who handed it to the men, and then the crowd went away. This was apparently a ritual form of blackmail which always happened after funerals as the beggars knew the family would give something for fear of displeasing the person who had died and of being cursed by the beggars. How much they had to give depended on the skill of the negotiator. Some people, not knowing how to deal with the situation, would begin giving money to each individual and would end up by handing out a fortune. Ah Say apparently managed very well and beat them down to a reasonable sum.

I was away from school for a week. On my first day back I was preparing for an English composition lesson, so I put my braille things away in my bag and sorted out some typing paper. Miss Wong would write the title or titles for our composition on the blackboard and see the class start work; then she would pick up my typewriter and go with me to the staff room where she would give me the same titles and leave me to type my composition there. Of course I would much rather have done it in braille so that I could read it back and make corrections as I went along, but if I did that, it meant reading it out to the teacher afterwards and this took too long. The teachers said that when I wanted to cross things out I could back space and put x's on them, but I tried to do this as little as possible because I was always working in a hurry and it was hard to count accurately and not cross out too much.

That day I heard Sister Margaret's footsteps coming towards our classroom. She told us that Miss Wong was on sick leave for a day or two so she was taking us instead. She said we could do "free composition," which meant we could choose our own topics. Then she helped me to take my things to the staff room and left me there to work. She was a most kind and thoughtful person; she never forgot I needed special help. Some of the teachers did and I hated having to remind them.

For written composition we had a double period—one and a half hours. I typed away as quickly as I could. When the bell rang and Sister Margaret came to collect my work I had done two pages in double spacing and felt quite pleased with myself. When Sister Margaret took my papers she stood without saying anything for so long that I began to feel worried. Normally she would just say thank you and promise to let me know the corrections later. I could not believe she disliked my composition as I had written on "My Wonderful Companion" (Ah Wor). At last she said she was so sorry to have to tell me that something had gone wrong with the typewriter and my work was unreadable; most of it was just blank. She then looked at the typewriter and told me there was a hole in the ribbon. Something had stopped it winding on properly and for one and a half hours I had been typing on the same spot. I was so disappointed and frustrated that I began to cry, although I tried not to. She put her arm round me and tried to comfort me, saying that it would be all right because, as it was a free composition, I could do it again whenever I had the time. I asked her to let me do it after school and she agreed. She told me to leave the typewriter with her and she would have it repaired and ready for me at the end of the afternoon. She also said that whenever I had to use the typewriter she would make a point of checking it and she would ask other teachers to do the same, especially during tests or exams.

After school that afternoon I stayed in the empty classroom to do my composition. I did not feel like trying to re-write what I had done in the morning so I decided to try to describe what it would be like if I were given the chance to see for one day. In the composition I said that when I first opened my eyes and could see, I found the daylight so strong that it hurt my eyes. I looked round and saw people standing in the room, smiling at me, but I did not know who they were until, one by one, they spoke. Then I knew them—Ah Wor, Father, Mother, my brothers and sisters. I looked at their clothes and everything in the room, amazed at all the colours but not knowing which was which and having to be told. I had always disliked the very idea of green because I associated it with the plants which destroyed my sight, but I wrote that when I could see, I found the colour very beautiful and loved it. I went on for two whole pages of imaginary visual experience, banging away to work off my frustration over the morning's episode. When time was up I gave the composition to Sister Margaret who assured me that all was well.

This unexpected disaster was upsetting at the time but it is probably a good thing that it happened when it did. After all, it might have happened during an exam. After that day I always concentrated on the sound as I hit the keys and if I thought I detected anything unusual, I asked someone to look at it for me and check. With experience I found I could usually tell if there was something wrong, though I still have an occasional calamity.

In our English class the following week Sister Margaret said she was giving back our compositions. I was afraid she would say I had written a load of rubbish. I had begun to regret writing it, but to my relief she did not mention any bad work. She said they were quite good on the whole and there were two she would like to read to the class. The first one was an imaginary trip to the moon. It was beautiful, describing streets and buildings all of gold. Then she started on the other. It was mine. When she finished reading it, the girls said it was lovely, and Sister Margaret said I ought to send it to the student section of a Hong Kong English-language newspaper. During the recess she asked me whether I would have time to type it again if she read me the corrections she had made, but she added that if I felt I really had not got the time, she would ask someone to type it for me and then I could send it to Hong Kong. I honestly did not think it was all that good, but Sister Margaret seemed determined so I accepted her offer of getting it typed by someone else, sent it off to the student newspaper and forgot all about it.

Several weeks passed. One morning as I walked into the classroom a group of girls told me my article was in the paper. Later Sister Margaret told me that the paper had asked the school to write an article about how I coped with my school work. This they did and that too was published. The result of all this was that I received a large number of letters from secondary school pupils in Hong Kong; one letter came from three boys—John, Peter and Paul —saying they would like to have me for a pen pal. I answered all of them with very short notes of appreciation, explaining that as I needed every minute for my school work I was afraid I would not be able to manage extra correspondence. However I received another letter from the three boys. They said they wanted to keep in touch with me because they found the way I coped with my life and studies a spur and an inspiration in their own lives. They said

they would write to me from time to time and I need not answer
their letters if I had too much to do. They even said they hoped I
would go to Hong Kong someday so that we could all meet. After
that the school sent several more of my compositions to Hong
Kong, to the *South China Morning Post*'s Sunday edition, and they
too were printed. There were four or five in all.

It must have been in March of that year that Sister Margaret one
day put a book with big pages into my hands. She told me it was a
scrap-book with the newspaper cuttings of my compositions pasted
in it. She said I should show it to my parents as they would be very
proud of me. I explained, shyly, that my parents knew no English.
However, she said that would not matter because even if they
could not read what I had written, they would certainly recognise
the fact that having the compositions published meant that I had
done a good job on them. I took the scrap-book and said I would
show it to my parents.

Of course I showed it to Ah Wor and she was pleased with me. I
never showed it to Father but this had nothing to do with the fact
that he knew no English or with his lack of interest in my education. He was by this time much more sympathetic—he had shown
this in many ways, from paying my fees to washing up the supper
things so that Ah Wor was free to take me to my readers. But his
rigid adherence to traditional attitudes had not softened; he still
felt it necessary to withhold praise from his children, whatever
their achievements, in order that both they and he should appear
properly modest according to the precepts of customary Chinese
behaviour. He might feel proud of me but in no circumstances
would he ever admit it to himself or to me. On one or two occasions in the past I had made the mistake of telling someone, in Father's hearing, that I had got good marks for something and had
been told off for boasting and immodesty. So I could not possibly
have shown him the scrap-book.

But I kept thinking of Seventh Auntie. She always took such an
interest in me and my little achievements. I had not forgotten how
pleased she was when she found I could read the English words on
the cards of dots and when I answered the telephone and spoke to
her for the first time, and how she often enquired about my school

work with genuine interest. But how could I show her the scrap-book? If I sent it to her in Hong Kong, even she might think I was asking for praise and was showing off. I had been pondering this, on and off, for a couple of weeks when one day I received a letter from America. I asked a friend to read me the address on the enve-lope, but when she did it meant nothing to me. I opened the letter and asked my friend to read the signature: it was "Aunt Alice." Still it did not ring a bell. Finally I asked my friend to read the whole letter. To my surprise it was from Seventh Auntie who said she had just arrived in America. She wrote that decisions had been taken and arrangements made so quickly that she had had no time to get in touch with me before she left Hong Kong. She said she had found a job and was prepared to work hard so that one day she could bring her family to America.

Although I had not seen Seventh Auntie much since we left China, except for the short period when they lived in Macau, I had not really missed her as she had not been very far away. But now, the sudden realisation that she had gone to America made the loss much more acute. She asked me to remember her to my parents and especially to Ah Wor, and hoped I would write to her. I was thankful I could use a typewriter, for although I had to have letters from other people read to me, I could now write my own letters privately. I wrote and told her how sad I felt that she had gone so far away and said I wondered when we would see each other again. It was many years before we met again, although we man-aged to talk on the telephone when I was in Boston and she was in Michigan.

The scrap-book lay in a drawer. It made me think more about writing and its possibilities. Dr. Chappel and I corresponded fairly regularly, and he encouraged me to write short articles and stories. He said I need not worry about my English as he could help me with that. So, full of enthusiasm, I started on a story called "Under-standing and Light," in which I wrote about a blind girl and her difficulties and how eventually, with her Christian faith and help and encouragement from friends, she obtained enough education to enable her to teach other blind people to read.

I knew that the story was too long to go on an airmail form so

Ah Wor said she would pay for the stamps to send it in an envelope. We posted it and I never thought of publication until I received a letter from Dr. Chappel about three weeks later. Inside was a corrected version with all the tenses put right and the sentences reconstructed. My younger brother read it to me while I took it down in braille. When I read it through I could see that his corrected version was much more smooth-flowing and better expressed than my original, but contained all my original material. He asked in his letter if he could send the corrected version to a magazine in Canada. He said he would also like to put it in *Discovery*, a magazine for children published by his Society. I wrote back delightedly, giving my permission for him to use the story in whatever way he thought best.

One afternoon when I came home from school Father told me there was a registered letter for me from America. I opened it and asked my younger brother to read it. As I took it out of the envelope I noticed that there was a thin sheet of paper, the sort used for typing, which I guessed was a letter from Dr. Chappel, but there was also a small piece of paper, much thicker than air-mail typing paper. My brother read out the English words, but none of us knew enough English to know what they meant. However, he found a dollar sign and the figure "25." I took it to Father and asked him what it was, as I thought that if it had to do with money, he might be able to help. He immediately said it was a money order for twenty-five dollars. He looked carefully and spelled it all out and said it was made out to me in my name—Lucy Ching. I still could not understand what it was all about so I asked my brother to read me the letter, spelling out the words so that I could take it down in braille. In this roundabout way I discovered that my story had been published by the magazine in Canada which had sent twenty-five American dollars in payment.

Dr. Chappel also said in his letter that Miss Schaeffer had written to the Society about me, and asked if they could help her contact me. He said that she had left Canton and was teaching in the Hip Woo Middle School in Hong Kong and hoped that perhaps one day she and I could meet. I was overjoyed and excited beyond words by all this. At that time one American dollar was equal to about $6.50 in Macau money, so the exact equivalent of the US$25 was $162.50 in Macau money. This was a fortune to me and totally unexpected at that. I realised that it meant that Ah Wor and I could go to Hong Kong to see Miss Schaeffer without having to worry about the expense.

The more I thought about going to Hong Kong, the more thrilled I got. Then, all of the sudden, my heart sank. Suppose Father and Mother said it was a waste of money. Father's pay was very little; money was a constant problem. He was always worried about how to manage and he might well think that my windfall could be put to better use than the financing of a trip to Hong Kong for Ah Wor and me. As usual I consulted Ah Wor and as usual she had the answer. Why not share it with the family, she suggested: give Father half and keep the other half which would still be enough for the Hong Kong trip. So we set off confidently to go to a money changer to cash the money order. I took my identity card and little did we guess what we were in for.

We went into a money changer's and Ah Wor whispered to me to speak to him. I was always nervous of speaking before I had heard the other person's voice, but I knew I must do it. As I was thinking of what to say, I carefully put out my hand and touched the counter to see how high it was. I wondered if the man was sitting or standing. I guessed he was probably sitting because I could hear the click of the abacus he was using.

Trying to sound calm and to speak carefully, I explained about the money order from the United States and said I wanted to cash it. I reached out my hand to put the money order and my identity card on the counter and he took them so quickly that our hands touched. He said nothing. I began to wonder if he would ever speak. Finally I repeated my request and then I could sense he was sitting down and that he lifted his head and stared at me. At last he spoke and asked if I could see at all. I said no. He then asked why a society in America should send me a money order. I explained about my story being published in a church magazine.

The money changer called to two other men, who came over to the counter. He told them about the money order and how I said I got it. One of them, who must have been the boss, explained to Ah Wor that they could not take the risk of cashing the order in case it was stolen or forged. For, as he said as he pushed it and my identity card against my fingers, everyone knew that there was no way a blind person could receive education so how could I possibly have written a story? I nudged Ah Wor and we left the shop. This humiliating scene was repeated at four or five more places. They all said the same. I was ready to give up but Ah Wor said she knew of one more, so we might as well try it.

Everything happened as before up to the point where the boss was called. He came and looked at the money order and said that, as it was a cash order, the money had already been paid to the issuing bank in order to purchase it, and as it was made out to my name which was the same as the name on my identity card, he could accept it. Ordinarily, he said I would need to have a guarantee from a shop but I did not know of one that would vouch for me. At last he said that if I agreed, he would take the money order, but would not give me the money until he had sent it to America to be cashed there. He would give me a receipt for it and I could go back in about three weeks' time for the money. I agreed, relieved that even though I had to wait three weeks I would have about a hundred and sixty dollars, more than I had ever handled in my life. Then he pushed a pen into my hand and asked me to sign my name. Horrors! I had never learnt to sign my name. I asked if I could give a finger print or any other substitute but he said that nothing but my signature would do, so that was that. But he was a kind man and did not seem to doubt that the money order was mine. He suggested that the best way might be for me to write to the people who sent it, explaining the situation and suggesting that they make it out to Ah Wor.

Feeling thoroughly discouraged, I said to Ah Wor as we walked home that this suggestion seemed to be the only solution. She said that before sending the order back to America I had better talk to Father and see whether he thought it would be all right to ask Third Uncle about it. Third Uncle had his business in Hong Kong and might have an idea what we could do. So that evening I told

Father what had happened. He agreed that Third Uncle would be the person to ask, and as luck would have it, he was coming to Macau the following weekend.

Third Uncle came to see us on the Saturday and I waited as patiently as I could for a chance to tell him the history of the money order. He was pleased to hear that something I had written was being published and for money too. He was as careful as Father in his regard for modesty, but for some reason he made an exception in my case and allowed me to know that he was really pleased with me. I told him that Dr. Chappel had made some corrections to my story so that I could not honestly say it was entirely my work, but he said that if the story had not been good enough Dr. Chappel would not have gone to the trouble of correcting it or of offering it to the Canadian magazine. He gave me the money straight away and took the money order, saying he was sure he could get it cashed in Hong Kong. However, he told me something I had not known before—that I ought to sign my name at the end of all letters I wrote. He said this was the correct way to end a letter and that I had better learn how to do it; it might not be a very accurate signature but it would serve as my personal sign. So, as soon as I could, I asked my younger brother and sister to help me to write my name, and I practised and practised till I could do it, using the edge of a card as a guide. I still do it in this way.

As Ah Wor suggested, I offered Father some of the money. I kept enough for the trip to Hong Kong and gave him the rest.

CHAPTER 25 ••

THE PROBLEM OF finding people to read my textbooks to me grew worse and worse. During my Form IV year I do not think that more than a third of any of them was ever read to me. Examinations were approaching and I had not heard one word of the Geography book. I asked my readers to try, but with only a week to go before exams I had less than two chapters of it in braille. Ah Wor and I racked our brains but could not think of anyone else to ask. The worst part was that I knew the exam would include a question on the map of North America, about which I knew nothing. I dared not bother my classmates to explain the map to me. They were all edgy and nervous and needed every minute of their time for themselves. Then suddenly I had an inspiration.

An American missionary, Miss Lovegren, came to our church. She was friendly and often stopped to speak to me. We knew that missionaries are always busy people with many demands on their time but, as Ah Wor said, I had nothing to lose by at least asking her for help. Ah Wor knew where she lived because one day, on her way home from market, she happened to see her letting herself into a house with a key. So that evening, after supper, Father said he would do the dishes while Ah Wor and I went to look for Miss Lovegren. Ah Wor said there were several houses looking alike and she was not sure which one it was, but after knocking at one or two doors and describing to the amahs who we were looking for, we found the right house. The amah said Miss Lovegren was just having supper and as she had left the house very early that morning she was very tired and would probably not want to see visitors.

Feeling disappointed, we turned and began to walk away when we heard the door open again and Miss Lovegren came out and asked who it was. I turned round and said my name. To my delight she ran out and took my hand and asked us to come in. She said she was just having some cake for dessert and asked if we would like some too. I said I would love to, before Ah Wor could stop me. She hissed at me, as Miss Lovegren left the room to tell the amah, that the polite and proper thing to do was to say "no, thank you" instead of "I would love to." I felt ashamed that I could so easily forget the manners I had been taught all these years, but we could never afford cakes at that time and I just could not resist them. The amah brought us plates and offered us pieces of cake, but Ah Wor said "no, thank you." I knew it was because she felt that, as an amah, she ought not to sit at the table with the misses. Miss Lovegren was evidently aware of the situation too and kindly suggested that she might like to take her cake home. When Ah Wor saw that the American lady was genuinely treating her as an equal she finally came and sat at the table and the three of us had our cake and tea together.

I told Miss Lovegren how desperate I was to have the Geography book read to me and especially how I needed help with the map of North America, as that question carried a great many marks. She took the book and, there and then, read to me for nearly two hours and then suggested that as it was in print and I would not need it that night, she would keep it so that she could work out how to give me the description I needed of the map.

In my three years at an English school, that evening was the first time I had had a book read to me by a *completely* English-speaking person. Even Norma, good though she was, was not that. I would never have believed what a difference it could make: instead of stopping and spelling out words as all my Chinese readers did, she read them fluently with correct pronunciation and only spelled out the ones I asked her to. I found it much easier to grasp what it was all about because her voice had the right English speech tones and inflexions.

Next evening we went back again. As we went into her living-room Ah Wor told me that on her desk there were several maps, pieces of paper covered with writing and my book open at the map. Her amah told us that she had worked on these until very late the night before. At this point Miss Lovegren came into the room. She said cheerfully that she had worked out how to describe the map and suggested that she dictate notes on it to me. We settled down to work and the notes she gave me were so clear and vivid that I really began to feel I knew something about North America as I pricked away on my handframe.

When we had done that and she had read me some of the book, we had a rest and a cup of tea and she told me about a blind classmate of hers back at her seminary in the United States. His name was Edwin Wilson and I was amazed to hear that he used a machine to write braille—a sort of typewriter called a "Perkins Brailler." She described it and explained that instead of pricking one dot at a time as I did, it could do up to six dots at a time, which of course speeds up the brailling process immensely. She said that she thought I worked very fast with my stylus and frame and I told her that most of the time, instead of brailling complete sentences, I tried to take down the important words and make very short notes. She told me another thing about Mr. Wilson—that when time did not permit him to braille everything, he asked his readers to read into a tape recorder. I had never heard of a tape recorder and asked what it was, so she explained; these sounded like things from another planet. Certainly, I thought, I shall never have a chance to use any of these wonderful things. Never in my wildest dreams could I have imagined that in just over one year from that evening I would be flying to America alone, to learn to use these machines with the help and understanding and experience of people who made a profession of educating blind people.

At last the dreaded exams were over. Our Form IV year was finished. We had handed in our last papers, and now we were hanging around in the playground, waiting for the bell so that we could go home. In September we would be in Form V and at the end of that—what? Some of the girls were talking about their plans —Form VI, secretarial college, teacher training. I listened but avoided getting involved. I knew and they knew that none of these could apply to me. How could I hope to go into Form VI? It was not just the fees—Father might manage them—but how could I get textbooks read to me? In fact, I was not sure I could manage even for Form V; and what would happen then? What hopes had I of getting a job of any kind and of being able to help my father by contributing to household expenses? It was my ambition to teach other blind people, but who was going to pay me to do that? Back in Canton Miss Dodson of the Mo Kwong Home and Miss Schaeffer of the Ming Sum School had both said that they would employ me as a teacher if I finished secondary school. But what good was that in Macau, where there was no school or home for blind women?

I was so lost in these thoughts that I did not hear some of the girls calling me. Someone banged me on the shoulder and made me jump; it was Karen, pushing a letter into my hands and saying it was from Hong Kong. I asked her to read me the name and address of the sender: it was from Miss Schaeffer. I opened it and gave the letter to Karen to read. Miss Schaeffer said the first news she heard of me ever since I left Canton was from Dr. Chappel, and then she had read my article in the students' newspaper. She asked if I could go to Hong Kong for a few days during the summer and said she would gladly pay for the boat tickets for Ah Wor and me. There were things she wanted to talk to me about, including my future after Form V. "Would you like to continue your studies?" Karen read out. I could not believe my ears. I asked her to read that sentence again and then read the whole letter through again. I knew it by heart now, every word, so I put it back in the envelope and tried to work out Miss Schaeffer's meaning. Continuing my studies was impossible—or was it? Or was I misunderstanding her? Whatever she meant, I could hardly wait to go to Hong Kong and find out, so I dashed back into the classroom and typed her a letter saying that Ah Wor and I were planning to go to Hong Kong anyway, as a result of hearing about her from Dr. Chappel's letter, and that we would ring her when we arrived. I also said I had enough money for the fares.

I had quite a job persuading my parents to let me go to Hong Kong but finally they agreed, so I wrote to my ham radio brother and sister-in-law to see if they could put us up. They lived somewhere on Hong Kong Island in those days. Within a few days I received a reply from Sister-in-law saying they could manage and would make us welcome. They had only one room, she said, but my brother could sleep in the passage so that she and I could share their bed, and Ah Wor could sleep on a camp bed in the same room.

Oh yes—I passed in Geography.

CHAPTER 26 ••••••••••••••••••••••••••••••••••••

IT WAS THE DAY we were actually going to Hong Kong. The boat left in the afternoon. In the morning Ah Wor went to the market and bought enough food to last for a few days. We had bought our tickets the day before and Sister-in-law had written to say that my brother would meet us off the boat.

We were anxious to arrive in good time so we took a pedicab to the pier. As some people were already boarding, we decided to follow them. Ah Wor showed our tickets to the ticket inspector and we were walking past him when someone seized my arm and pulled me back. I thought it must be a thief and I was about to shout for help when a man's voice said, "Can you see at all?"

"No," I replied and tried to walk away, but the hand would not let go of my arm. Ah Wor whispered to me that it was the ticket inspector; out loud, to him, she said we had already shown him our tickets and he should let us through, but the man insisted that if I could not see I could not be allowed on the boat. I was completely taken aback and said angrily that he had no right to stop me. To my fury he still held my arm while we argued. I felt my face becoming hotter and hotter as I became aware that we had gathered quite a crowd of onlookers. The man asked why we were going to Hong Kong—were we going to take up permanent residence? I resented very much being questioned but said shortly, "No, a visit." He still held me so I insisted on seeing whoever was in charge. I heard him calling for his senior, and he pushed me to one side, presumably to clear the way for other people. We then had a long, infuriating wait.

When at last the senior man came, things began to improve. By sheer luck he happened to have read my article in the students' paper and guessed at once who I was. He was very pleasant and agreed that there was no reason at all why I should not go to Hong Kong, especially as my own brother and his family were there. I listened with satisfaction while he reprimanded the man who tried to stop me. We started once again to walk towards the boat, but the wretched man, after receiving such a public ticking-off, was not going to let me go as easily as that. He held me back for a moment and muttered maliciously that he had tried to stop me as he thought Hong Kong already had enough blind women singing in the streets and would not want to have another one from Macau. I longed to answer him back but decided it was more important to get on the boat, so we turned our backs on him and walked away.

Apart from making me angry with the man, the incident made me wonder anxiously whether I would have the same sort of difficulty at the Hong Kong end. Suppose the officials there would not let me in? For three hours on the boat I prayed that nothing would stop me from entering Hong Kong. Ah Wor tried to cheer me up but I was so despondent that she did not have much success. I was trembling like a leaf as we went through Immigration, but all was well and no one said anything to us. As we walked out into the street I was delighted to hear my older brother's voice. I decided not to tell him about the unpleasant episode; it was over now and I was much more interested in finding out about him and Sister-in-law and where they lived.

In the taxi I bombarded him with questions as we drove along. They lived in one room in a flat shared by three families. The landlord and his wife lived in one room and let the other two bedrooms. There was a living-room, a kitchen and a bathroom which everyone had to share, but Brother said they did not use the living-room except on very special occasions. He explained that most people had to live in crowded conditions like this because rents in Hong Kong were much higher than in Macau and only rich people could afford to have a whole flat to themselves.

The taxi stopped and Brother said we were in Happy Valley. The flat was on the ground floor and as we went in, Sister-in-law was waiting for us and introduced us to Mrs. Kwok, the landlady. Mrs. Kwok greeted me cheerfully and said she hoped I would enjoy my visit to Hong Kong. She insisted that we should have our supper in the living-room. Our visit was evidently a special occasion. After that first evening we had all our meals and did everything in Brother and Sister-in-law's bedroom.

After supper I asked whether it was too late to go to a shop to telephone Miss Schaeffer. Unexpectedly Sister-in-law said that there was a telephone right there in the living-room. She said nearly everyone in Hong Kong had one, in contrast to Macau where they were found only in well-to-do houses. Sister-in-law took me to it and I dialled the number. The bell rang a few times and then Miss Schaeffer answered. At first I did not recognise her voice; it was several years since we had last met in Canton and then we had talked in Chinese, not in English as we were doing now. But after a few moments her voice sounded familiar again. I could hardly believe we were really talking to each other again after so long. She said she was particularly glad to know that Ah Wor was still with me. It was arranged that we would go to see her the following morning.

Next day we crossed the harbour on the Star Ferry and found our way to her flat in Tsim Sha Tsui in Kowloon. I told her all my worries—that I could not find readers for my Form V books, and if I could not get the books read, what point was there in going into Form V at all? And then there was the problem of finding a job; what could I do in Macau? With no Ming Sum School and no Mo Kwong Home there seemed no hope of realising my ambition to teach blind people or of doing anything to earn my living and lessening the financial burden on my parents and on Ah Wor. After a moment she asked me if I would like to do my Form V studies in Hong Kong. I said surely that would not be possible; I had heard that there were not nearly enough school places for people wanting them and that it was terribly difficult to get into any of the good schools. Miss Schaeffer agreed, but said that it was still worth thinking about. She had the Diocesan Girls' School, in Kowloon, in mind, she went on, and if I could get into this school, she could read to me for several hours a week and probably some of her friends would be glad to help too. She said she realised that the reading help I needed would probably be much more than she and her friends could give me, but she thought it would be easier to find paid readers in Hong Kong than in Macau. Then she said she wanted to make a telephone call. I can still remember that conversation almost word for word.

"Hello, Nancy," she said. "Remember Lucy that I talked to you about?" I quickly realised that Nancy was a teacher at the school and that Miss Schaeffer was asking her to talk to the Headmistress about me to see if she would agree to take me. "She can't do Form V in Macau, there's no one to read to her. Yes, I know, but that does not mean that it can't be done . . . There's what's called the integrated programme in England and America . . . Well, yes, of course, blind pupils in schools over there have all sorts of facilities and aids that Lucy doesn't have . . . Yes, it's a miracle that she manages as she does . . ." I listened to Miss Schaeffer pleading my case with her friend and I hardly dared to think what it might mean. I thought of Miss Lovegren and of the revelation that her reading had been to me—an English-speaking person reading English and, understanding it herself, making me understand it. If I could have Miss Schaeffer and her friends read to me, the difference in time and effort would be tremendous.

Miss Schaeffer said goodbye to Nancy and rang off. She told me to call her the following day as she hoped that by then she would have heard about the Headmistress' reaction from her friend. As we were leaving, Miss Schaeffer put a *lai see* packet into my hand. I was very surprised and tried to refuse it but she insisted, so I took it and told her how grateful I was for everything she was doing for me.

Deep in thought, Ah Wor and I made our way back to Brother's place. Problems loomed on every side. Supposing the school would take me, how on earth could I get the money to pay the fees? Above all, how and where would I live? Ah Wor agreed that this was the most daunting problem. How I wished that Seventh Auntie had not gone to America! Then Ah Wor had an idea; she said I should ring up Third Uncle and Aunt. They had a little flat in Kowloon and perhaps they would let me stay with them for the school year. Anyway, whether they agreed to that or not, courtesy demanded that I get in touch with them. Uncle had been very good to me, not only in the good times when he was prosperous and important but even recently, when he had paid for my readers.

Poor Uncle. He no longer had any official position or any influence and he was hard up like the rest of us. He kept a little office to which he went each day, ostensibly to carry on some sort of import and export business, but I think he really kept it on so that he had an escape from Aunt and the flat. I do not think he did much business. His small income came from the rents of two houses he owned (they had belonged to Third Auntie). It was enough to live on but Aunt firmly managed all the money matters and let him have only very little spending money for himself, and systematically starved the business of money too. It was all in sad contrast with the great occasion of the visit to us in Canton seven years ago.

I rang them from my brother's place. Third Aunt answered and sounded pleased and surprised to hear that I was in Hong Kong. She invited us to go and have supper with her and Uncle that evening. It took us a long time to get there but we were all glad to see each other. I told them about my visit to Miss Schaeffer and about her telephone call to her friend at the Diocesan Girls' School. Uncle was most interested. He said this school was one of the best English schools in Hong Kong and most of its pupils were from rich families. Because of its high standard there was great competition for places. I said honestly I did not think I had the slightest chance of being accepted—it was only Miss Schaeffer's idea. Then to my amazement Aunt said quite spontaneously that if the school accepted me, Ah Wor and I could stay with her and Uncle for the school year. I could not believe my ears; it was more than I had dared to hope for. I knew Uncle would not be able to help with the fees but to promise us a place to live in was too good to be true.

I felt elated as we started the long journey back to Happy Valley. One of my two big problems was solved. But the matter of school fees and all the other expenses was not. The more I thought about it, the less elated I felt. Now that I began to think seriously about it, it looked more and more impossible.

Ah Wor refused to regard it as an insuperable difficulty. She said she had been keeping a look-out wherever we went and had seen women doing all kinds of handwork, sitting on the steps of houses or in groups on the pavements. This was obviously outwork from factories and she could see no reason why she could not find some and earn enough money for the fees. I did not know what to say to this. For one thing, I did not think that this would be enough to pay the fees of such an expensive school, and in any case she had already given up everything—time, money, her entire life—to me. In addition, accepting help from her meant that she was not saving money for her own future. She was already in her fifties and had no savings left; she had used them all for me. How could I agree to her spending even longer hours at dull, repetitive, ill-paid jobs that strained her eyes? It seemed we were destined always to play the same parts—she the giver, I the taker.

I told her I wanted to find a telephone to call Miss Schaeffer. She did not ask why; she led me into a shop and put my hand on the telephone. To my relief Miss Schaeffer was in. Trying to sound calm and unemotional, I said I had thought it all over very carefully and realised that I would never be able to afford the fees and there was therefore no need for her friend to tell the Headmistress about me.

"Oh, there's no great problem about the fees," said the voice in my ear. She had some money, she said, given to her by the John Milton Society to use for blind people in Hong Kong. She thought my school fees would be just the sort of project that the Society would think worthwhile. The amount she had would not be enough for the whole year but she would write to the Society to see if they could provide additional help. She also said that if I were studying in Hong Kong, I could go to visit the girls at the Ebenezer Home for the Blind, and perhaps the Superintendent might want me to teach the women there. She said she would telephone me the next day as soon as she had news from her friend.

I did not know where I was or what to think. I had gone from hope to despair and now back to hope again. I went to bed that night too confused and excited to sleep properly. I dared not fidget for fear of disturbing Sister-in-law, whose bed I was sharing, and it seemed as if the night would never end. In the morning I listened for the telephone. There were several calls, all for other people; then at last Mrs. Kwok called out that I was wanted. Miss Schaeffer said Mrs. Symons, the Headmistress of the Diocesan Girls' School (D.G.S.), would like to see me. I asked if she thought this meant that I had a chance of being accepted. She said she could not be sure, but the fact that Mrs. Symons wanted to see me must mean there was a possibility.

Next morning Ah Wor and I set out for the D.G.S. I had telephoned and had been told to go at eleven o'clock. Here I must digress briefly. When I said earlier that I kept only enough for the boat tickets out of my American dollars I meant exactly that. I handed the rest to my father and I literally brought no money with me. I knew that Brother and Sister-in-law would be pleased to give us our food. Ah Wor had a little money of her own but not much, and as our visit was now becoming longer than we had intended, we dared not spend a cent if we could help it. I now had Miss Schaeffer's *lai see,* but I did not want to touch that as I felt strongly that I must save it for something important and not use it for casual expenses. Wherever we went, therefore, we walked. In those days there was, I think, no Wan Chai ferry. People who know Hong Kong's geography will read with surprise that when we went to supper with Third Uncle and Aunt we walked from Happy Valley to the Star Ferry in Central and from the Star Ferry in Tsim Sha Tsui to Kowloon City, where they lived not far from Kai Tak airport, and back again after supper. We certainly had blisters. When we went to D.G.S. we again walked from Happy Valley to the Star Ferry and from the Star Ferry in Kowloon up to Jordan Road. Ah Wor had been told it was near a particular cinema which she remembered from when we lived in Hong Kong in 1949, so she knew the general direction, but even so she still had trouble finding the school itself, which lies off the main artery of Nathan Road. We finally walked through the gate in good time for the appointment, having been about two hours on the way. We had started out very early in order to make sure we were not late and we were only too glad to have a short while to get our breath back.

In the first building we came to Ah Wor said there was a lady sitting at a desk. I told her who I was and said I had an appointment to see Mrs. Symons. The lady was pleasant and helpful and let me hold her arm as we walked to a room. She asked Ah Wor to come along too, and said that Mrs. Symons would be there in a few minutes.

I stood up when brisk footsteps came into the room. She came straight to me and took my hand and introduced herself. Then she gave my shoulder a little pat and a press to indicate I was to sit down. She sat next to me. She asked me about my school work and which were my strongest and weakest subjects. To my surprise she did not refer to my blindness, nor ask how I managed about textbooks, tests and exams. When she asked me what form I would like to go into, I said that as I had finished Form IV I would like to go into Form V. She said that in the normal way she did not accept admissions into Form V but that my case was exceptional. If my school reports were good enough and if I could pass a test to satisfy them that I was up to Form V standard, they would consider admitting me. I told her my grades in the Form IV exams at Sacred Heart and explained about being able to study only a part of the syllabus. She said she understood my problems, and that in order to assess my standard in general English she would like me to take a test that would be like an entrance exam for Form V. I could take the test the following month, just before term started. However, when she asked if I was spending the summer in Hong Kong and found out that I was only staying with my brother for a few days and about the American money order making the trip possible at all, she said she would see if they could arrange to give me the test the next day, to save another trip. I was so grateful for her understanding and consideration, and felt more eager than ever to be admitted to the school.

Mrs. Symons left us alone for a few minutes and then came back and confirmed that I could do the test the following day. I gave her my Sacred Heart report and we said goodbye.

Next day we repeated our walk to the school. At least Ah Wor now knew the way and exactly how long it would take, and we made sure I would have a little time to sit and wait before doing the test. Mrs. Symons introduced me to Mrs. Lodge, form mistress of Form V, who sounded very gentle and kind and that put me at my ease. I had my handframe and stylus with me and for the first time in my school life I did not have to explain about taking down the questions: Mrs. Symons and Mrs. Lodge both seemed to understand without being told what needed to be done. However, when she read the questions to me, I found Mrs. Lodge a little difficult to understand; some words sounded different and I had to ask her to repeat things or spell out some words. But they were all brailled eventually and I settled down to answer them, using the school office typewriter. It was an Imperial office machine, much bigger than the portable I was used to. The keys seemed to be larger and stiffer to press. It also sounded so different from the portable that I could not tell by the sound whether the ribbon was moving or not. I hoped for the best. I was working in the office with Mrs. Lodge at another desk doing her own work—I could hear her pen as she wrote. The unfamiliar sound of the typewriter bothered me so much that I stopped and of course immediately forgot what the last word I had typed was. Mrs. Lodge came over to me. I heard her speak, but thought she was talking to someone else as her voice was so quiet. I was trying so hard to remember what I had just written that I did not take any notice. Then she touched my shoulder to attract my attention and said that if at any point I forgot what I had just typed she would be glad to read it to me. It was the first time I had ever had such an offer and it was a great help.

After the test I went to see Miss Schaeffer. I told her all about it and asked her why I found Mrs. Lodge hard to understand. I did not always understand everything that Miss Lovegren or Miss Schaeffer herself said to me, but I found Mrs. Lodge much more difficult, as her whole way of speaking seemed to be different. Miss Schaeffer explained that people of different nationalities all speak English with different accents; she and Miss Lovegren, both Americans, spoke alike, but Mrs. Lodge was English and was perhaps the first person I had met to talk to properly who spoke "orthodox" English, with the accent one would hear in London or Oxford. She agreed that there were big differences and suggested that I try listening to broadcasts from the BBC to make myself familiar with the English accent, as I would have to learn to understand it.

Mrs. Symons telephoned me next day to tell me that the teachers had read my test papers and my Sacred Heart reports and considered that I had reached the required standard for Form V. She was therefore willing to admit me in the September term. I stammered my thanks, feeling dazed, and went to see Miss Schaeffer. She was delighted and said she would write to Dr. Chappel about the fees. She then gave me some money to be going on with and said that Ah Wor and I had better go straight back to Macau to break the news to my parents and then make preparations for September.

One thing remained to be done before we went home to Macau; we again made the long trip to Kowloon City to tell Third Uncle and Aunt the news. I think it came as something of a shock to Aunt. She admitted that she certainly never expected to have to take me and she evidently repented of her rash offer. However, she said she would not go back on her word; Ah Wor and I could stay with them for my year at the school. So that was settled, though we were under no illusions that Aunt was pleased at the prospect.

The following day we packed our belongings and caught the ferry back to Macau, arriving home just before supper time.

Father and Mother listened speechless to my recital. When I finished Father made me go right through it all again, step by step, as he wanted to be sure he had really understood it all. Then he asked me if I thought I had acted properly. Clearly what worried him most was the thought of accepting financial help from Miss Schaeffer and from the John Milton Society in America. He reminded me of the Chinese saying that we should never accept an advantage which we have done nothing to earn. Also, I must realise that I could never repay these obligations. I explained that Miss Schaeffer hoped, if I got adequate education, that one day I could teach blind people. I was sure, I told him, that this was her reason for helping me. As for the John Milton Society, their support for the Ming Sum School in Canton proved that they were interested in helping blind people in China and the Far East.

Father replied that none of this altered the fact that it was a disgrace to him and to the family that I should have to receive outside help. He wanted me to refuse the offer.

My family's pride (right or wrong) versus my chance of education—what could I do? Tearfully I took my dilemma to Ah Wor in the kitchen, where she was doing the washing from our trip. For the second time in my life I heard her in tears too. There did not seem anything either of us could say. After all our hopes and plans . . . then Father suddenly spoke, close to us. I had not heard him come in.

"Ah Wor, you want Little Girl to have whatever she wants, don't you? If she wanted a piece of your flesh you would give it to her, wouldn't you? All right, go ahead, the pair of you, and make your plans. I know that whatever I say will not stop you." And making no attempt to conceal his displeasure, he left the kitchen.

I asked Ah Wor what I should do. She said that although Father was clearly not happy about it, he had given me his approval . . . after a fashion. As my studies in Hong Kong mattered more to me than anything else, there was nothing I could do but carry on and make preparations. She pointed out that Father was displeased because his pride was hurt; the need for his daughter to accept outside help showed that he was incapable of providing what was necessary. Perhaps later, he might feel less upset and become more reconciled to the whole thing.

The next few days were neither easy nor cheerful. Father and I hardly spoke to one another. I felt depressed and uncomfortable at mealtimes and drank water to wash the food down. I could understand how he felt and yet I just could not give up the chance of a lifetime to go through with the Hong Kong plan and all it involved. I prayed for Father's understanding—of me and of the motives of all the people who wanted to help me. And I prayed for the soothing of his hurt pride too.

Five or six days of these strained relations passed. It was midnight and I was lying in bed, awake; Father was still in the living-room. He was coughing. For the past two days he had not stayed long at the table at meals and I suspected that he was not feeling well, but was afraid to ask for fear of irritating him. Now I suddenly felt an impulse, almost like an instruction, to go and speak to him. I was on edge; we children, myself especially, seldom took the initiative to start a conversation—normally we spoke only when we were spoken to—but I had the sensation of being directed by a force outside myself, so I left my bed and walked slowly to the living-room, which was only a few yards away. I walked up to Father and asked if he was feeling all right. When he spoke I realised he had a terrible cold. I felt panicky, expecting a lecture and reproaches. Trying to keep calm I pulled up a chair near to him.

For quite a while he said nothing; I sensed he was looking at me. Then he spoke. He had been thinking a great deal about my affairs, he said. If Miss Schaeffer, who had worked with blind people for so many years, had offered to see that my school fees were taken care of, that must mean that in her opinion I had done well in my studies. In that case, he said, he could be proud of me instead of feeling humiliated by my acceptance of financial help. The fact that a school with such a fine reputation as D.G.S. should be willing to accept me was certainly also an honour and so, he said, he wanted me to know that I had his approval and blessing to go and study in Hong Kong.

How I wish I could have told Father how grateful I was for his understanding of me. But we had never expressed our emotions to senior members of the family. At that moment I could understand how he felt. It really was bitter for him that, after working hard and building up his business in Canton, he had lost everything and had none of the enjoyment of possessions. He just had to work harder than ever and endure being poor and having difficulty keeping his family. I could not think of anything to say to him though I searched for words, but I think he understood. It was not easy for Father to do what he had just done. In his culture a grown-up, especially the head of the family, would never admit to a junior member that he was wrong or admit that the junior member was right. I tried to find some words of appreciation to tell him how grateful I felt, but the words did not come.

He must have understood, for he said that he felt better after putting his thoughts into words, and he knew I must feel better too, and that we should both go to bed and have a good sleep.

CHAPTER 27 •••••••••••••••••••••••••••••••

ONCE FATHER HAD given me his permission, I went to Sacred Heart to see Sister Margaret. I walked up to the school with mixed feelings. The whole place was silent and felt deserted, except for a few office staff. While I waited for Sister Margaret I thought back on all the happy memories of my three years of English education, especially of the kindness they had shown in taking me with so little hesitation when other schools were reluctant. How could I tell Sister Margaret, after all she and her school had done for me, that I now wanted to leave and go to Hong Kong? And how could I thank her for all she herself had done to help me?

I was thinking about this when I heard her familiar footsteps. As usual she greeted me cheerfully and we went to the school office and sat down. I said there was so much I wanted to tell her that I did not know where to begin. She told me to take my time. Her voice, as always, was warm and smiling and it put me at my ease. I told her about all that had happened in Hong Kong.

"Sister Margaret," I blurted out, "I am very sorry that I shall not be able to continue my studies in this school, but—"

"Sorry?" she said delightedly, "but God has worked this out as another step towards fulfilling your desire to help blind people. You have been chosen as the special instrument of His divine plan." She went on to say that everything pointed to the fact that I was intended to go—money and readers being offered to me which I could not have in Macau. She told me about the Honeyville Home for blind women in Mount Davis Road on Hong Kong Island, a home founded and run by the Canossian Sisters, and suggested that I should go and see the Sister in charge and arrange to meet the girls. She thought that the Sisters would probably be glad to have me to teach when I left school.

This certainly was good news. Not long ago I had been worried whether I would have a chance to work with blind people as there was no home or school for them in Macau and now, within a few days, I had heard about the Ebenezer Home and the Honeyville Home, both in Hong Kong.

"I am sure that some day you will come back to help the blind people here in Macau," Sister Margaret said confidently. It was good to hear her say that, though at the time I felt that there was little hope. I could not have guessed then that five or six years later I would be using my spare time to teach braille to a would-be braille instructor and training other people in teaching methods and techniques with the visually handicapped. This was when I took under my wing a project, headed by Mrs. Ruby Ko and sponsored by the American Foundation for Overseas Blind, to set up a training centre in Macau. But all this was for the future.

One day I read in an American braille magazine that blind people in England and America were taught to find their way about not only indoors but outside too, starting from their homes and going first to nearby shops and then gradually going further and further until they could go to bus stops, board buses and go wherever they wanted to. This was called "Orientation and Mobility" and had to be taught by trained instructors.

I thought and thought about this. It tied in with an idea that was slowly taking shape in my mind. If I could be taught to do this and find my way from Third Uncle's home to D.G.S. it would free Ah Wor to work as a full-time amah. There was so much talk about the high wages of amahs in Hong Kong and how they were in demand; it would be wonderful if Ah Wor could find a well-paid job like that. I knew I would miss her and be terribly lonely without her but it was important for her to earn some money while she was still able to, so that she could provide for herself in her old age. I had learnt my way in Macau and could go from home to school and from home to church by myself. It would be more difficult in Hong Kong with longer distances and much heavier traffic, but Miss Schaeffer had received her training in blind work in America and perhaps I could ask her to help me. If Ah Wor could see that I was able to travel on my own, then she would not have to worry about me and perhaps I could persuade her to take a job.

I spent the entire day typing a long letter to Miss Schaeffer about this. Ah Wor, seeing that I was turning out pages and pages of typing, asked what I was writing about. She thought I was writing a composition. I said no, I was writing to Miss Schaeffer. I was afraid she would ask what I was writing about but she did not. She was never inquisitive, but whenever I wanted to discuss anything with her she was always ready to listen and to understand my point of view and would go out of her way to help.

I posted the letter and waited anxiously for a reply, which came in about a week. Miss Schaeffer urged me to give up any idea of finding my way about in Hong Kong. She gave a number of reasons. One was that I had to spend much more time and effort than any blind pupil in America on listening to textbooks being read, taking notes and putting it all into braille so that I would never have any time for relaxation. Therefore, she said, I should conserve my energies for my school work and not squander them on unnecessary things. She also pointed out that Ah Wor, who had devoted herself entirely to me, certainly would not want to leave me as I was all she had. It would break Ah Wor's heart, Miss Schaeffer said. She also assured me that I would probably be able to support Ah Wor when I finished secondary school, for even if I could not find a job teaching in either of the homes for blind women in Hong Kong, I could give classes in conversational English. She added that she could probably help me to find some work of this kind so I was not to worry about all that at this stage.

All this was reassuring and made good sense to me. I certainly would need every minute for my school work and it would be a bad use of time to try to find my way about. This was, after all, to be my last year at school so it seemed wiser to concentrate on my work and to go on enjoying Ah Wor's loving help and companionship.

I was overjoyed to receive a letter from Dr. Chappel congratulating me warmly on being accepted by D.G.S. He said he was delighted to hear this good news from Miss Schaeffer. He told me he was leaving the John Milton Society to take up a new job with the World Council of Christian Service and would like to introduce his successor, Dr. Dwight Smith, who said he would continue to correspond with me. In fact, he enclosed a letter from Dr. Smith who said he had taught at the University of Changsha in China and felt the loss of all his Chinese friends. He said he would be glad to correspond with me and he also assured me of the Society's continuing support for me. I was deeply moved by this. I thought of these good American people who had so much important work to do, and yet could find time to write to me and take so much interest in me and my schooling.

I decided there and then that I would follow their examples of love and concern for others and would do whatever I could for blind people whenever I had the opportunity.

A short time later I received another letter from Dr. Smith asking me how much money I thought I would need every month. The correct answer, with my background and upbringing, was that I did not need anything except the school fees. I thought about Ah Wor working away into the late evening, wearing herself out and ruining her eyesight over tedious, fiddly beadwork; I thought about the year ahead in Hong Kong and how she would have to go on doing the same sort of thing; I thought about Miss Schaeffer's letter; I thought about my father and his pride and his standards. I replied to Dr. Smith that I did not need anything except the fees.

I took this decision on my own for once, without asking Ah Wor. I told her afterwards and she said I had done the right thing. So now, in the time that remained, we had to concentrate on preparations and packing.

My braille notes bothered me most. My three years at Sacred Heart had filled our small flat with vast piles of folded newspaper. They were stored in dozens of cardboard boxes which Ah Wor had found discarded outside shops. Long ago the boxes had overflowed from the room I shared with my sisters, and Father and Mother complained as they took up more and more floor space. But how could we take them all to Hong Kong? I told Ah Wor we could not pack too many sheets in one box as it would damage the dots. In fact, no matter how loosely we packed them, the sheets near the bottom became almost unreadable, but even these squashed ones

were better than none at all and I could make out something from
them.

When Father saw us piling boxes one on top of another and
tying them together, he exclaimed with horror that even if we managed to get them to Hong Kong, we certainly could not expect
Third Uncle and Aunt to find room for them. He said I should get
rid of some, take only the most essential and leave the rest at home.
I protested that I needed them all as I had no idea what the
teachers might want to refer back to, and I would never be able to
get parts read again. In the end, as Ah Wor was as determined as I
was, Father gave in and he and Mother decided to help us take it
all to the pier. Mother even told Ah Wor not to worry about going
to market that morning; she went herself while Ah Wor and I
finished packing, and bought the things she knew I liked best for
lunch. Lunch was delicious but a little subdued, and later we set
off in a procession of pedicabs for the ferry pier.

And so, at last, Ah Wor and I were once more sitting on the boat
heading for Hong Kong. It was the realisation of so many ambi-
tions, but I felt sad. It was the first time I had left home. Hong
Kong was not far away but I knew there was little hope of afford-
ing the fares to go home at Christmas or Chinese New Year, so I
probably would not see any of my family except my brother in
Happy Valley for the whole school year. What Ah Wor's thoughts
were I do not know; she kept them to herself. But she can have
had few illusions about the problems she was facing for my sake.
We sat in silence thinking our own thoughts, surrounded by my
school books. People must have stared curiously at the pair of us
and our luggage, but I could not see them.

When we reached Hong Kong, the only trouble we had was in
carrying the boxes off the boat. We had to make several journeys
and finally pushed them past the Immigration Officer. To go by bus
was out of the question, so we decided to take a taxi. One stopped
by us and as we got in Ah Wor whispered that a man had got in
with us, and was sitting in the front seat by the driver. She said she
had no idea why he was sitting there, but he did not say a word.
The driver grumbled as Ah Wor struggled to cram all the boxes
into the taxi and asked impatiently where we wanted to go. I gave

the address and we started off. When we reached Happy Valley Ah Wor paid the driver, but then the other man suddenly demanded a larger amount of money, about ten dollars. We argued, saying we had no reason to pay him anything, but he insisted that we had to pay him for the time he had taken to accompany us all the way from the ferry pier. He was evidently a small-time racketeer, in league with the driver; presumably the pair of them thought (correctly) that they could easily bully us. I continued to argue with him, but Ah Wor said we had better pay him, otherwise he might force his way into the house and swear and make a scene, which would make us very unpopular with the landlord and landlady. I am sure she was right, but I could not bear to see her pay the wretched man what represented days and days of her sweated labour—and all for nothing.

We stayed the night with Brother and Sister-in-law and spent the next day or two taking our luggage and my braille boxes, piece by piece, on foot, to Third Uncle and Aunt's flat in Kowloon. I can remember my blisters to this day!

Uncle's flat was self-contained but small. They gave me their box-room for my bedroom, where there was just room for a bed, a table and a chair, and Ah Wor had to sleep in the living-room. Poor Ah Wor! Aunt insisted on having the living-room door locked at night. She said it rattled in the wind and might wake her up, but I think it was just one of her ways of making life difficult for Ah Wor. The catch was on the passage side of the door so when we went to bed I had to go and lock her in. It used to worry me dreadfully wondering what would happen if she needed to go to the bathroom. Somehow she managed for a year without a crisis, but I do not know how she did it.

We left some of the braille boxes at Happy Valley and I packed as many as I could into my bedroom. We took some to Miss Schaeffer's flat and even left a couple with an amah friend, Ah Ying, who cooked for an English lady and had some spare space in her living quarters. I numbered and labelled all the boxes and kept a record with me as to where each one was. As time went on, I was very thankful that I had brought it all to Hong Kong; it was quite often necessary to refer back to these earlier notes and extracts from textbooks, and although they were scattered all over Hong Kong and Kowloon, I could at least dig them out when I needed them, whereas they would have been of no use to me in Macau.

There was still a couple of days before school began, so I asked Miss Schaeffer to look up the telephone numbers of the Honeyville and Ebenezer Homes for me so that I could make appointments to go and see them. Ah Wor and I visited both of them. We met Sister Victoria at Honeyville and Miss Morgenstern at Ebenezer. It was like an assurance from heaven when both supervisors said they would be glad to have me to teach their girls when I had finished secondary school.

Our first effort to visit Ebenezer was not a happy occasion. Ah Wor and I walked all the way out to Pokfulam. I have since worked out the distance and found it to be the best part of eight miles altogether, three miles in Kowloon and the remainder on Hong Kong Island with the short trip on the ferry across the harbour between the two. I had made an appointment on the telephone with Miss Morgenstern, so we rang the bell confidently. The door was opened by a member of staff (not an amah) who asked suspiciously what we wanted. I said we had an appointment to see Miss Morgenstern but the woman clearly did not believe this and refused to let us in or to go and tell Miss Morgenstern we were there. After saying she supposed I wanted to come and live there, she shut the door in our faces. What could we do? We walked back to Kowloon City.

I telephoned Miss Morgenstern and told her what had happened. She was most distressed: she had been in the house all the time, expecting us. What she did about her member of staff I do not know but the appointment was rearranged. Ah Wor and I did the long walk again and this time we found Miss Morgenstern waiting outside for us. And this time she had a car available to take us back.

That visit was very important for me. Miss Morgenstern told me that she was a missionary who had become involved, more or less by accident, with blind work and knew little about it apart from what she had learnt from experience. She was evidently interested in my plans and hopes to use my education to learn how to work professionally in this field, and it was actually she (I discovered later) who first suggested that I be given a scholarship to go to the United States.

We met the residents at both the Homes. Most of the young women were older than I, but we had much in common and I was glad to find some girls of my own age and even younger at Ebenezer. At that time both Homes worked on the same system as the Ming Sum School and the Mo Kwong Home in Canton: it was the older girls who had learned more who worked as teachers and taught the younger ones. I lent them some of my braille notes and tried to explain the lessons to them so that they could use them for teaching. I did this whenever I could at weekends and on public holidays. They had an insatiable hunger for knowledge. Teacher Lau, who taught elementary English to the younger girls at Ebenezer, became one of my good friends, and remains so to this day. She now resides at the Ebenezer Home for Elderly Ladies.

In fact, several of the present residents in the Home were teachers at the time I was studying at D.G.S. As I was accustomed to addressing them as "Teacher Lau," "Teacher Chan," etc., it was with some difficulty that they recently succeeded in persuading me to call them "Lau Tse Tse" and "Chan Tse Tse," meaning "Big Sister." I shall never forget that when I came back from the United States in 1959 and started working with blind people, Teacher Lau had hand-brailled some of both the English and Chinese language textbooks which I needed for my first classes. That was real friendship of the most practical kind.

CHAPTER 28 ●●●●●●●●●●●●●●●●●●●●●●●●●●●●

MISS SCHAEFFER HAD given me enough money for my fees, which had to be paid on the first day of term. She asked if there was anything else I needed and I said no. I felt I could not ask her for bus fares for the two of us. Ah Wor agreed, so we decided to allow one hour to walk from Uncle's place in Kowloon City to Jordan Road. In fact we found it took us a little under an hour, but all the walking we did every day on hot pavements with traffic roaring by was terribly tiring.

D.G.S. was the third school I had gone to, and on the first day I braced myself apprehensively, expecting the confusions and embarrassments that seemed inevitable. But nothing of the kind happened. As we went through the school gate I was greeted by two girls who told me that their names were Doreen and Lily. They said they were in Form V and they would take me to the classroom. One of them offered me her arm. As the girls were so helpful, I told Ah Wor that it looked as if I was going to have all the help I needed and that she could leave me. She said she would go and find some outwork to do and would bring me something to eat during the lunch hour.

The girls spoke English so I tried to do the same. From the way they spoke I could tell that neither was Chinese. They walked with me to the classroom and showed me my desk; I found I was sitting between them. We sat down and I put all my braille things and my wad of folded newspapers in the desk. As the girls were so friendly, I asked one of them if she would give me a little nudge to let me know when it was time to rise for the teacher. She did this and we all stood up. When the teacher said good morning I recognised Mrs. Lodge's voice. This was a relief, as I had already met her. At first I found I had to listen very hard to catch what she said, because of her English accent, but after a little while I found I could follow her quite easily.

When the lesson—General English—was over she came to speak to me. She said if there was anything I was not clear about, I must not hesitate to tell her. The other teachers who took us that morning were Miss Mansfield who taught Biology, Mrs. Kvan who taught History, and Mrs. Symons who taught Geography: all gave the same offer of help.

Doreen and Lily introduced me to the other girls during break. In the short change-over period between classes the girls offered to read me the class schedule and any notes written on the blackboard, and began to show me my way around the school.

When the bell rang at the end of the last class I asked them to show me to the gate so that I could wait for Ah Wor. Two of them said they were day pupils and had amahs coming to bring them their lunch, so we could all wait together. Within a few minutes several more girls joined us. We were there for just a little while until Ah Wor arrived. "Oh how very nice," she said with a broad smile in her voice, "you are surrounded by all these good misses. I am so glad."

Cars were arriving and stopping and doors were slamming. There was chatter all round us. Ah Wor told me that the amahs who brought lunch for most of the girls came in chauffeur-driven cars. We were shown the way to a big, airy room which was used for lunch by the day pupils and for some special occasions. Before we started lunch Ah Wor asked me to move away from the others for a moment as she wanted to say something to me. When we were out of earshot she said she was bothered about what she had brought me for lunch; it was only a small bowl of rice and vegetable and looked very meagre, she said, compared with what the other amahs were setting out for their girls. She wondered whether I would rather we looked for somewhere to eat where we would be alone. I told her not to worry. The chances were that the others would not notice, and if they did, I could say we usually had a light lunch because we had our main meal in the evening. I said I was afraid it would look unsociable if we went and ate somewhere else when they were all being so friendly.

Ah Wor agreed but I could tell she was uneasy. We went back to the others and I started to have my lunch. I noticed Ah Wor was not eating, but she said she had had hers while she was in the shop buying mine. I strongly suspected (correctly, I found out later) that she had given me hers to increase the quantity of mine. In fact, the girls must have noticed but they were very tactful; one said she had more chicken than she could eat and another asked if I could help her out with some fish. Ah Wor nudged me and I knew she was reminding me to refuse in a proper, polite way. But I was hungry and the food smelled good, so I am afraid I could not resist saying, "Yes please, just a little." They were all so good-natured and generous that Ah Wor finished up by having some too.

I soon came to know more girls, both in my own class and in other classes. Most of them were natural and at ease and spoke to me directly: a few were evidently nervous of me and kept away, but most were friendly. They even worked out a rotation of their own accord so that every day someone read to me for about an hour and a half or two hours after school. Later on I asked them how they knew I needed readers, as they offered their help on the second or third day of term, before I felt I knew them well enough to ask. They said Mrs. Symons had spoken to them during a drawing period when I was not there, telling them how urgently I needed to have books read to me and asking them to come direct to me and offer, if they wanted to help. She also pointed out at the same time that I would want to make friends like anyone else, but that they must be careful not to treat me differently from other people or as if they pitied me.

My reader would read to me as soon as school was over. Then she would go home or to her room if she was a boarder. Ah Wor, who had been doing whatever handwork she had found, would come for me and we would have some supper in a shop or cheap café and then go on to Miss Schaeffer or one of her friends for another two hours of reading. Some of my readers were from other classes. Dolly, who was in Form IV, offered to be a reader and this started a friendship which we have kept up ever since. I became a social worker, she a primary teacher, and on many occasions she has offered to help as a volunteer teacher with some of my blind trainees.

All the readers were English-speaking, a fact which made all the difference in the world. They understood what they were reading and therefore I could understand it. Many problems remained, but the dreadful process of trying to make sense out of having nearly every word spelt out, letter by letter, was now just a bad memory. Miss Schaeffer and her friends did as much as they could in the time they could spare, and I renewed acquaintance with another missionary I had known in Canton—Jaxie Short. When I knew her in Canton she was learning Cantonese and I remember how she would try to say my name in Chinese, making the tones and pronunciation as accurate as she could. I found out her address from our church in Hong Kong and Ah Wor and I went to see her and we had a great reunion. She joined the ranks of my readers and gave me much help with my work.

The actual day-to-day grind of school work never let up. The sheer effort of being read to and making never-ending notes in braille, trying to read dots which almost immediately went flat in the soft, unsuitable newspapers I used, brailling laboriously with the handframe, never having as much of the text as the other girls, always studying far into the night, always struggling to keep up, always being short of sleep—these were wearing and exhausting. However, the year at D.G.S. proved to be the best school year I ever had in spite of some financial worries at the beginning.

Three weeks went by and we would soon have to pay our fees for October. I began to feel apprehensive. Ah Wor was working long hours to earn as much as she could. If necessary she could probably manage the fees, but what she earned was going towards other unavoidable expenses, such as food, and she could not possibly work any more than she was already doing.

Then, one evening, I went to see Miss Schaeffer for reading and she said that there was some money for me from the John Milton Society. It was US$25, so she gave me about $160 in Hong Kong money. She told me that starting from November they would send her a money order at the beginning of each month and she wanted me to know this so that Ah Wor and I could work out our budget. I said I really did not need that much. In previous conversations with her and in my letter to Dr. Smith, only the school fees had been referred to, and they were less than one third of what she had just given me. She said that Dr. Smith had written and asked her to tell him, approximately, what she thought my monthly expenses would amount to, so she had worked it out. She had budgeted for fees, bus fares for both of us, including going to readers' houses, lunches, money to pay for some of the readers and the hire of a typewriter, and a little pocket money. She had also allowed for about $40 a month which she said I could use for piano lessons or in whatever way I thought best. All that came to about $160 a month.

I listened to all this with astonishment. She went on and said that the reason Dr. Smith had asked her advice about this was because when he wrote to me and asked how much I thought I would need, I had replied that all I would need was my fees. As he had worked in China, he realised that a family such as mine would have taught me that I should not accept financial assistance from anyone outside the family—but that if I did, I ought to accept only enough for the barest necessities. The Society understood this, but they were anxious that during this school year I should be free from any financial worries. She then handed me a letter which she said was written to me by both Dr. Smith and Dr. Chappel and addressed to me care of her. I asked her to read it to me. In it they told me that it had been decided at a board meeting of the Society that I should be a recipient of part of their overseas scholarship fund. This fund was designed to help people in financial difficulties, but it went further than that; recipients had to be people who demonstrated a real desire to work for blind people and who also appeared to have the necessary academic ability and mental attitude. I was overwhelmed and did not know what to say.

For the first time since we left Canton I could stop worrying about money. And so could Ah Wor. She need no longer do her handwork day and night to try to ensure that I had enough money to carry on. Above all, I could go back to having my beloved piano lessons. In Macau I had only been having occasional ones when

Father or Ah Wor could spare the money for it—a fairly rare occurrence in our household. I was glad too that I could offer to pay something to the girls who read to me. I knew they did not mind doing it as a friendly act, but no schoolgirl minds having a few extra dollars and it would show them that I appreciated the time they were giving up for me. From that day onwards I told the various girls who read to me that the John Milton Society had offered to pay for my readers. They all said they did not expect to be paid, but as I insisted, they finally agreed to take the money.

Next day, feeling on top of the world, Ah Wor and I boarded a bus to school. At break I went to see the music teacher, Miss Edwards, and asked her if she could arrange private piano lessons for me. She said she did not give private lessons herself, but she could refer me to a good teacher, a Mr. Lee. She also said I could practise on the school piano any time it was not in use. I had felt sure I would have to use my pocket money for practice time.

Another of my cherished dreams looked like being fulfilled and I walked back to the classroom feeling very cheerful. But out of the blue two unwelcome facts thrust themselves into my mind. One was that I would need someone to read the music from the page so that I could take it down in the braille music code, and I did not think any of my particular friends were learning music. The other was that Miss Edwards had spoken of *Mr.* Lee, a man. I had not learnt from a man before; both my previous teachers had been women. It would be necessary for my teacher to touch my hands to show me what to do and most people would not want to touch a blind person's hand. My two women teachers had not objected, luckily (one of them had been blind herself), but Mr. Lee, as a man, might be expected to feel more strongly about it on account of the inhibitions and superstitions attached to blindness, especially in women. Rarely in my life had I touched the hand of a boy or a man, apart from holding my younger brother's arm going to church.

As soon as possible I went back to Miss Edwards and tried to explain the problem. This was not easy as it was very much a matter of Chinese social behaviour. She did not take it nearly as seriously as I did and said she could not see where the difficulty was since men and women would normally shake hands when they met. What, she asked, was the difference? However, she said that if I would much rather have a woman teacher she would look round for one for me but it might take a little while.

Miss Edwards' reaction and her confident assurance that the problem did not exist made me think again. I hoped she was right. She was certainly correct about people shaking hands on meeting. Perhaps Mr. Lee would have a Western education and would never think twice about touching my hands. In any case, as I was going to pay for the lessons by the month, we could easily stop if he did not like it. Finally, I asked Miss Edwards to refer me to Mr. Lee, on condition that she told him that I was a totally blind person so that he could say straight away if he did not want to teach me. She said she was sure that it would make no difference, but in order to satisfy me she called him there and then on the telephone. His reply was completely reassuring; he said he would be glad to take me and I was to go the next Saturday afternoon for my first lesson.

On the Saturday afternoon we accordingly went to find Mr. Lee's place. It was at a church in Ho Man Tin. We found it without much trouble and Mr. Lee was actually waiting outside for us. I had spent the morning rehearsing what I hoped were tactful speeches about physical contact with a blind pupil, but Mr. Lee took the wind out of my sails completely by saying that his studio was upstairs and offering me his arm to go up.

This was so unexpected that for several seconds I stood where I was and did not even reply. Then, mentally shaking myself, I thanked him and took his arm. But before we started up the stairs I asked how long the lesson would be. He said he was free for the next two hours and he could read me some music for me to braille for my lessons if I would like this. This was another surprise. It would certainly be a great help to have him read the music to me, as he would know what he was reading. Trying to take it down from friends who did not know much about music was very difficult and always led to endless mistakes. However, I suddenly thought of the money side of this offer—I had only a limited amount to spend on the lessons and it certainly would not cover this extra time, even if he charged less than for the actual lessons.

After some hesitation as to how to explain this to him, which must have made him wonder why I was so slow answering a simple question, I managed to say that I would not be able to pay him for the time he would spend reading music to me. He just laughed and said he would not expect to be paid, so Ah Wor said she would come back for me in two hours.

Mr. Lee and I went upstairs. Instead of feeling nervous, as I thought I would, I felt completely relaxed and thoroughly enjoyed the time, even when he asked me to play something I knew. He said we would not regard this first time as a proper lesson—it was a time for getting acquainted. We discussed what pieces I could learn and he then dictated them to me. It was so easy taking it down from him: it was like the first time Miss Lovegren read to me —a revelation that something could be so much clearer and simpler than it had ever been before. And of course I realised that Miss Edwards had been right when she had just laughed at my fears about him touching my hands. It all seemed nonsense now.

This experience did much to increase my confidence. From that time, I worried much less about all these things and learned to shake hands with men without thinking twice about it. The following year when I went to America for my studies and had piano lessons from a man, I never gave it a thought. Men taught me cane travel and a whole host of subjects, including weaving and pottery, all of which involved much guidance of my hands, and they all took it for granted as part of the job.

My music lessons were probably what I enjoyed most of all, but next to them came English lessons; language and speech are subjects where blindness makes little or no difference. I still love both the Chinese and English languages. In General English we had a choice of whether or not to take Drama. I enrolled for Drama and enjoyed it immensely. Our teacher was Mrs. O'Connell who was herself deeply involved in the whole range of Speech and Drama teaching and worked for years in connection with the famous Hong Kong Schools Music and Speech Festivals. She taught us to develop our voices and to try to use them and project them effectively.

One day she announced that we were going to prepare a play

and asked who would like to be in it. With one accord the girls said I must take part. I protested and said I certainly could not be in a play; I thought Mrs. O'Connell would be glad, but she seemed genuinely to want to include me, and though I stuck to it that I did not want to, she asked me to think it over and let her know the following week. At break she asked me why I had refused. She said that judging from my class work I really enjoyed it and was doing quite well. I agreed that I did love Drama but that because of the problems of movement I did not feel I could cope with actually appearing on the stage with fast-moving sighted girls. Mrs. O'Connell said she was not going to accept this as final and insisted that I think about it for a week. She also said I could choose any part in the play, if that would help. I had made up my mind but I promised to think about it and to let her know at the next class.

When the time came Mrs. O'Connell asked the girls to choose their parts, but they all said I was to choose first. I said firmly that I was not going to be in it, so they asked why. I said I had explained to Mrs. O'Connell but they were so insistent that Mrs. O'Connell could not quieten them down. I hated having to give such a personal explanation to the whole class: telling Mrs. O'Connell had been bad enough but to shout it out in front of everyone was mortifying. However, it was obvious that nothing was going to be done until I said something, so I blurted out that I did not think I could move fast enough on the stage to act with the rest of them. They all said, "Rubbish! Nonsense!" and there was lots of rehearsal time in which I could practise. Then one girl, Annie, raised her hand and said, "Why doesn't Lucy play the king, then she wouldn't have to move about—all she'd have to do is sit on the throne." All the girls clapped and joined in a chorus, "Lucy play the king. Lucy play the king." It made me feel good that they really wanted me in the play. I raised my hand and Mrs. O'Connell asked me to speak. I stood up and said, "Yes," and sat down again. So that was settled and we could get on with the class.

Rehearsals took place after school several times a week. Naturally Mrs. O'Connell had to spend more time showing me exactly what to do than she did with the others. But she was patient and kind and encouraging. The girls helped as well and explained all about the stage. They seemed to enjoy doing it instead of finding it a nuisance. They laughed with me but not at me when I made mistakes. The play was a success. The parents of many of the girls congratulated me in a kind and genuine way, without condescension, and all this made me feel that I need not be ashamed of being a blind person.

CHAPTER 29 ●●●●●●●●●●●●●●●●●●●●●●●●●●●●●●●●●●●●●●●

THE PLAY HAD occupied much of my precious reading time and I had a job to catch up. After one longer-than-usual session with Dolly, Ah Wor and I went to a small restaurant to have some rice before going on to an American lady's home for another session. While we were eating we heard the announcer on the radio calling for special attention. The place was so noisy that I could only hear parts of it, but I did catch the words ". . . blind . . . to a Christmas party . . . Social Welfare Office." I could not hear any more. We moved closer to the radio. I listened hopefully and sure enough, after a long while, the announcement was repeated. This time I heard the entire message.

It seemed that the Social Welfare Office (it was not a Department at that time) was going to give a Christmas party on the Saturday afternoon, a week before Christmas. Any blind person who was interested and their friends and relatives were to telephone for tickets.

I was excited when I heard this. I told Ah Wor that I would like to go to the party so that I could meet more blind people, especially those like Tse Tse, my blind friend of long ago in Canton. But how could I telephone the Social Welfare Office during office hours? I had never asked to use the telephone in the school office and in any case the break between classes was too short for me to make a call. I asked Ah Wor to do it for me, but she said she had never made an official call in her life and was afraid that she would not make herself understood. I knew that this was true; she was by nature shy and never talked much with anyone apart from me and a few close friends. However, as both the telephone number and the address of the Social Welfare Office had been given over the radio I decided to write them a note and enclose a stamped addressed envelope, asking them to send a ticket to me. Ah Wor thought that a good idea so I typed the note that evening and Ah Wor posted it the next day.

I was working in my little room one Sunday afternoon when the doorbell rang. Ah Wor opened the door and I heard an unfamiliar voice asking for me. I introduced myself to the stranger who told me that she was Daphne Ho from the Social Welfare Office. I realised that this must be the result of my letter. I was not sure what to do. If I asked her to come into the living-room, that meant that Third Uncle and Aunt would have to retreat to their bedroom, but I did not know her well enough to ask her to go to my bedroom where there was only one chair. Finally I decided to invite her into the living-room. Uncle and Aunt greeted her as I introduced them. They then left the room, leaving us by ourselves.

Miss Ho was friendly and comfortable to be with. She said they had received my letter and were surprised to learn that I was a blind person studying at D.G.S., so she wanted to see me. She said she had called several times on her way home from work but I had been out each time. I told her that I was out every day after school for my reading sessions and did not get home until quite late. She asked what I meant by "reading sessions" and when I explained she offered to read to me sometimes in the evenings or at weekends. This was another gift from heaven as I could never have too many readers. She was a former D.G.S. girl so we were on familiar ground about teachers and other aspects of school life. At last we returned to the reason for her visit—the Christmas party. She said it was to be held at the Southorn Playground in Wan Chai and asked if I would like someone to come over and fetch me. I said there was no need; Ah Wor would take me there if Miss Ho would explain where it was. I was glad to learn that Miss Ho lived in Kowloon Tong, not very far from Kowloon City. That would make reading sessions with her easier.

There were so many things I wanted to ask her, knowing she was a social worker, but it was time for us to have our supper. I knew that Uncle and Aunt would not want to have their supper delayed, so even if Miss Ho was willing to give me more of her time I must try somehow to bring this visit to an end. I was at a loss how to do this, but fortunately at this moment Ah Wor came in and said supper was ready and asked if she would like to have supper with us. Miss Ho tactfully took the hint and said she must go. Before she went she gave me her home address and her phone number, both at her office and at home. She asked me to call her Daphne, as we were friends, but I said I would not feel comfortable doing that.

From that day on Daphne Ho became one of my great friends. She gave me boundless practical help and encouragement, and through her I learned that the job of a social worker could not always be limited to official hours. It was a continuing process of helping people who were in need, no matter at what time their need arose. In the weeks that followed, I sometimes went to her home for reading and at other times she came and read to me in my little room, sitting on my bed. I felt I could talk to her about my dreams and desires of working with and teaching blind people. She was pleased and interested that I wanted to do this. She told me that until that time the Hong Kong Government had been providing handicapped people with relief goods only—rice, tea, other daily necessities—but that now the Government was exploring the possibility of education and training for handicapped people, including blind people. She said it was good that I wanted to live a useful life working with blind people, but she warned me that I must be prepared for the fact that, if I was able to do it at all, I would be a pioneer worker in this field and it would not be easy. It would mean gaining acceptance from the sighted world, whose deep-seated prejudices would be very hard to overcome. They would have to be persuaded by degrees that even though a person has one disability, that does not invalidate her other abilities. However, she said this was not the only problem; there was also the matter of trying to induce blind people themselves to recognise that there might be other ways of earning their living, apart from the time-honoured, traditional ones. That would mean attacking their intense and understandable conservatism. All this, she said, meant that life was not going to be easy for me. This I did not doubt for one moment—all my experience hitherto confirmed it— but I had confidence in my faith in God and had no fear that I would give up completely.

These talks with Daphne Ho were a very important and formative part of my life. She was a decisive influence as well as a wonderful friend and guide. Much of what she said was too advanced for me then and only gradually did I come to understand the full implications, but one thing she said early on took root in my mind: "If the pressure is too great and you fail," she said, "blind people in Hong Kong will fail." That was like a challenge; perhaps she meant it that way, because it had the effect of strengthening my determination not to be defeated by the obstacles in my path.

Soon after Miss Ho left on that first Sunday, Ah Wor set the table for supper. During the meal Uncle asked if I was thinking seriously of going to the Christmas party. The living-room and their bedroom were adjacent and obviously he and Aunt had heard our conversation. I said yes. He asked whether I realised that the blind people at the party would be beggars and prostitutes. I said I had a feeling they would be because they had no other way to earn a living. Uncle asked if I had thought what I would look like sitting there talking with people of this kind. To this I did not reply. I knew I should not argue with Uncle, the head of the family. We dropped the subject. I was glad to notice that he did not appear to be angry or even displeased with me, and he did not ask me to promise not to go to the party.

The long-awaited day of the party came. We made our way there early and I asked Ah Wor to find somewhere for us to sit among some blind women. I listened to their conversations; they were talking about ways to improve their cries for money when begging, and what tactics to use to attract customers at night. Then the woman on my left suddenly touched my arm and asked if I was blind. I replied that I was, so she asked what I was doing to earn my living. When I told her I was a school pupil she repeated this loudly for the benefit of the whole group and many of them burst out laughing, saying that I must be joking as they had never heard of a blind girl going to a sighted school. Another woman asked why I went to school. They roared with laughter when I said I wanted to earn enough to make my living. They were emphatic that their age-old traditional ways of earning money could never be changed. They did not seem to see any reason why they should be changed.

The party began with a programme of entertainment and the last item was refreshments and the distribution of gifts. When it was over, Ah Wor and I were walking to the bus stop when someone came up to us and asked if she could talk to me for a minute. She said she was Mrs. Ip and she had a daughter who was blind. She wanted very much to know how I was able to go to an ordinary school as she would like her daughter also to receive a school education. This cheered me up considerably after what the blind women said. It was good to know that people like Mrs. Ip did exist, who believed in educating blind people. I said I would like very much to meet her daughter, Irene, and she suggested we go to her house for tea the next day, Sunday. I knew I really should be studying to make up for the party afternoon, but I wanted so much to go that I decided to do so, even if I had to stay up all night to make up the time.

The next day Mrs. Ip and Irene collected us in their car as arranged. Irene and I climbed into the back while Ah Wor sat in front beside Mrs. Ip. As we drove off, I was longing to talk to Irene but was, as usual, inhibited from starting a conversation in front of an older person. However, Irene swiftly dispelled all such worries by beginning to tell me about herself and her family and what they did and where they went. She chatted away, occasionally asking her mother for a name or a detail, until finally she stopped for breath. Mrs. Ip carried on by telling us what we were passing on the road—a huge crowd at a bus-stop, Christmas decorations in the shops, funny things she could see people doing or wearing. I felt at ease even before we reached their flat; we had a lovely afternoon with them. The whole family had tea together and I was reminded of my stay at Seventh Uncle and Auntie's house where the children were relaxed and informal with the grown-ups in just the same way. It turned out that Mr. Ip was a senior inspector in the Hong Kong Police and they lived in a furnished Government quarter. They often spoke English among themselves and I soon realised that their Western culture and education accounted for the fact that Irene was treated in exactly the same way as the other children. They were kind and good people. Irene was attending Ebenezer as a day-pupil and I found out that the Ips often gave presents of food to the ladies in the Ebenezer Home.

Irene took me to her room and showed me the braille texts she used for her lessons. They were all Cantonese braille. (I later taught her the English alphabet in braille so that she could learn English braille.) When we went back to the living-room Mr. and Mrs. Ip asked me how I had managed to enter D.G.S. They were eager to know if there was a possibility of Irene going there too. She had learnt to read Cantonese braille at Ebenezer, but there was not a lot more they could teach her and her parents were very anxious for her to have as full and as normal an education as possible. There would be no problem about reading to her, as they could all do that, but they wondered what else they could do to improve her chances of being accepted. I remembered something I had read in a braille magazine about American and English parents learning braille to help their children in their education. I also remembered the discouraging results of trying to teach braille to the church ladies in Macau, and I must have made a face at the recollection because Mrs. Ip asked what I was frowning about. I explained and was delighted to hear that both she and her husband were enthusiastic about learning braille, so that they could transcribe books for Irene. In the end I promised to tell Mrs. Symons about Irene and find out if she could go into Primary 5 or 6 the next year. (Mrs. Symons did accept her, and from the primary school she went into the senior school, up to Form V, and then to Perkins, in Boston. She now lives and works in Australia, as her family moved there.)

This visit was the beginning of a lasting friendship with the Ip family. I think they were fond of Ah Wor and me and they were certainly good to us. During the next eight or nine months of our stay in Hong Kong, their flat became almost like a second home to us and they included us in many of their family activities. When Mrs. Ip found out that Ah Wor made most of my clothes by hand, she made me some dresses on her sewing machine. And although

Irene and I were several years apart in age, we became great friends. She had a very good brain, and we had many things in common.

The day after the first visit I went to Mr. Lee for a music lesson. He played two pieces and asked me to choose the one I would like to learn. I picked the one I liked best and Mr. Lee said he was glad that I had chosen that one—it was a Beethoven rondo—as it was the set piece for one of the classes in the Schools Music Festival. He wondered whether, as I was going to learn the piece anyway, I would like to enter for the Festival, which would take place in a couple of months' time. I did not know what to think or say. Being watched always made me nervous and the thought of playing the piano in front of a crowd horrified me. But Mr. Lee was keen and Miss Edwards had also said on several occasions that I ought to compete in the Festival. Finally I agreed to think about it. Mr. Lee advised me to make my mind up quickly, as the closing date for entry was near. I promised to telephone him the next day.

I talked this over with Ah Wor as she took me to a reading session that evening. As always, she was very diplomatic. She never tried to persuade me to do things in one way or another, but she did say that as hardly anybody knew that blind people could receive an education, there was a chance that if I entered and played in public, the family of another blind child might hear about me and do something about educating their own child. This decided me—I would enter, no matter how nervous I felt. Next day I telephoned Mr. Lee and said I would do it.

When we arrived home, the people who lived on the ground floor of the building said there was a letter for me. Because Aunt and Uncle lived on the fourth floor and Aunt worried about the postman climbing up all the stairs with heavy braille books which came by post from libraries in America and England, I had arranged with the family on the ground floor to receive my mail for me. As the lady handed me the letter, she said she could see from the stamps that it was from Macau. Her husband could read Chinese but he was out, working on a late shift. It was the first time I had received a letter from home. I knew that, if it was from Father, it would be in the old Chinese literary style that many of my friends in the English school would not be able to read and that we would have to wait until we found a street letter-writer to read it for us.

Next day, after school, we found one. There were only three amahs in front of us so we did not have too long to wait. I was in school uniform, of course, and I heard one of them say (not very quietly) that it was really useless for a blind girl to go to school if she could not even read her own mail. When it was my turn, I handed the man my letter and was surprised to hear him say it was an English letter, and so he could not read it. I handed him the envelope and found out that it was indeed from my Father from our home address. He said he could direct us to an English letter-writer but the charge would be much higher. However, there was no need to pay anyone to read it, as we were on our way to a reading session. We paid the letter-writer and left.

We could not understand why Father should send me an English letter. Even if he was ill, Mother or my younger sister could have written. I asked Ah Wor if the letter was long or short. She said it was a foolscap sheet, covered all over with writing. We grew more and more worried. As soon as we reached Winnie's house, I asked her to read it. The mystery was quickly solved; it was from my three pen friends in Hong Kong, John, Peter and Paul. They wrote that they were going to Macau in the New Year, and would look me up. Winnie said that I must write to them at once and tell them that I was already in Hong Kong, but I was not so sure. Normally it must be very exciting for pen friends to meet, but I had mixed feelings. I had often thought about them since coming to Hong Kong, but knowing how most people felt about blind women, I did not want to risk spoiling our friendship by actually meeting. I was afraid they might find me a social embarrassment and this was why I had not let them know that I had already moved to Hong Kong. But now what was I to do?

I pushed it firmly to the back of my mind while Winnie read to me, but at home that evening I knew I must make up my mind. I decided to write to them. As Ah Wor said, it did not matter whether I wanted to see them or not—I had to let them know that I was in Hong Kong before they went off looking for me in Macau.

It was too late to use the typewriter in my room; Uncle and Aunt were already in bed and it would disturb them. So we took the typewriter up to the roof where there was an open space. It was mid-December and very cold, but I managed to type. I told them that I was studying at D.G.S. in Hong Kong and apologised for not letting them know before this. I explained that my time was entirely taken up with brailling and reading sessions and going from one house to another; I arrived home late nearly every evening and then had to do my homework and reading. I hoped they would understand from this how difficult it would be to see them.

It must have been four or five days later that Ah Wor and I were walking away from school, debating where to go for something to eat, when I heard footsteps running towards us and a voice—a man's voice—asking if I was Lucy Ching. I replied that I was, wondering what was coming next, but the next moment he introduced himself as John, my friend. He said that his car was close by and asked Ah Wor and me to come with him. He took my hand and I asked where he was going to take us. He said with an audible grin that he was taking me somewhere to be sold. This expression was accepted as a general way of teasing and Ah Wor and I laughed, but a moment later, to my surprise, he apologised most humbly for saying it. I was still giggling but Ah Wor grasped the point of his sudden apology—he had remembered about blind women being sold and exploited. She whispered quickly to me and I assured John he need not worry, I was not in the least upset by it.

Once we were in the car I asked again where we were going. He told me that Peter's mother had invited us all to supper, and that Paul was already at Peter's flat waiting for us. I suddenly felt out of my depth. Of course I had met boys from time to time; I had met them at church and I had known some of my younger brother's friends. But I had never been to their homes and I felt very unsure of myself, especially as we had only just met. In a whisper I asked Ah Wor what we should do; her answer was that if I wanted to join them, she could go somewhere else and would come back to pick me up later, but John heard this and said that Peter's mother was expecting both of us for a meal. I asked why they should think of preparing supper for us. John explained that they knew from my letter that we usually went to have something to eat when I had been read to for two hours after school, and decided it would be the best time for us to come and visit them. I protested that I had reading sessions arranged for the evening and could not stay, but the boys offered to read to me after supper, so I telephoned my other readers and told them that I would not be coming.

It was a delightful evening. At first I felt shy and awkward, but everyone was so friendly and natural that before long I stopped feeling self-conscious. Peter's mother was Chinese, but was born and brought up in Canada, and his father was a Canadian. We talked and talked and at one point were comparing notes about what books we had read for our General English. I said I loved *The Mill on the Floss*, one of our set books, and remarked that it would be so nice if it were made into a film. Peter said it had not only been made into a film but it was actually showing at a cinema in Kowloon and he was going to see it on Sunday. He asked if I would like to go along. He included Ah Wor in the invitation, but she said she did not want to go, so Peter said that he and I would go together.

Waiting for the bus to go home I chatted excitedly with Ah Wor about going to the film. I remembered *Pride and Prejudice* in Canton and how much I had enjoyed that. When the bus came, it was packed with people and we had to stand. After a while a man offered a seat to Ah Wor, but instead of taking it herself she steered me into it. A disapproving voice immediately commented that the seat was offered to the older woman, not to a schoolgirl. Ah Wor explained that I was unable to see and was safer sitting down. Another woman remarked that since I was blind I should not be out and about. This reminded me of what, in my excitement, I had momentarily overlooked—the sort of comments that Peter and I were bound to hear at the cinema on Sunday and the embarrassment that this would mean for Peter.

When we reached home I telephoned Peter and told him I had changed my mind. He sounded surprised and disappointed and of course asked why. I did not want to tell him the real reason, as I felt it was difficult to put into words, but he insisted that he would not hang up the telephone until I told him, so I made myself say that we were sure to hear remarks that would be embarrassing for him. He just laughed. "Why should we worry about what other people say—they would only be showing their ignorance," he said, sounding as if he really meant it. Of course I wanted to believe him and, as I knew Aunt would not like me using the telephone for too long, I changed my mind and agreed to go.

To reach my bedroom from the living-room I had to pass Uncle and Aunt's bedroom and I heard Aunt say urgently to Uncle, "Tell her! You must tell her!" I stopped at the door of their room and greeted them, but nothing was said so I went on to my own room. However, before long Uncle came and asked me to go with him to the living-room. He asked whom I was talking to on the telephone so I told him what it was all about. He asked me if I realised that going to a cinema with a boy of my own age was "dating" and said that Aunt wanted to make it quite clear to me that a blind girl had no business dating anyone, especially a sighted boy. I did not say a word. Inside, I was seething with resentment at the narrow prejudice and the injustice, but I knew that I must not contradict him. Fortunately he did not actually ask me to promise that I would not go out with Peter. It was like the time when he showed disapproval about the Christmas party for the blind but did not forbid me to go. I think he hoped to make me feel so guilty that I would comply with his wishes without forcing him to take a definite stand. He said nothing more and the interview was evidently at an end. I left the living-room in silence and returned to my bedroom. He had succeeded in making me feel guilty, not about having a date and going to the cinema but about being tacitly disobedient to him. He made me feel rebellious also and the rebellion won.

Sunday came. We went to the cinema and I thoroughly enjoyed it. Peter introduced me to his school friends and subsequently they joined my group of readers. This benefitted me in two ways: I gained more readers, but more important I learned to be with boys in an easy, casual way and found that I could be just as relaxed with them as with my girl friends. This was a great help when I went to Perkins where everything was co-ed.

After the cinema Peter took me home. We said goodbye at the

entrance to the building and I went up the familiar stairs and rang
the bell. Ah Wor let me in and whispered that Uncle and Aunt
were in the living-room. I greeted them politely as I passed the
door but there was no reply. I suspected that I was in disgrace.
Next morning when we were out in the street, Ah Wor told me that
as soon as she got home after taking me to meet Peter, Uncle had
asked her if I had "gone out with that sighted boy." She had managed to avoid giving him a direct answer and merely said something vague about coming home to do some sewing and Uncle had
not said any more. However, a few days later I received a letter.
Ah Wor said it was in Chinese and was in my Father's handwriting, so I decided that I would ask Peter to read it the next day,
as we had planned to read English Literature together after school.
I had honestly forgotten about my visit to the cinema with Peter
and Uncle and Aunt's displeasure, so it came as a shock when Peter
read me a long letter from Father, several pages of it, scolding me
for displeasing Uncle and Aunt, especially Aunt. He also said I had
better decide whether I wanted to study or go out with boys because I could not do both. I was embarrassed and assumed Peter
must be too, but as soon as he reached the end he hooted with
laughter and asked which I would choose. I said I wanted both,
and then we both laughed. I thought I had better reply to Father
immediately, so Peter wrote as I dictated. I explained that Peter
and I were friends, that we were the same age and were doing the
same work at our different schools and liked to study together. I
told Father that I often went to Peter's home, where we did our
work and Peter read to me, and that his parents were good to me.
Before long another letter arrived from Father, quite different from
the first one. He said he knew all the time that Peter and I were
just friends and said that it was kind of his parents to let me go to
his home. This confirmed what I suspected, that neither Uncle nor
Father was that narrow-minded; the truth of the matter was that
Uncle had to rebuke me to please Aunt and Father had to do the
same to please Uncle.

CHAPTER 30 ●●●

As THE DATE of the Schools Music Festival drew ever closer, I practised as much as I possibly could. Mr. Lee and Miss Edwards both
seemed quite pleased with me and I began to hope that I would at
least pass. I was doing my very last hour of practice on a piano at
school on the day before I was due to compete when someone
came and, standing behind me, asked if I had any difficulty locat-
ing the various keys. I said no, not particularly, as I knew the inter-
vals between them. Then she asked how I could be sure of finding
the right key to start. I explained that first of all I would find middle C which is always slightly to the right of the key-hole of the
piano. She asked me to show her how I did this and suddenly I felt
self-conscious and nervous. I found the key-hole and for the first
time felt doubtful about middle C. I had a moment of panic and
finally had to strike a note softly to make sure where I was on the
keyboard. This really terrified me as I had to do it in public the
next day. I spent the rest of my hour trying to make sure that I
could find the right note without striking one. It seemed incredible
that something I had done so easily for so long could suddenly
become difficult, just because I had made it a conscious action. I
was so afraid that I would get it wrong next day that I burst into
tears when I told Ah Wor about it. She said sensibly that I was
probably very tired so the best thing to do was to cancel my reading sessions, forget about work and go to bed early. This I did and
felt much better next day. I arrived at school in very good time,
went straight to the music room and ran through my piece with no
trouble at all. The previous afternoon was like a bad dream.

Later in the morning Mrs. Symons sent for me and asked me to
choose a friend to go with me. I chose Lily. I wanted to be there
early to listen to one of the earlier classes, so at about half past

eleven we slipped out and walked over to Grantham College of Education, where my class was being held. It was not far from our school. We found the hall and sat down. I noticed that some candidates were very nervous and played wrong notes while a few became hopelessly lost. I began to feel jittery, especially when one or two competitors who had finished playing told me that the piano was rather stiff. I wished I could have tried it but there was no time for that now.

The class finished, the Adjudicator gave the results and then we all left the hall. Lily and I were not sure what to do and we were walking along a passage when footsteps came towards us and stopped. Then a man's voice greeted me by name and asked what I was doing there. It was Mr. Law, the Principal of Grantham and a friend of Father's. I told him I was due to compete in the piano class at two forty-five that afternoon. He asked if we had had any lunch and when we said no he at once offered to send out for some sandwiches for us. We said we really did not want anything to eat, so Mr. Law suggested that we go to his office and have some tea and sit and talk. His office was quiet and we sat in comfortable armchairs drinking tea. I told Mr. Law how nervous I felt of playing on a strange piano and how I wished I could have tried it first; he said that if he had only known, he could have arranged for me to practise on it. It was too late for that now, but he was so kind and the tea was so welcome and refreshing that I began to feel a little less nervous. Lily and I agreed that we would go back to the hall in good time to be sure of getting seats near the front as I did not want to have too long a walk to the piano. Mr. Law wished me luck and we said goodbye.

There were two other short classes before mine—sight-reading and piano duets. Then at last it was time for Intermediate Piano Solos—my class. I was number seven on the list of sixty-three competitors. The first six went up and played and were clapped by the audience. Then it was my turn. Lily walked me to the piano, which was on a stage. I can still remember the loud squeaking of my shoes as I walked up the wooden steps on to the stage—I wanted to walk on tip-toe to stop them. The audience clapped so much that as I bowed I felt relaxed enough to smile at them. They clapped again at this and went on while I sat myself down on the piano stool. They only stopped when I actually began to play. I forgot about being nervous, about the strange, stiff piano, about not being able to find the right keys to start. I began without any difficulty and as I played I really enjoyed it, as if I was hearing the music for the first time. Only when it was all over and Lily and I were safely back in our seats did I think about being nervous. At last the class ended and the Adjudicator, Dr. Sidney Northcote, went to the front to talk about our playing and give us the results. I could not believe my ears when I heard my name among those awarded merits, but I had to go and take my mark-sheet from Dr. Northcote and that proved it.

This was the only time I ever went in for such a competition (by the following year I was in America), but it made me realise just how good it is for the morale and confidence of any disabled person to be able to enter an open competition on equal terms with non-disabled people. I genuinely enjoyed the experience.

But there was another very valuable aspect to that day. As a result, parents of blind children and young people contacted me, so I visited these families and eventually all these blind people went to Ebenezer for their studies. My friend Jaxie Short told me that one of her Sunday School pupils had confided to her that she had a blind sister, so I went to see her too. Her name was Wai-yee and she was anxious to learn. Her parents were kind but conservative in their outlook, and they took a great deal of convincing about their daughter's need for education. I often went to see them and in the end they agreed; in September, just after I reached Perkins, I received a letter from Jaxie saying that Wai-yee had gone to Ebenezer and was doing very well.

When we returned to school after the Easter holidays I became aware that my classmates were often discussing something in low voices but stopped and changed the subject as soon as they saw me approaching. I could sense that they were uncomfortable. This was worrying and I could not think what I had done to make them so distant and secretive. It could not be my handicap, as they had accepted me long ago and treated me as one of themselves. After a while I asked Doreen, one of my close friends. She was very reluctant to tell me, but I begged her to and finally it all came out. They were all talking about what they would do after Form V, but as they thought it very unlikely that I would be able to go to college or find a job, despite working so hard, they did not want to emphasise the differences between us by talking of their plans and hopes in front of me. So that was it! They were all being so kind and thoughtful, never realising how much they were upsetting me. I asked Doreen to tell them all that they need not worry about me because Miss Morgenstern of the Ebenezer Home had promised that she would have me to teach the girls there.

Despite these confident assertions, the old nagging anxiety about not being able to find a job crept back into my mind. It never occurred to me for one moment that I could consider going on studying after Form V. The John Milton Society had offered to help me financially for just one year, and although they said they did not expect me to pay them back, I hoped to do so even if it took me years, but the crucial question was—would Miss Morgenstern really keep her promise to employ me? Miss Schaeffer had assured me that she could get some private pupils for conversational English, but deep down inside me I wanted to keep my promise to Tse Tse, and to God, to teach blind people whatever I learned. At last I decided to go and see Miss Morgenstern. It was wonderfully reassuring to hear her say that she would take me whenever I was ready to start work. She also told me what my monthly salary would be and I knew that Ah Wor and I would be able to live on it. It was agreed that I would start work early in September. With this settled, I felt freed from gnawing anxieties about the future and concentrated on my school work for we had end-of-year exams looming ahead.

One day—it must have been about the second week in May—I received a registered letter from Dr. Smith of the John Milton Society. By this time I had learnt to sign my name—not very accurately, to be sure, but it served as my personal sign. The postman accepted it when I also showed him my identity card and my student's card. I could not imagine what the letter could be. It was

quite thick. I knew it would not be a cheque as I had asked the Society from the outset to send my monthly cheque to Miss Schaeffer
who took it to the bank and cashed it for me. I opened it and
found that, apart from one page of typing, there were several
thicker pages. Ah Wor told me they were printed. I took the whole
thing to my next reading session and asked my reader to read it to
me.

What she read was so totally unexpected, so far beyond anything
I had ever dared to hope for, that I could not believe it. I asked
her to read it again and then a third time. I still could not be quite
sure if I was dreaming so I asked her to read it to me slowly so
that I could take it down in braille.

It was from Dr. Smith. He said that from time to time when
funds were available and they knew of a suitable person, the Society offered a scholarship to a person interested in doing blind welfare work, irrespective of whether the recipient was sighted or
blind. He said that on the strength of my school reports, which I
regularly sent to them, and in the knowledge that I was hoping to
teach blind people, they had discussed my future with Dr. Edward
J. Waterhouse, Director of the Perkins Institution for the Blind,
and the Society and the Institution together had decided that I
should be offered a scholarship to receive professional training in
blind work. If I would accept the scholarship, I was to fill in the
forms and return them. Dr. Smith explained that they needed to
know my decision so that they could make plans accordingly. That
evening I made a bad job of taking braille notes. I kept trying to
push this bombshell into the back of my mind but it would not stay
there.

Out in the street after the reading session I told Ah Wor the incredible news. She was as thrilled as if she had won a million dollars, but suddenly, in the middle of our excitement, I found myself
crying. Surprised, she asked me what was the matter but it was a
while before I could pull myself together sufficiently to tell her I
just could not bear the thought of leaving her alone. She said she
would be all right as she could find a job and work till I came
back. However, I was afraid she might find herself with nowhere to

live if she did not get a job at once, because Uncle and Aunt had said all along that we could only stay in their flat until the term ended. I knew Ah Wor would not want to stay there without me anyway, as she knew she was only there on sufferance. I asked her if she would consider going to Macau to my family for a while but she said no, it would only mean Father having one more mouth to feed. She assured me that she would not starve as she could certainly find something to do and she believed that God helps those who help themselves.

Father, Mother, Uncle and all my friends were very happy to hear the news. Everyone congratulated me, Miss Ho and Miss Schaeffer helped with the various formalities that had to be seen to, and Miss Schaeffer took me to the American Consulate General for my interviews.

After a few days of initial excitement I came down to earth again and began to think about it all realistically. All my life Ah Wor and I had always been together. The first anxiety I had felt about her future was to some extent allayed by her confidence that she could find a job and keep herself going until I returned. Having decided that she would be all right without me, I then had to face the question, "How shall I get on without *her*?" All these years I had tried to learn to do as much as I could for myself, such as putting my things away and identifying my own clothes as much as possible, but there was always the comforting knowledge that whenever I forgot the colour of a dress or was not sure if two stockings matched, Ah Wor was there to tell me. Now, in only a few short months, I would be on my own with no one to turn to for help.

I pondered the situation as objectively as I could and came to the conclusion that lack of vision was, undeniably, a great limitation but if other blind people could manage I must not allow myself to say "I can't." What I had to say was "How can I do it in my own way?" As ever, Ah Wor had sensible ideas. For a start, we settled on certain places for my clothes and other personal articles and I tried to remember always to put them there. It was difficult at first as we did not have a wardrobe or drawers, but we used different sized bags for identification, though we soon realised that there was a limit to the number I could identify: beyond that it just became confusing. Little by little I found that I could memorise colours of clothes and accessories by making mental associations with texture, style or trimmings. Ah Wor explained which colours went well together and suggested that as I had only the vaguest idea about colour combinations, it would be safest to stick to simple ones. She made my clothes with this in mind and devised ways of indicating colours by putting little French knots, beads or crossed threads where they would not show; for example one knot, bead or cross might mean blue, two black and three pink. I kept a braille key which I could refer to when I forgot what was what. I learned to recognise different tops, lengths and textures of stockings and discovered that it helped to tie a pair together before washing. Ah Wor sewed tags inside the tops for identification and I tied them together again when they were dry. This way I could tell which were everyday ones and which were for special occasions. To save worrying about colour, Ah Wor suggested that I wear neutral ones that would go with anything.

Another scheme she thought up was a system of marks to tell me which items in regular use—underwear, etc.—had been bought at the same time so that I could use them in rotation and give them equal wear. We knew that in America I would probably have a wardrobe and drawers in my bedroom and I would save time and trouble if I put my best clothes on the right and everyday ones on the left in every case. I could keep things I did not use very often in a bag to save them from becoming soiled by needless handling.

At first when we started working out this system, I found it very hard to learn. I had to refer to my braille key constantly, but as time went by it became easier and after a while it was almost second nature. I felt really triumphant when I could find things and identify colours all by myself. Ah Wor sighed with relief and said she would not have to worry any more. At that time I innocently thought we had invented something unusual. At Perkins I discovered that blind people were all taught how to do this under the regular rehabilitation programme.

While we had solved one problem, another was quickly becoming more acute. One evening Uncle reminded us that he and Aunt could not keep me once the school term was over. This was daunting. It was useless to plead with poor Uncle, who was in a difficult situation. He was fond of me and in a most uncharacteristic fashion had shown his pride in me by talking to all his friends and acquaintances about me during my whole year at D.G.S. I am sure he would gladly have let us stay, but later that evening, while Aunt was having a bath, he came to my room and whispered to me with tears in his voice that he could not go against Aunt's wishes. Worried as I was and having no idea where we could go, I felt I had to comfort him and tell him that he need not be anxious about me as I was sure I would be all right. With a sinking heart I promised him that we would leave his flat the day school broke up for the holidays.

Uncle went quietly back to his room; Aunt was still in the bathroom. I had secretly hoped that Aunt would relent and let us stay until my departure in September. Now it was clear that there was to be no reprieve. I dreaded telling Ah Wor. She was planning to use her handwork money to buy me clothes, including some Chinese silk and brocade dresses which would have to be tailor-made and would cost a lot of money. If we went back to Macau and had to make additional journeys at the behest of Immigration and the American Consulate General, she would kill herself trying to earn the money needed for fares. But what alternative was there to Macau? I sat on my bed, elbows on knees, head in hands, listening to the living-room clock striking the hours and wondering if Ah Wor was lying awake too, on the other side of that locked door. She must have heard Uncle come to my room even though Aunt did not. She probably guessed what he came to say.

Poor Ah Wor. Ever since I was born she had stuck by me. Things had never been easy for her, even when Father was prosperous. Fighting my battles had left her with no friends and no savings. She had spent her savings and earnings on my needs and she secretly supplemented the housekeeping when vital things like rice ran out and Father had no money. Other amahs would ask her about her wages and, when they heard how long she had been working with our family, would remark that she must have saved many gold coins or even bought herself a flat, as many amahs of her age had done. She just laughed and said nothing.

Recently she had been losing weight. I noticed that climbing the stairs to the fourth floor left her badly out of breath and I could feel her shaking as we stood arm-in-arm outside the front door. The shaking may well have been due to nerves, as Aunt made no secret of her dislike of having us there and vented her spleen on Ah Wor. Ah Wor never complained to me about this and, knowing I could do nothing about it, I did not mention it. But the strain of all this was affecting her health. We could not afford to go to a doctor, but my friends told me she looked pale and thin. She talked of going to work as an amah for another family—but would her health stand it? She needed a rest, not more work. Suppose I went off to America and something happened to Ah Wor while I was away, how could I ever forgive myself?

America—my golden opportunity, the dream-come-true of which I had never even dared to dream! But if I did not go, I could still keep my promise by working at Ebenezer. I could tell Miss Morgenstern I was ready to start work there as soon as school ended; we could leave Uncle's place and go straight to Ebenezer and not have to worry about finding a place to live for the summer. Was this the decision I was meant to take?

I tried to convince myself that I had found the solution to our problem. I would tell Ah Wor and she would be glad to know that there was no more to worry about.

I waited until the clock struck six and tiptoed to the living-room door. I hesitated with my hand on the catch, in case it squeaked and woke Aunt, but Uncle's snores reassured me and I turned the catch as quietly as I could and opened the door, wondering if Ah Wor was still asleep. She was beside me instantly, whispering to me to dress so that we could go out.

We crept out of the flat and down the stairs. Once outside the building we could talk at last. I told her I had changed my mind and wanted to stay in Hong Kong. We could go to Ebenezer as soon as school ended and I would start work. The American idea had been exciting at first but I did not really want to go. I tried desperately to convince her that I was really happy with this decision, but it was no good—despite all my efforts I wept. I never could hide my feelings from her.

Calmly and sensibly, she told me not to be upset and not to be silly. She said of course I must go, and reminded me of how the example of my education had acted as a lever to get other blind children into schools. I could not go back on it now; it would undermine all that had been achieved. She pointed out that many families ran themselves into debt to give their children an education abroad and yet here I was actually talking of refusing a scholarship. If I would accept it and come back to work in Hong Kong, perhaps some day the John Milton Society would help another Hong Kong blind person to do the same. So we were back with our problems.

The next thing we talked about was her state of health. She admitted that being in Aunt's flat made her terribly nervous. Aunt made it all too clear that she could not bear having her around and was constantly rude and unkind. If Ah Wor was cleaning vegetables, Aunt would snatch them from her; if Ah Wor swept the floor, Aunt would seize the broom and march off with it. Ah Wor said she was sure she would be all right with another family: it was the incessant strain of putting up with Aunt and keeping her temper under provocation that was getting her down. I hoped she was right. She promised to write to me as often as she could, through a street letter-writer, to tell me how she was. This sounded fine.

We went into a small restaurant and ordered some food, and as we were sitting waiting for it, it suddenly dawned on me that we could not correspond through street letter-writers. Probably no one at Perkins would be able to read Ah Wor's letter in Chinese, and if I sent her typewritten letters in English the street letter-writer would not be able to read them. Yet another difficulty. I was so busy trying to think how we could get round this one that I neither heard nor smelled the food when it arrived and Ah Wor had to tap me on the shoulder. I did not want to worry her with yet another problem but we had to discuss it. She said she could go to an "English" letter-writer, which would be much more expensive but that could not be helped. I knew that the so-called "English" letter-writers charged at least five times as much as the ones who read and wrote Chinese. But that was not all: although they claimed to know English the letters they wrote were often incomprehensible. I had seen a few, shown to me by amahs in houses where I had gone for reading sessions. However, I decided not to worry Ah Wor about this for the moment. It could wait a little while.

When she left me at the school gate she told me not to worry too much—we still had a month. However, for the next week, although neither of us referred to it, we both knew very well we were worried sick because we still had not found anywhere to live. There were only three weeks left.

At least we solved the letter-writing problem; we decided to ask one of the blind ladies at Ebenezer to help. That way letters could go in both directions in braille in the normal Cantonese dialect, which would be natural to Ah Wor—more as if we were talking to one another. Unfortunately she would have to go all the long way to Pokfulam every time, which would be time-consuming, especially if she was living on the other side of the harbour, in Kowloon, but that could not be helped.

The days passed. There were only two weeks to go and we had still not found a place to live. We mentioned our trouble to various friends, hoping someone might offer us a refuge, but no one did. Most of the people we knew lived in the crowded conditions that are so typical of Hong Kong, where fitting in two extra beds is a physical impossibility. The days were not so daunting; we could visit people or sit in parks or other public places, but we were desperate for somewhere to sleep.

And once again, money—or the lack of it—had to be thought about. Wherever we found to sleep (and we assumed we would find something, somehow), it almost certainly would not include anywhere to cook and we would have to have all our meals out. I wondered about writing to the John Milton Society and asking them to help, but Ah Wor firmly disagreed, saying that they were paying my school fees and other expenses, and it was unfair to ask for more. I knew she was right, but it was hard on her. Her handwork was poorly paid and prices of everything were rising all the time. I remembered Miss Schaeffer saying she knew some people who wanted to learn conversational English. I asked her to contact them for me. She found seven; some wanted three hours a week, some two. This was most welcome, providing both occupation and some money and I could start work as soon as school finished and go on until the end of August. But it did not provide us with a room.

We were so desperate by now that we were resigned to putting up with bed-spaces, if we could find any. Ah Wor had to do the searching which meant taking time from her handwork. Once she did find a place, a cubicle in a divided room, and agreed terms with the landlady; but when she took me along to show it to me and the landlady saw I was blind, she at once changed her mind and refused to let it to us. I pleaded with her saying I was only a schoolgirl but it was no use—I was a *mang mui* and would bring embarrassment and bad luck, so that was that. We were back where we started. And that was not an isolated incident; Ah Wor found other places, four or five in all, and the same thing happened every time.

One evening as we got off the bus on our way home a woman's voice asked if I was Bee Nui. Bee Nui was my home name, so I knew that the speaker was someone who knew me as a child. I was delighted to find that it was Amy, the daughter of a Mrs. Li, who was a good friend of Miss Six, Third Uncle's former concubine, and of my mother. She lived with her mother and sisters only two blocks away from Uncle's flat. She urged us to go and visit them that evening as they would all be delighted to see us. Miss Six was with them and she would like to see us too. I wanted very much to go, but I knew that Aunt would not like to be disturbed by the opening of doors after ten o'clock at night. I told Amy this and said I did not think we could come, but to my delight she said they could put us up for the night. They did not have a large flat, but she slept in the living-room and said we were welcome to sleep there as well.

At first I was afraid of the prospect of telling Uncle and Aunt that I wanted to stay away for a night. But then, I thought, we would be leaving their flat very soon so what did it matter if we did displease Aunt? We were only going to have to put up with

each other for another week or two. So I told Amy we would go
and collect our nightdresses and toothbrushes and then come to her
flat. Ah Wor was very shocked at my agreeing so readily to spend a
night in someone else's flat, a thing I had never done before. She
said we should not go. I said we were going. I won.

CHAPTER 31 ●●●●●●●●●●●●●●●●●●●●●●●●●●●●●●●●●●●

WHEN WE REACHED their home we found Amy, her mother, whom I called Auntie Li, Amy's sisters Doris and Helen, and Helen's husband. Amy's husband was away, but Miss Six was there and it was lovely to see her again. We talked and talked of old times in Canton and I told them about my scholarship. They asked what we were going to do when term finished, at which point I burst into tears and wept uncontrollably. They were stunned and asked why, so Ah Wor told them. To my inexpressible joy they said we could stay with them until I left for America. Upon hearing this I was almost hysterical with relief, laughing and crying at the same time.

Next day before we set off for school Amy gave me a red packet which she said was lucky money for me. I would not take it, saying that as they were so generous as to offer to have us, I just could not accept more from her. In the end she gave the packet to Ah Wor. Seeing that she really wanted us to have it, Ah Wor took it, thinking it must be a token gesture. However, she told me later that at lunchtime she opened it and found two one hundred dollar notes in it. We then remembered Amy had said I ought to have one or two Chinese brocade or silk dresses for special occasions, such as Visitors' Days at college or when I had to speak to a group. We were so touched: Amy had two children at boarding school and she really did not have a great deal of money. We had told her about my English lessons and about Ah Wor's handwork, but she must have realised that it would not add up to very much.

The routine of long hours of study had created its own momentum which had kept me working hard through this period of intense anxiety. End-of-year exams were only a week or two away now, and although the anxiety about where to live was relieved, I had to confess to myself that despite all my efforts and labours I could not cover as much ground as the other girls, especially in supplementary and newspaper reading. All I could hope for was that my intensive knowledge in some subjects would make up for my extensive ignorance in others.

The exams came. Tense and sweating in the summer heat of Hong Kong, I picked my way through the papers, doing what I could, having to leave some questions unanswered. Even at D.G.S., with its enlightened attitude, I did not have any extra time for exams. And when it was all over my results were not brilliant but they could have been very much worse. My eight years of schooling were over.

When exams were finished I was given a going-away party. This in itself was heart-warming but even more so was a gift I received. The girls who had read to me and whom I had paid daily for the entire school year, thinking they would be glad of a bit of extra pocket money, gave it all back to me. It was almost four hundred dollars and they said I was to use it for something I needed for the trip. I cried when they gave it to me: the confusion of gratitude, pleasure and excitement mixed with sorrow at leaving so many friends was too much for me. With the money I bought myself two good suitcases, some Chinese dresses and other necessities.

Immediately term ended we moved to our new home. Aunt watched us go with undisguised relief, but I know Uncle had regrets. Auntie Li and her family were very kind people but we did not want to be a burden to them or be on top of them the whole time. We had received another eleventh-hour offer of help from Wong Wing-tze, my friend from school in Canton who became an ophthalmologist and who was by this time living and practising in Kowloon. I met her quite by chance one day: she had a small flat not far away and was able to squeeze us in, so we alternated between the two places, trying not to overstay our welcome at either. We had some meals at wherever we were sleeping, and some with Irene Ip's family, but most of the time we ate out. All these friends were very good to us and we did not want to risk putting any strain on their friendship.

I decided not to take on all the seven people who wanted conversational English lessons but to accept only four—four who did not live too far away because we had to go to their homes. The reason for this was that I wanted time for Ah Wor and me to go to visit the homes of blind people, children and adults, whom I had heard about from Miss Ho. I particularly wanted to try to get the children into Ebenezer. Miss Ho took me with her on her official visits to some of these homes. She was very pleased to see that although the people we visited were at first hostile, when they found out I had studied at D.G.S. and was leaving for America soon, a number of parents changed their minds and agreed to send their children to school. She said she then realised that my wish to work with blind people was not just a passing fancy and that I had the makings of a social worker. But she was afraid that when I was in America, I would change my mind about coming back. I tried to convince her that I meant what I said about keeping my promises.

After a week or two Auntie Li said that we could have a room to ourselves. It happened that the couple who rented it from her were leaving, so instead of letting it to someone else she said we could have it until I went away. It was a big room with cupboards and drawers, so I was able to work out how to arrange my things and practise putting them away and finding them, as if I was already on my own at Perkins. Helen asked Ah Wor to work for her, to take care of her two children, when I went away. This was wonderful; most of our problems had been solved at last.

We came home one evening to learn that Third Uncle had dropped in unexpectedly that afternoon. He had known for a long time where the Li family lived: Amy had met him in the street several years previously and had pointed the place out and invited him to call. In fact, when Miss Six was with Uncle, they were all good friends, but the friendship was broken after Third Aunt was reluctantly accepted into the Ching family. We all knew Uncle was fond of them, especially of Amy, but Third Aunt naturally would not want to have anything to do with Miss Six's friends, which made it impossible for Uncle to go on seeing them.

But that afternoon Uncle actually paid them a call. Mrs. Li described what happened. As he walked into the living-room and sat down, he asked curiously where each of them slept at night and how each room was used. Mrs. Li showed him round the flat and explained who slept where. She also pointed out the empty room left vacant by the couple who had left. When they returned to the living-room she noticed that Uncle's eyes were fixed on a pile of my braille papers which I had left on a little stool. He then asked who was asleep on the couch, with her face turned to the wall. When he heard that it was Amy he asked Mrs. Li to wake her up; he greeted her and very shortly afterwards he left.

I asked if Uncle had seen Ah Wor's and my things in the "vacant" room. Mrs. Li answered that as the door was closed, he could not see in, but although she did not tell him anything, she had the impression that he must have been worried about me. We all realised that he would not want to enquire outright where I was, as this would amount to an admission that he was unable to keep me under his roof and would mean loss of face. Mrs. Li thought that since he had seen the pile of braille, he would know I was connected with them and had somewhere to sleep. Actually, I had tried to find an opportunity to tell him where I would be staying after I left his flat, but I never had a chance to see him alone and he dared not talk to me when Aunt was there.

The days passed in a hectic rush. When there were only two weeks left, I asked Amy and Helen if they could think of anything I ought to do which I had overlooked. They said I ought to do something about my hair. I would look much better, they thought, with my plaits cut off and my hair permed. Amy offered to treat me to a perm at her hairdresser's.

The "beauty salon" was a new world to me. We had always made a sort of soap for washing our hair by boiling part of a special kind of tree. I do not know exactly what it was but it cost only a few cents from a herbalist. Now people round me were talking about shampoo, hair spray, hair lotions—things I had heard mentioned in stories on the radio but had never come into contact with. They smelt lovely and were much more pleasant than our old-fashioned way of hair washing.

When it came to my turn, the hairdresser asked how I wanted my hair done. As I had never seen how people did their hair, I was at a loss, but Amy came to the rescue. She said I had told her what I wanted and gave the hairdresser some instructions. I just nodded and agreed to everything. I was a little sad as the scissors cut off my long hair: it seemed so final. Then, when he rolled my hair up and began to put a big machine on my head, Amy came and said I had told her I would not want a machine perm, but a cold one. The man said it was much more expensive, and although it would be a more comfortable process, it was not worth spending that much. Amy quickly said that I had given her the money. I did not know what was going on so I just said yes to everything except when she said I had given her the money; I started to say no, but she nudged me, so I said yes.

Amy was having the same done to her hair. Suddenly the hairdresser asked me in which area of the city I was working. I did not understand what he meant but he repeated the question again and again. I tried to repeat it to Amy, but I was told she was under the dryer and could not hear me. The hairdresser kept badgering me to answer so in the end I yelled at Amy as loudly as I could. To my surprise I heard people laughing; I did not know what I had said wrong and felt very uncomfortable. Amy had heard me that time and shouted back with displeasure in her voice that I was not working anywhere in the city, that I was a school student and was leaving for further studies in America. Then I knew what it was all about and was really embarrassed.

After the hairdresser combed out my hair he handed me a mirror. I laughed and said the only mirror I could use was my hand. He laughed too. Although I examined my hair with my hand, I could not tell whether it was done the way I wanted since I had no idea how it should be done. I was relieved when Amy said it looked very attractive.

As we were walking home talking, a man stopped us and asked Amy how much he would have to pay her if he wanted me for the night. Amy was angry and told him he had come to the wrong person. I did my best not to show my embarrassment, but I could not stop my face from getting very hot.

During the time that remained, Amy and Helen showed me how to manage my hair. Combing and brushing were easy enough, but I was mystified about setting it after I washed it for the first time. Amy showed me the rollers and the pins and how to use them. It seemed easy enough, so I started rolling it up, but Amy soon noticed that I was rolling it all in the same direction and told me I had to do it according to the way the hair grew. I did not quite grasp what she meant, so in an effort to explain it to me more clearly she blindfolded herself and rolled up her own hair. She made a very good job of it. I felt a bit dashed. If she could do it without seeing, why couldn't I? She soon realised that she could do it because for years she had watched hairdressers at work and knew what the final result should be, whereas I had nothing but touch and imagination to guide me. In the end she put the rollers in for me, then I took them out again one by one and rolled them back in again. This worked.

Making-up was not so easy. I could not tell whether I had put on too much or too little. Amy said I usually did quite a good job, but might find it easier to use powder cream and wet rouge as with these it was much easier to know exactly how much was being applied. Lipstick was not so difficult: I could follow the line of my lips and if I thought I had gone over the edge it was easy to straighten it up with a tissue.

One week before my departure date Miss Schaeffer told me that there was some money left from my scholarship fund and she asked what I would like to do with it. I asked how much it was and found that it was enough for Ah Wor and me to go to Macau and back, so we went home to spend three days with my family.

Every minute of those three days was precious. The rule that a junior member should not talk in front of the senior members was broken; we talked and talked and talked—Father, Mother, my youngest sister, Ah Wor and I. Father and Mother wanted me to have the kind of food I liked most, as they thought I probably would not get much Chinese food at Perkins. They even bought some meat and cooked it as nearly as possible in Western style and showed me how to use a knife and fork.

Every time neighbours and friends called in, Father and Mother would tell them how I had studied at school, about my scholarship and about going to America. Some people said I had brought honour to my family name and it had all been well worthwhile: others said it was foolish for me to go abroad as many sighted people could not make the adjustment to different places and customs and were very miserable, so what hope could there be for me? Anyway, my parents were evidently proud of me and that gave me great pleasure and satisfaction. True to Chinese custom, they would not praise their children in public, but the fact that they talked about me with their acquaintances and seemed eager to introduce me to them showed that they took pride in what I had done. Also, they told their neighbours that if their children needed help with their English lessons, they could come and ask me for help. I had qualms every time another anxious enquirer arrived, book in hand, in case I might not know the answer, but mercifully all of them were either in lower forms in English schools or in higher forms in Chinese schools, so my English was adequate. Furthermore, I took some of these young people to visit Po-yuk, the daughter of the pedicab driver, and through Po-yuk they visited other blind people in Macau and became genuinely friendly with some of them.

Again, the problem of correspondence arose. Again, it was no use for me to type my letters to them as Father and Mother did not know English and my youngest sister was only in Chinese primary school and would not be able to read English letters. And it was no good their writing to me in Chinese—at Perkins. In the end we agreed to write to each other in braille with the help of Po-yuk.

Ah Wor and I returned to Hong Kong and the last four days were a confusing succession of invitations, packing and last-minute jobs. I was invited out for nearly all meals by friends, who gave me all sorts of useful presents. And I had to pack my two suitcases and make mental notes of where I had put certain things so that I could find them without too much difficulty. It was a great relief that my friends had promised that they would keep all my braille notes for me until I returned—unless they had to move house. Only Ah Wor and I knew the true cost of those braille notes and books: the miles and miles we had walked to readers' houses in blazing sunshine and in rain; the endless brailling; my aching hands and head; my bleeding knuckles.

When at last the time came for my departure, Father managed to come from Macau to see me off. My plane left early the next

morning. I knew better than to ask why Mother and my youngest
sister did not come. That night Father, Ah Wor and I all shared the
one room at Auntie Li's. None of us, including the Li family, slept
much. It was after midnight when we decided we must have some
rest. I lay in bed quietly but I could not sleep. I kept praying and
praying as I had never prayed before that God would take care of
Ah Wor. I was so afraid that something might happen to her while
I was away. Of course I thought of Father and Mother and my
sister, but I must admit I was much more anxious for Ah Wor, who
had given me as much as any human being has ever given to another. Suddenly I heard someone creeping to the bathroom. I listened carefully and recognised Helen's step. I slid out of bed,
opened the door silently and waited outside the bathroom. Helen
must have had quite a fright when she opened the door and found
a figure there! She gasped but I whispered to her to come back into
the bathroom and closed the door. I found myself weeping with all
my emotion for Ah Wor and it was a minute or so before I could
speak. Then I pleaded with her to take care of Ah Wor for me, and
if at any time she was not well, to write and let me know. Helen
had been a registered nurse before her marriage and her husband
was a medical laboratory technician at one of the Government hos-
pitals; this, and their genuine kindness, made me feel much better.
She promised to do as I asked and told me that Ah Wor had already said that she would come back to me as soon as I returned.
Then we both went back to bed.

CHAPTER 32 ●●●●●●●●●●●●●●●●●●●●●●●●●●●●●●●●●

IN THE CAR going to the airport my mind was a jumble of different kinds of feelings: happiness, yes, because the opportunity of going to America was more than a dream come true; sadness, also, at leaving Father and Mother and my youngest sister. My heart ached when I remembered Father saying she cried for two nights because he could not bring her to Hong Kong to see me off. I was afraid too; afraid I might not do well in America, that I might not be able to keep up with my studies, that I might be a misfit. But most of all, how could I bear the thought of leaving Ah Wor behind? In all my seventeen years of life the only time I had been away from her was when I spent those few days with Seventh Auntie. How I wished I could put my arms round her; how I wished I could say "I love you." But I just could not.

When we got out of the car it seemed as if everyone I knew had come to say goodbye and wish me well. There were my school-mates, my church friends, my ham radio brother and my sister-in-law and some relatives I had not seen for a long time: Miss Schaeffer was there, and Miss Ho, and my three pen friends, John, Peter and Paul and Peter's parents; Third Uncle was there. Ah Wor said there were tears in his eyes and he did not speak. I tried to compose myself and introduced all these friends to Father and Uncle.

Somehow the necessary formalities with tickets and luggage were dealt with and a little time remained before I would have to go. One of the ground staff of the airline suddenly approached me, bringing a wheelchair with him. He wanted me to get into it, say-ing that I should board the plane ahead of the other passengers to avoid the rush, but I said I did not need a wheelchair because I could walk. Also I knew there were still twenty minutes before we had to board, so I wanted very much to stay with my family and friends until the flight was called. We argued for a few moments until finally Miss Ho rescued me by asking him to allow Ah Wor to walk with me to the plane. He hesitated and then agreed.

I tried to be calm and made my way round the group saying goodbye to everyone. Suddenly, Uncle asked me to have a word with him away from the others. I excused myself from the group and took his arm. It was the first time I had ever taken his arm. I felt a surge of affection for him; he had done so much for the family as well as for me and I felt sorry for him; he had been the head of the Ching household, the man whose word was respected and carried out, but for the past six years he had been dominated and browbeaten by Aunt who pursued her own ends ruthlessly without regard to his feelings or interests. I could feel tears coming into my eyes and tried hard to control them.

When he spoke I heard his voice quivering a little and he had to clear his throat. He said he was sorry he had not been able to keep me in his home until I left for America. He hoped I would not feel too bitter towards Aunt for, whether or not she had been willing to keep Ah Wor and me for the past nine months, the fact remained that she had actually done it. I told him I was really grateful to him and Aunt for keeping us, and if in the future I could get a job, I would do all I could to make both of them happy. Uncle said he had set aside a flat in my name: in the future, he said, no matter what happened I would have the income of the flat to help me out. I said I hoped that when I returned I would be able to find a job and keep Ah Wor and myself and that I would not need financial assistance. Uncle said Ah Wor would probably not want to stay with me on my return if I was unable to pay her well—domestic helpers' wages, he pointed out, were rising all the time. Uncle of course knew nothing of the real situation between Ah Wor and me, nor that she had been doing handwork all the time to provide for my needs. (So little did he or Aunt understand of what was going on that when friends gave us cast-off clothes and Ah Wor altered them to fit me, Aunt said Ah Wor was deliberately cutting up my good clothes to spite me because I did not pay her enough. She never missed an opportunity to ridicule Ah Wor, but Ah Wor never once bit back.)

Father came over to us and said I should think about settling in America because even if I could get a job on my return to Hong Kong, it would be very difficult for me to gain acceptance among sighted people in this part of the world. I wanted to tell Uncle and Father that Ah Wor and I would be together after my studies in America and that I meant to keep my promises to Tse Tse and to God, but at that moment I heard the first call for my flight. I quickly returned to the group and said goodbye. Peter's father and mother actually kissed me. I wished I could kiss Ah Wor.

The airline official let Ah Wor take me to the plane. We walked in silence. There were so many things we wanted to say to each other, but they went beyond words. Also, we were not in the habit of speaking of these things. We climbed a long flight of steps and reached the entrance of the aircraft. I handed the officer my ticket book and my boarding pass and he flipped through them and called out to someone, saying they had a special passenger coming on board, a blind one. A stewardess came over and said I could walk with her.

I knew it was time to say goodbye. At that moment all we managed to say to each other was "Ah Wor," "Miss Three." We repeated this three times. Passengers were coming in past us so I said, "Ah Wor, you must go," and she said, "Yes, Miss Three, I must go." We did not touch one another. Then I heard her familiar footsteps going away down the steps.

I was on my own.

EPILOGUE •••

I WAS ON my own among strangers, in strange surroundings—an aeroplane that gathered speed and rushed me headlong into a strange new life. The contacts with friendly people during the flight provided a link with reality, but all the time I was aware of the increasing distance between me and everything that was familiar and everyone I knew and loved and trusted. I tried to keep thoughts of Ah Wor out of the front of my mind.

My neighbour—a Frenchman—was interested in my braille book (ironically, he seemed never to have heard of Louis Braille) and a small crowd gathered to watch me read; I had to wrestle, with only partial success, with the mysteries of the washroom; the stewardess (who turned out to be a friend of Amy's sister Doris) promised to tell the airline about the problems a blind person has with all the equipment and gadgets; I ate; I slept; we went through Customs and Immigration at Anchorage and I slept again; time passed . . . and eventually I was in New York being met by Dr. Smith and his son. I spent the night at the house of some kind people, the Szedens, on Staten Island. Next day I met, at last, the man with whom I had corresponded for so long and who had become like a sort of godfather to me—Dr. Chappel. It was a wonderful moment when he came in and said my name and I heard his voice for the first time.

Later the same day another godfather, a Mr. Avery, took charge of me. He was rich, generous and very kind and he was a good friend to me during my two years at Perkins. He died in 1956. That day we travelled in his chauffeur-driven car from New York to Boston where he delivered me and my luggage to Dr. Waterhouse, the Director of the Perkins Institution for the Blind, in whose house I spent my first night at Perkins. He and his wife, who is blind, looked after me most kindly. I was there at last, the realisation of the dream that began on that May evening five months before when I received the letter from Dr. Smith.

Other people have written about their experiences in that remarkable place. When I think back on it all, a few outstanding incidents and impressions always come to mind. I was given a braille watch; I had a room to myself and was able to put into practice all the systems Ah Wor and I had worked out; I learnt to use a Perkins brailler instead of my familiar handframe and stylus and, more important, I painfully unlearned my inaccurate self-taught braille and learned the correct forms of standard English braille, the music code and the maths code; I was almost intoxicated by the library, with its thousands of braille volumes covering every imaginable subject, including even some of the Chinese classics; above all, I met Miss Carpenter, the Dean of Girls at Perkins, who had for years worked with Miss Schaeffer at Ming Sum and was the closest link with home that I had, as she was familiar with Chinese life and customs and understood a great deal about the problems I encountered.

I did have problems. It was not difficult to alter such details as table manners, once I was told what I should do, but I found it far harder to adapt to an entirely alien, free and uninhibited social life. After a few attempts to go to parties and to dance—things that I knew would have shocked my family—I gave up and decided just to follow my own instincts and behave according to my own upbringing instead of forcing myself to do things that were contrary to it. Miss Carpenter encouraged me in this and said I did not have to copy the others.

But my worst problem arose unexpectedly over one of the things I had most looked forward to—O and M (Orientation and Mobility) and cane travel. All went well until one day a friend, in all innocence, asked me how I would feel using a cane back in Hong Kong. Once the seed of doubt was sown in my mind, I could not root it out. It grew and grew and overshadowed everything. The old spectres of beggars and prostitutes and canes and their attendant bad luck haunted me. I made no progress and was miserable and finally was referred to a psychiatrist. By good fortune the psychiatrist had once visited Hong Kong. This gave us some common ground, and with remarkable insight and some penetrating questioning, he grasped my problem and its implications in relation to Chinese social attitudes and prejudices. He made me see that I did not have to behave like a crusader back in Hong Kong, defiantly going about alone with a cane, inviting comment and opposition; I could travel with a companion. But he said that in order to change the prejudices, I should need every possible weapon and that the ability to demonstrate to people that I could, if necessary, move about independently was one of them. If I felt that this was imposing too much of a strain, then I could just stop learning O and M, but I should be depriving myself of one of my weapons and placing myself at a disadvantage. Faced with this choice, I decided to carry on.

In the spring of 1955 Dr. and Mrs. Waterhouse told me they were going to the Far East and would be in Hong Kong for two days. I was most anxious that my family should meet these two wonderful people who had done so much for blind people all over the world, but the plan was fraught with problems, linguistic and financial. I wrote to Ah Wor and to Third and Seventh Uncles. In the end, all was arranged: Third Uncle invited them to tea in a hotel restaurant. Seventh Uncle went along to interpret and dear Ah Wor sent $100 in Hong Kong money to Father in Macau to enable him to travel to Hong Kong to join the party. Ah Wor herself, alas, was not at the tea. She found her way with difficulty to the hotel but as she was in amah's clothes she was not allowed in. She met them afterwards. Father and my uncles were shown a copy of the Perkins 1954 Annual Report, which had a photograph of me in it. As might be expected, they took care not to appear too interested and did not ask for copies, though they later said in letters to me that they would like to have them to show to our friends and relatives.

There was one curious result from this meeting. When Dr. Waterhouse returned to Perkins he enquired closely about my work—which the teachers all said was good—because Seventh Uncle had told him I was careless in my typing, with frequent back-spacing and erasing. This was discussed and analysed and Miss Carpenter defended me, saying I had little time for letter-writing and would naturally spend less time and effort on letters than on my school work. It all simmered down, leaving mild traces of anxiety on all sides, but I knew the real reason: it was just further proof that Seventh Uncle, despite his American education, was still intensely Chinese and was comforming yet again to tradition by finding fault with younger members of his family in the interests of modesty. He would certainly never have realised the trouble he caused me. The end result was that he did not receive as many letters after that!

One other unforgettable experience was meeting the legendary Helen Keller. We first met at a function in New York in the spring of 1955, when she was about to set out on her tour of the Far East, and later in the year I spent a day at her house in Connecticut. She could not read my speech on my lips easily so we sat at two braillers and hammered out our conversation that way. It was she who first put the idea into my head of writing my life story, but she said I would need a dependable and hard-working friend to help me.

I was in America for a total of four and a half years. The first two years were at Perkins where I did the Specialised Training Course in Work for the Blind. I was the only blind student on the course. I spent the rest of the time at the Baptist seminary at Fort Worth, Texas. This came about as a result of contacts I made during my first summer vacation, in 1955. I went to several conferences and camps that summer, but the one I enjoyed most and which had the most effect on my future was the National Church Conference of the Blind at Louisville, Kentucky, where I was the guest of Mr. Edwin Wilson, Director of the Braille Evangel. He is the blind man Miss Lovegren had told me about when she read me my geography book in Macau.

The conference was a stimulating experience. It was attended by about a hundred blind people, all Christians, all deeply involved, professionally and privately, in service to their churches and their communities. They had problems but they were certainly not social outcasts. The whole atmosphere of vigorous activity was a revela-

tion to me and reinforced my determination to go back to Hong
Kong and fight for a better life for blind people there.

Mr. Wilson offered to help me in any way he could and I told
him how much I would like to learn about church music, in terms
of the piano. I still had a year at Perkins in which to think about it.
I wrote to Miss Ho and Miss Schaeffer for advice and both said
that it was a good idea and that any training I had would be of
value. So I worked at my music during my second year at Perkins
and in September 1956 I went to Fort Worth as a scholarship student of the Braille Evangel.

I had a wonderful friend and teacher in my Professor of Voice,
Joe Ann Shelton. She not only taught me to sing, she overcame the
problems of imparting the essentially visual aspects of the tech-
nique of voice production to me; she also taught me much about
life and even had me as a guest in her home. I am still in touch
with her. She now runs a business but is in constant demand all
over the world as an evangelical singer.

I am grateful to the Baptist seminary at Fort Worth for two
other friendships which have meant—and still mean—much to me:
Carol Burns (now Mrs. Wesley Smellie) and the Messer family.

Carol attended the seminary summer course in 1958. She is a
woman of deep purpose and conviction. She has started many
homes for disturbed and delinquent youngsters and always says
that God gives her the strength to carry on against impossible odds.
I found her friendship inspiring and I am still in close touch with
her and her parents, Mr. and Mrs. Burns. They have taken great interest ever since in me and my Christian projects in Hong Kong
and Macau and have treated me like one of the family.

The Messers had a daughter, Beverly, who was both blind and a
cripple, but she had an infectious joy in life and in the love of her
parents and they all took such a warm interest in me that they
drew me into their family circle. They were wonderfully happy
people. Beverly and Mrs. Messer are both dead now but I am still
in close touch with Frances Messer and Beverly's father.

All through those exciting, stimulating, varied and challenging
years Ah Wor had never been out of my thoughts and my prayers.

We had corresponded as arranged, with the help of the ladies at Ebenezer. She sent me all sorts of things—silk and brocade *cheongsams* for special occasions and little gifts, such as pins, bracelets, earrings and ivory carvings, which I could give to my friends. She also sent a great part of her wages to Father in Macau. She did this so that I could concentrate on my studies without having to worry about the hardships suffered by my family. Throughout the four and a half years that I was away, she stayed with Helen, taking charge of her children and the housekeeping. And thank God she was never ill.

I was at Fort Worth from September 1956 to February 1959. As the end of my course approached I faced one of the most difficult decisions of my life: whether to go home or stay in America. I was pressed to stay in America, with agencies writing to offer me jobs; my father and my uncles also wrote saying that my life would be impossible in Hong Kong and I should stay where I was; even my fourth brother and fifth sister arrived in America to live and they joined the chorus urging me not to go back. By this time, more mature and more experienced, I was beginning to understand the warning Miss Ho had tried to give me, late in 1953, when she said I would find the going hard and it would test my faith to the limit. But I had made my promises—to Tse Tse, to God and to myself. If I broke them, I would never again feel any self-respect, tempting though it was to accept the easier alternative.

I wrote to Ah Wor and asked her what she thought about it. She already knew most of the arguments, but I pointed out that if I stayed in America I was much more likely to earn a salary which would enable me to repay her savings which she had spent for me, and to honour all Father's IOUs from Macau. She wrote back saying she would back me up in whatever I decided to do and that as to money, we did not have to worry about such things between us; she said I owed her nothing and that she had burnt all Father's IOUs long ago.

Jaxie Short came to Fort Worth during 1957–58 and it was she who finally helped me. The breaking point was reached one night when she had read me yet another offer of a job. I asked her what

I should do. I was torn with doubt and indecision and in the end we prayed, both of us, for a long time and Jaxie asked God to make my path clear.

Then I knew I was returning to Hong Kong.

I returned in February 1959. Father and all my relatives met me at the airport; except for Ah Wor, they all made it clear what they thought—that I should have stayed in America. I took Ah Wor's arm and longed to hug her (after all, I had become accustomed to American ways) but we preserved our habitual, lifelong reserve. For a few nights I slept at the YWCA, then Helen and her husband, Kuk, kindly made room for both of us and we stayed with them while we started on the all-too-familiar search for a room. We found one in the end; an elderly lady with a flat in the Bonham Road area of Hong Kong Island was willing to rent us a room, so at last we had a home of sorts and I could concentrate on starting work.

Many people might think me unlucky because I am blind, and of course they are right in one way, but I prefer to think of myself as one of the lucky ones, which I am in relation to many blind people. Despite having been born into a highly conservative society and deprived of my sight by a combination of ignorance and superstition, I have nevertheless had the satisfaction and fulfilment of education and a profession—things which are denied to millions of women, blind and sighted, for a multitude of reasons but all too often because of economic and social backwardness. Indeed, I am lucky. The opportunity to make the best of things is held out, if we would only work for it. To quote Helen Keller, "I thank God for my handicaps, for through them I have found myself, my work and my God."

❋   ❋   ❋

In 1977 one of my dreams really came true. I was offered a scholarship by the John Milton Society to go to America for a three-month study tour, and thanks to the efforts of a few people it was made possible for Ah Wor to come with me. At long last she was to have the trip of her life. She went everywhere with me, saw everything, was received in people's houses and was loved by everyone, especially by Dr. and Mrs. Chappel, Dr. and Mrs. Waterhouse, Mr. and Mrs. Burns and our new friends Mr. and Mrs. Lyon. Few people can have worked as hard or as long or as selflessly as she has; no one can ever have deserved a reward more richly. Whatever I may have achieved, whatever I am able to do, whatever I really am, it is Ah Wor who made it possible.